Modeling Messages

Modeling Messages

THE ARCHITECT AND THE MODEL

Karen Moon

THE MONACELLI PRESS

First published in the United States of America
in 2005 by
The Monacelli Press, Inc.
611 Broadway, New York, New York 10012.

LIBRARY OF CONGRESS CATALOGING-IN-PUBLICATION DATA

Moon, Karen.
Modeling messages : the architect and the model / Karen Moon.
p. cm.
Includes bibliographical references and index.
ISBN 1-58093-128-6
1. Architectural models. 2. Architectural models—History—20th century.
3. Architecture—Designs and plans. I. Title.
NA2790.M597 2005
720'.22'8—dc22   2004025130

Printed and bound in China

Designed by Miko McGinty

CONTENTS

The use of models, and their importance in the architectural process, has grown exponentially in the twentieth and early twenty-first centuries; the last few decades in particular have culminated in a wealth of spectacular and diverse productions, many of which fill the pages of this book. Yet although recent studies have explored the model's use in the Renaissance and Baroque periods, the contemporary model has as yet attracted surprisingly little attention.[1]

Models are a means of expression; they are often objects of great beauty and charm. The creative abilities of architects, designers, and craftsmen are equal to those of painters and sculptors. While this is not a call for models to be considered "art" in some rarefied, abstract sense, the products of the architectural process hold as much interest as preliminary studies in the fine arts—and also deserve attention as works in their own right. Preliminary studies, or process productions (be they sketches, drawings, computer renderings, or models), intimately relate the story of the final artifact.

Models have always reflected the maker's skills and the architect's purpose, but over the course of the twentieth century, their agenda was enlarged. Good architects typically respond to developments in the visual arts; now the model has become a vehicle for the expression of their personal artistic concerns. New materials and changes in technology have brought with them a new breed of modelmaker, with different, more broadly based skills, vastly augmenting the model's capacity for articulation of ideas.

Just as models seem at a zenith of their power, however, changes are taking place. A new order of architectural representation, in the form of virtual three-dimensional renderings, computer modeling, and walk-throughs and fly-bys, presents a challenge to the model's traditional role; simultaneously, computer-controlled manufacturing processes are altering the meaning of craftsmanship in the model. What this signifies for the future is unclear, but it prompts important questions. Is it possible that within a decade or so, the virtual will supersede the physical in the creation of architecture? How will this affect and change our buildings? What will be the result of imagining, studying, and developing architecture solely on the two-dimensional plane of a computer screen? And what effect would the loss of the only physical part of the architectural process have on the design of what are essentially hand-crafted structures? Only by understanding the model's contribution to architecture and exploring its role in design, in conveying ideas, and in the germination of the architect's vision can these questions be answered.

My principal concern in this book is with models made as part of the process of designing an architectural project, with models produced by or under the direction of an architect while the project is "live"—that is, while the building is still in some sense an idea rather than a reality. I have occasionally included after-the-fact models, but replicas of historic structures do not form part of my discussion.

It has to be acknowledged that considering models in photographic form necessarily compromises their three-dimensionality. Indeed, reproductions of models can be almost indistinguishable from reproductions of highly realistic drawings or computer renderings. Thus imagination, required to comprehend all forms of representation, is also needed here.

ACKNOWLEDGMENTS

My first thanks must go to the Graham Foundation for Advanced Studies in the Fine Arts for its very generous grant in support of this book, to my publisher, The Monacelli Press, and to my editor, Andrea Monfried.

Many people helped me as I prepared this book. Kym Rice encouraged me to develop my ideas on models. Joe Rosa suggested I turn my material into a book. Carolyn Goldstein consistently provided support. I am grateful to my husband, Allister, for his apt advice and always positive critical comments; my family—Allister, Sam, and Ben—more than any others have helped me believe in what I am doing.

I am particularly indebted to modelmakers Richard Armiger, Kenneth Champlin, Mike Fairbrass, Alec Saunders, Christian Spencer-Davies, Richard Tenguerian, Alec Vassiliadis, and Chris Windsor; to architects Jonathan Leah, Keith Mendenhall, Peter Pran, Hani Rashid, and Michael Sorkin, who have untiringly provided information and help throughout the process of writing this book; and also to Bonnie Duncan, Mariko Nishimura, Kendell Cronstrom, George Rome Innes, Henry Millon, Victoria Newhouse, Sasha Porter, Evan Schoninger, Elizabeth White, Miko McGinty, Wolfgang Stockmeier, and John Wilton-Ely. Others have provided practical help and friendship: Andy Cantwell, Debbie Crall, Annelise Højhus, Susan Jacox, Takako Mizuno, Frode Neergaard, and Lynda Tanner.

I am grateful to the following individuals and offices for supplying material and providing assistance: Alsop Architects, A Models, Jarrod Arellano, Asymptote, Atelier 36, Michelle Barger, Beam Dynamics, Ruth Berktold, Aaron Betsky, Sherry Birk, Gunnar Birkerts, Roberta Britt, Pat Brugh, Angelo Cardillo, Leo Castelli Gallery, Brian Clarke, Richard Coleman, Catherine Cooke, David Coon, Coop Himmelb(l)au, Jonathan Coss, Roderick Coyne, Chuck Crisp, Horst Dagenstadt, Leo Daly, Odile Decq, Spencer de Grey, Richard Doerer, Steve Doubek, Kenneth Drucker, Christophe Egret, Amanda Eicher, Peter Eisenman, Michael Fischer, Jana Foit, Foster and Partners, Kenneth Frampton, Cathy Frankel, Future Systems, George Gabriel, Gehry Partners, Adriaan Geuze, Montserrat Gili, C. G. Girolami & Sons, Jennifer Gorman, Michael Graves, Lisa Green, Michael Gross, Michael Gruber, Zaha Hadid Architects, Mig Halpine, Caroline Hancock, Ivan Harbour, Katie Harris, Courtney Havran, Zvi Hecker, Hellmuth, Obata + Kassabaum, Sascha Hendel, Cyndi Hoffpauer, Kimberley Holden, Steven Holl, Sian Imber, Arata Isozaki & Associates, Toyo Ito & Associates, Clare Jacobson, Philip Johnson, Kandor Models, Jan Kaplicky, Wayne Kempton, KMCA, Jan Knikker,

David Knoll, John Koga, Kohn Pedersen Fox, Rem Koolhaas, Balthazar and Monica Korab, Annette Kriemeier, Ileana LaFontaine, Willy Leichter, Stuart Leuthner, Studio Daniel Libeskind, Nina Libeskind, John Lodge, Deirdre Loftus, Ian Luna, Jonathan Makepeace, Stephen Malmberg, Joachim Mannebach, Jeffrey Manta, Gayle Markovitz, Peter Marshall, Craig Martin, Duane Martinez, Jürgen Mayer H., Thom Mayne, Richard Meier & Partners, Christin Minnotte, Anna Moça, Martin Moeller, Monath & Menzel, Morphosis, Carolann Morrissey, David Morton, Eric Owen Moss, NBBJ, Network Modelmakers, Marlene Norum, Vanessa Offen, Office for Metropolitan Architecture, Erin Palmer, Susan Palmer, Peter Papademetriou, Gregg Pasquarelli, Pei Cobb Freed & Partners, Cesar Pelli, Piper Models, Jock Pottle, Antoine Predock, Wolf D. Prix, Max Protetch, George Ranalli, Raymond Riccord, Ilona Rider, Kevin Roche, Richard Rogers Partnership, RoTo, Michael Rotondi, Michael Harrison Russo, Michele Saee, Janet Samples, Joseph Santeramo, Mark Schmidt, Michael Schumacher, SHoP/Sharples Holden Pasquarelli, Gunnar Sillén, Katie Sipthorp, Skidmore, Owings & Merrill, Lucien Smith, Marian J. Smith, Paolo Soleri, Wendy Sommers, Scott Springer, Chris Stanley, Sara Stemen, Erica Stoller, Yoko Sugasawa, Tomiaki Tamura, Thorp Modelmakers, Xandra Tober, Jennifer Trantino, Petra Trefalt, UN Studio, Tricia Van Eck, Melanie Ventilla, Selim Vural, Wes Wach, Elizabeth Walker, Scot Walls, Aislinn Weidele, Eryl Wentworth, West 8 Urban Design and Landscape Architecture, Ross Wimer, Michael Winstanley, Lebbeus Woods, Hannah Yampolsky, and Woody Yao. And to the following libraries, collections, and organizations: American Architectural Foundation, Washington, D.C.; American Institute of Architects Library, Washington, D.C.; Architect of the Capitol Archives, Washington, D.C.; Archives of the Diocese of New York; Association of Professional Model Makers, Lake Zurich, Illinois; Avery Library, New York; Bodleian Library, Oxford; Cosanti Foundation, Arizona; Irish Architectural Archive, Dublin; Library of Congress, Washington, D.C.; Montgomery Museum of Fine Arts, Alabama; Museum of Contemporary Art, Chicago; Museum of Modern Art, New York; Netherlands Architecture Institute, Rotterdam; Queens Museum of Art, New York; Royal Institute of British Architects, London; St. Paul's Cathedral, London; St. Peter's, Rome; San Francisco Museum of Modern Art; Sir John Soane 's Museum, London; and the Victoria and Albert Museum, London.

Alsop Architects (U.K.). BBC Broadcasting House, London, England, 2000. Competition model, 1:500, polyester resin castings, wood, acrylic: A Models (above); development sketch, oils: Will Alsop (opposite); photomontage: Andrew Murray (left).

Architects have a choice of media for representing their ideas. For the BBC Broadcasting House, a model, color sketch, and montage (combining a computer model and a site photograph) elucidate different aspects of the design.

CHAPTER 1

The Model Defined

Architecture has always required representation. Architects have ideas, and ideas must be visualized and communicated. Models are one of the architect's tools.

Any form of architectural representation—a working drawing, a perspective, a computer-generated or physical model—must make material a concept that begins as a chimerical image in the creator's mind. Of all these forms of representation, the model is the only physical, three-dimensional realization of the architect's idea—which, after all, is ultimately intended to be a physical, three-dimensional thing.

However much time we might spend looking at two-dimensional images, we live in a three-dimensional world. We can view, and move around, the model, much as we view and move around the objects of everyday life. Because models are closer to reality than other media, they are understood more easily by the eye, and are more accessible to a wider range of people. They are more readily comprehended than computer images, require less training to read than an architect's drawings, and can provide more information about a building than almost any number of perspective views. As a result, they facilitate understanding. Models have what architect Peter Pran of NBBJ describes as "a kind of universal language. Everybody can understand a model; that's the beauty of it. Freehand renderings and three-dimensional computer renderings have great appeal, but models speak to us all."[1] The directness and immediacy of models, aiding both visualization for the architect and communication to others, have ensured their popularity over centuries.

Models are extraordinarily versatile. They enable architects to convey a range of information about a project, which may be factual in character, or conceptual, or both. They are also, like drawings, a rich and vivid means of expression, offering an infinite range of possibilities. It has long been recognized that drawings are more than a simple visual record of their subject matter. Models, too, comprise far more than the surface realities of a bricks-and-mortar project, but have waited longer for such recognition. They can reveal their creator's

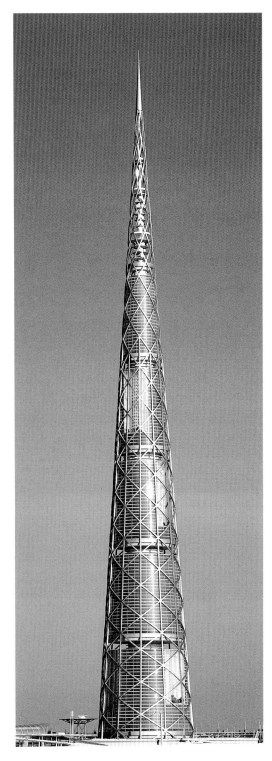

thoughts and imaginings, sources of inspiration, and underlying conceptual ideas. Today's models are extremely varied. They can be mesmerizing in their exactness as miniature versions of reality, or they can be wildly energetic representations of architects' visual and spatial concepts—essentially abstract sculptural form. This compound nature of the model, its ability to engage and respond on such a variety of levels, makes it intriguing and worthy of inquiry.

The complexity of the model is not easily understood. One basic rule to aid comprehension of the medium is this: no model can communicate everything about a project. Each one is a construct, the result of a series of choices about what to show and how to show it, in which many factors are intentionally excluded. The model's scale, its materials and color, and its degree of realism and finish must all be deliberately selected. Each separate decision affects how the model looks and the overall message it conveys.

The model communicates in a variety of ways that are interconnected. First, there is the aspect or part of the project it addresses. The focus can be on a tiny fragment, like a stair-rail profile, or on a building as a whole, in its surrounding site or urban context. But a model is not always concerned with representing how the building will look in reality. Often it shows something a viewer would never see—a slice through the building (a sectional or cutaway model, for example), the general relationship of building masses (a simplified block model), or perhaps an isolated feature of the design, like the floor arrangement, the mechanical services or transportation routes, or more abstractly, the imagined lines of movement through space that have inspired the architect's idea. The information offered in a model is often quite specific and limited, and no model can tell us everything about a design.

Every model has a particular purpose and audience. It may be made for the architect's own use, as a medium through which initial ideas are explored in

Foster and Partners (U.K.). Millennium Tower, Tokyo, Japan, 1989– . Model, styrene with brass, acrylic, and medium-density fiberboard, 1990.

Sprayed a uniform silver and eschewing detail, this model presents a perfect glossy image of a sleek, tapering tower. It gives limited information about the proposal, instead conveying a particular message about the design.

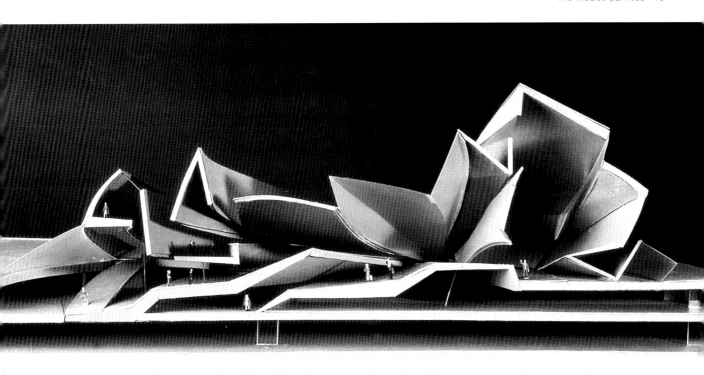

a purely experimental way, or as a tool for analyzing the success of a number of different solutions. It may be intended for the methodical testing of a design's acoustic or lighting effectiveness. It may help demonstrate the structure to a contractor or present the idea to the client. The uses of models are wide-ranging, but they can be conveniently summarized under two broad headings: study and communication. Most architectural practices use models in both ways, but some use them more to convey their ideas to outsiders, whereas others use them more for themselves, to form the design. These purposes are not always mutually exclusive, and a single model can have a series of different incarnations during a project's life, sometimes for study and sometimes for communication, or can incorporate public and private functions at the same time. Hani Rashid, of the firm Asymptote in New York, describes the dual purpose of a typical model made in his practice: "It

[is] one way to convey to others what you are trying to do, and one way to convey to yourself something you can meditate upon, enter into a critique [with], and develop more ideas from."[2]

Models tell us about project-related ideas, but they also communicate in other ways. Inevitably, through their form, they convey messages—not always intended—about the designers themselves: about their personalities and architectural approach. They demonstrate the image of the building the architect wishes to project and also an image of the architect—or of how an architect wishes an audience to see him or her. Models are also a product of the maker's choices: a maker who may be the architect, but may be—in fact, often is—someone else. Models reflect the maker's training, skills, and personality. Makers can be motivated by a love of craftsmanship or technology. Their technical skills can direct their decisions on whether to work in metal, plastics, or wood.

Eisenman Architects (U.S.). Natural History Museum, Staten Island Institute of Arts and Sciences, New York. Sectional model, 1997.

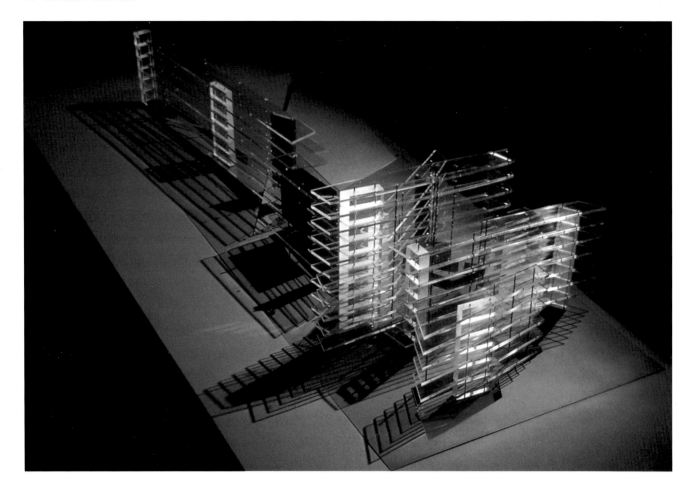

Zaha Hadid Architects
(U.K.). Zollhof 3 Media
Center, Düsseldorf,
Germany, 1989–93.
Model: Daniel Chadwick.

Hadid's model, made from
clear acrylic, gives very
specific information about
the arrangement of the
building's internal levels.

OPPOSITE
Odile Decq Benoît
Cornette (France). Banque
Populaire de l'Ouest,
Administrative and Social
Centers, Montgermont,
Rennes, France, 1988–90.
Model.

Zaha Hadid Architects (U.K.). Hafenstrasse Development, Hamburg, Germany, 1989. Painting: Zaha Hadid.

Like Will Alsop's colored sketch for the BBC Broadcasting House, Hadid's exploratory site studies for the Hafenstrasse Development illustrate her inspiration for the project in an expressive, two-dimensional format. But these gravity-defying images would be impossible to construct.

Models may be versatile and enormously varied, but they have limitations. They cannot confine the onlooker (as does a perspective) to a single, selected image of the most attractive view.[3] They cannot show every aspect of the architect's creative line of thought. Zaha Hadid's architectural paintings show her vision for a building but are not constrained, as a model would be, by gravity and the need to be constructible. A model's typically reduced scale can cause restrictions. Interior spaces cannot be explored as freely as with a moving two-dimensional simulation, such as a computer walk-through or a film or video; only a scale large enough for movement inside the model would make this possible. In most cases a model, unlike a plan or elevation, is not a convenient way to communicate specifications. Nor can it travel or be reproduced as easily as a drawing. All forms of representation have inherent advantages and limitations, and it is for this reason that most architects use the different media in combination.

While a model is one element in the process of architecture, it also has an independent existence as an object, quite apart from the project with which it is associated. The ambiguous relationship between model and building has endlessly troubled architects, and prompts the question: what exactly is a model? A model is not a miniature building, because the miniaturization makes it something else. A building is for human habitation: if a model were able to fulfill this role, it would become a building, not a model. Even so, for the architect, the difference can in practice seem small, as Luca Galofaro writes of Peter Eisenman: "Eisenman does not draw any distinction, except in terms of scale, between the model and the built object. He sees the model as an object deprived of the need to be lived in."[4]

Recognizing that models claim a relative autonomy from the building, some architects have considered them analogous to the activity of architecture, almost its equivalent. "Compared to a drawing on paper, the models are very real; they are the building," asserts Antoine Predock on his Web site.[5] Hani Rashid, who studied under Daniel Libeskind at Cranbrook in the 1980s, found that

> What was really interesting about [Libeskind's] approach, which became my approach, was that the model for us became a piece of architecture. There was no separation, really, in our minds at that time between making a model of a building and it being the building . . . and that's really the kind of exuberance and attitude we had to modelmaking . . . the feeling that the thing itself had all the . . . implications of a building.[6]

During that same period, a group of Russian "paper architects" went one step further, considering their models as sufficient unto themselves, in an approach so focused on the object that the idea of built architecture became superfluous.[7]

But a model is patently not equivalent to a building. It represents the idea of architecture, not the actuality—a manufactured object, built from

Asymptote (U.S.). The
Steel Cloud, Los Angeles
West Coast Gateway,
California, 1988. Model.

Gehry Partners (U.S.).
Guggenheim Museum
Bilbao, Spain, 1991–97.
Design process model,
paper, acetate, and
wood, 1994.

Just one of a vast number
of models made by
the Gehry office for the
museum, this study
explores the design of
the atrium.

ideas, or "an idea scaffold for the real thing," as
Jaquelin Robertson described it in the catalog to the
1976 exhibition "Idea as Model," ultimately con-
cluding, "finally, and most tellingly, [the model] is
about itself."[8]

The model, then, is an idea but also an object.
It is about the project, but it is also about itself. As
an object, it has its own identity and presence, which
demand attention, and which can take the architect
almost by surprise. Michael Graves ponders this dis-
turbing characteristic: "Once we have modeled or
represented an idea, that representation, the object
made, begins to have a life of its own, somewhat
separate from or beyond our original conception."[9]
Is there a suggestion here of the architect losing
control? Many architects have recognized the dangers associated with the model's ambiguous position.
Its independence is not always welcomed, which has
created a struggle (between architect and model)
that for some architects has never been resolved: a

conflict explicitly acknowledged by practitioners as
diverse in time and architectural convention as the
fifteenth-century Italian Leon Battista Alberti and
the twenty-first-century American Frank Gehry.
Alberti attempts to suppress the model's attraction:
models should be "plain and simple, so that they
demonstrate the ingenuity of him who conceived the
idea, and not the skill of the one who fabricated
the model"[10]; Gehry seeks to elude their power by
working on models of two or three scales at the
same time, because, he finds, "If you focus on one
scale, you become enamored of the object in front of
you, and [the model] becomes an end instead of a
process."[11] Alberti blames the problem on the maker,
while Gehry blames it on the scale.

The trouble with models is that they have their
own intrinsic attraction, which is not necessarily the
attraction of a building. While some architects
struggle against this quality, others—recognizing its
potential—use it to achieve their own aims. Some
treat the model as a totem, loading it with symbolic
significance, so it stands for far more than the project it describes. Others use it to woo the client
(through astonishing degrees of detail or tricks of
photomontage) to believe in its reality.

However long the autonomy of the model has
been recognized, it is only relatively recently that it
has been much explored. References to models
before the mid-twentieth century are small in number, indirect, and obscure. In the 1970s, along with
other forms of architectural representation, the
model suddenly began to attract attention as an
object in itself. Articles were written and exhibitions
opened; museums took fresh interest in the collection of models; and sale prices increased.

Exhibitions focusing on models were unusual
before the 1970s. Models had always been included
alongside other forms of architectural representation in the shows put up by architectural societies,
like the Architectural League of New York, and in
the architecture sections of broader shows such as
London's Royal Academy Summer Exhibition and

the Paris Salon. But they were included solely to help illustrate current projects. By the mid-twentieth century a new awareness of the model as object had begun to grow. One early exhibit, in Oxford, England, in 1941, declared that its chief aim was to "show the value of architectural models."[12] Twenty-four years later, also in England, John Wilton-Ely organized "The Architect's Vision" at the University of Nottingham to explore the history and functions of models in architectural design. This was introduced as the "first exhibition of architectural models to be held in [England]."[13] Another eight years on, in 1973, the Victoria and Albert Museum installed "Marble Halls: Drawings and Models for Victorian Secular Buildings."[14] So isolated or little known were these early exhibitions that a repeated claim to precedence, in a 1974 exhibition, may perhaps be excused. At that date a display of architecture of the previous twenty years was set up by the Sheffield Society, which called itself the "first body in the

U.K. to stage an architecture exhibition in terms of models."[15]

These exhibitions, like the recent and more widely accessible Renaissance and Baroque model shows at several international venues, recognized and highlighted the model's role in the process of architecture, significantly raising public consciousness of the medium.[16] The prime purpose of each of these exhibitions, however, was to elucidate a particular period of architecture, using models as the medium of study.[17] The idea of viewing them as objects in their own right (apart from their role in a project) and understanding their significance for the architect was barely considered.

In the 1970s, as model-based shows were appearing with increasing frequency in England, the initiative of inquiry began to shift to America. "Idea as Model" of 1976, shown in New York, might be described (tentatively, of course, in view of earlier inaccuracies) as the first exhibition that truly focused

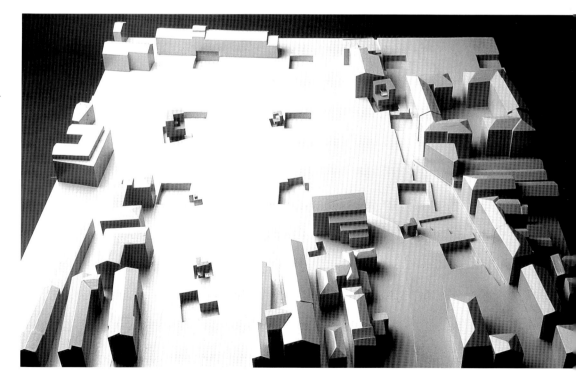

Eisenman Architects (U.S.). Cannaregio Town Square, Venice, Italy, 1978. Model.

Eisenman's model was featured in the 1981 exhibition catalog for "Idea as Model."

on the model itself. While intended to encourage the use of conceptual models in the design process, first and foremost, as explained in the catalog text's first paragraph, it was a response to Peter Eisenman's "intuition" that "models, like architectural drawings, could well have an artistic or conceptual existence of their own, one which was relatively independent of the project that they represented."[18] The nature of the model was considered in a number of articles and through the contributions of a group of invited participants, including Eisenman, Charles Moore, Raimund Abraham, Stanley Tigerman, Michael Graves, Diana Agrest, Mario Gandelsonas, and Rafael Moneo. Several of these architects explored the border between drawing and models, initiating a dialogue on architectural representation that still continues. For Eisenman, the model represented "an idea in itself and an idea about objects"; for Tigerman, it was "an idea about ideas rather than an idea about architecture."[19]

This was the point at which the model's independence became openly recognized. Models assumed a new self-consciousness. Just how large a part "Idea as Model" played in this awakening is difficult to determine. At the time of the exhibition, the attitude to the process of architecture was already changing. The catalog for "Idea as Model" was delayed; publication was not until 1981. Richard Pommer, looking back in his catalog commentaries, identified two influences in particular that he felt had prompted the show. The Museum of Modern Art's "École des Beaux-Arts" exhibition of 1975 was the first. According to Pommer, it had implied that drawings were conceptual and models

Arata Isozaki & Associates (Japan). House of Nine Squares, 1980. Model, lead.

This lead panel, "The Formal Principle in Relief," was shown by the architect at the Leo Castelli Gallery's "Houses for Sale" exhibition.

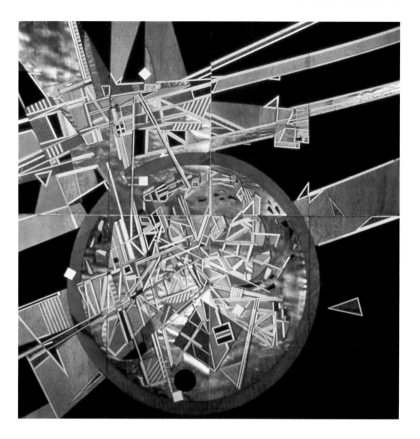

were not, a view that invited refutation.[20] He also posited that models, along with other forms of architectural representation, assume greater importance (or "reality") during periods of radical change, when architecture is shifting direction. Writing at a time "when buildings seem unreal, when the Beaux-Arts looks false, [and] SOM empty," he was alluding to the perceived failure of modernist architecture.[21]

The new attention lavished on the objects of architectural representation must also be linked to theories of modern art current at the time, and in particular to the movement known as Conceptual Art. The first American exhibition specifically devoted to Conceptual Art took place at the New York Cultural Center in 1970. Writing in 1976, Edward Lucie-Smith defined the movement as "first, the examination of what we mean by the concept 'art' and second, the concept itself as art." In all, he explained, the movement comprised

> a shift of attention from the physical embodi-
> ment to the art "idea" . . . the work of art can
> be seen as essentially the map of a thought
> process, a visible summary of all the steps
> which have been necessary for a particular end
> result to be achieved. Hence the frequent use
> of labels such as "process" and "system."[22]

For Conceptualists, it was no longer necessary for the final "art object" to be displayed; what became more important was the documentation of the process. In fact, the catalog of "Idea as Model" reads like a manifesto of Conceptual Art. Buildings are the "physical embodiment," drawings and

models represent the "idea"—the documentation that assumes a new significance.

"Idea as Model" was followed by several New York shows in which the investigation of the model's nature moved unambiguously from model as idea to model as art. "Houses for Sale," at the Leo Castelli Gallery in 1980, presented models by a group of architects in an environment traditionally reserved for the contemplation of the fine arts. Arata Isozaki in particular displayed a series of enigmatic and beautiful objects that any collector would have appreciated on his or her wall. As the catalog explained, "The involvement of an art gallery in this role is novel. For the first time, buildings are made available in a way formerly limited to paintings, sculpture, graphics and photography, bringing architecture into the realm of contemporary art collecting."[23] The 1981 catalog for "Idea as Model" was quick to note this change:

Michael Sorkin Studio (U.S.). Model City, Artists Space, New York, New York, 1989. Model, 16 by 16 feet.

This large-scale, semi-abstract model belongs to Sorkin's Urbanagram series. Sorkin says, "As a representation the model sits somewhere in a field bounded by architecture, topography, diagram, and plan." The model was "the first materialization of a city I have been trying to imagine." While primarily an exercise in urban design, it is also a work of abstract art created for a gallery exhibit.

Four years have passed since the close of the exhibition "Idea as Model." In the interval, architecture has changed in several ways . . . First, models and drawings have been taken up by the galleries. Architects have stopped pretending that they are above selling their ideas as works of art . . . house models are sold to the highest bidder just like the new works of Alice Aycock, or Siah Armajani, and Mary Miss.[24]

At traditional architecture exhibitions, too, models were being seen in a new light. At the Royal Academy Summer Exhibition in London, where fine art and architecture are judged side by side, their importance as art objects has grown. Richard Rogers Partnership's model of the European Court of Human Rights in Strasbourg was one of the final three at the Royal Academy in 1990. But what was being judged, the object or the design? Ivan Harbour, one of the firm's directors, explained that the model is judged in much the same way as other entries: "What is it as a piece of art? What is it conveying?" After all, he remarked of their Strasbourg entry, "That model's very much a sculpture."[25] Spencer de Grey of Foster and Partners confirms this notion: "It's not at all inconceivable that models might be chosen for their visual quality, their abstract quality."[26] More recently, in 1999, an Alsop Architects model of a pavilion for the Hannover Expo, made by A Models in London, was short-listed for the

Alsop Architects (U.K.). Pavilion for Daimler Benz, Hannover Expo 2000, Germany. Presentation model, 1:200, acrylic, cast resin, etched nickel silver, and aluminum mesh: A Models.

The shell of the building was to be assembled from three-foot-square ETFE-inflated "cushions" held together by a steel "spider" structure.

Morphosis (U.S.). Malibu
Beach House, California.
Model, 1986.

Zaha Hadid Architects
(U.K.). Landscape Forma-
tion One, Landesgarten-
schau, Weil am Rhein,
Germany, 1999. Model.

Charles Wollaston Award for the most distinguished
work in the Royal Academy Summer Exhibition,
one of the largest art prizes in the U.K. (David
Hockney was the eventual winner.)[27] The separation
between objects of architecture and objects of art
has become less and less defined.

Since the Castelli show, and others at New
York's Max Protetch Gallery, the format of
presentation has also changed. Models are hung on
walls like paintings or relief sculptures.[28] The
American firm Morphosis has produced artistically
considered stands or bases for its models as well as
box frames, like picture frames, in which to hang
them on walls. At Max Protetch's 1999 "Architectural
Imagination," Zaha Hadid reoriented one of her
building models vertically, distancing it from the
proposal and presenting it instead as a freestanding
work of sculpture.[29]

Models have also been seen from other perspectives. The Renaissance and Baroque model shows of
the 1990s associated models with the objects of high
cultural and aesthetic value in national collections,
drawing attention to craftsmanship and antique
qualities.[30] These exhibitions came at the climax of a
growing appreciation of models as craft. Models,

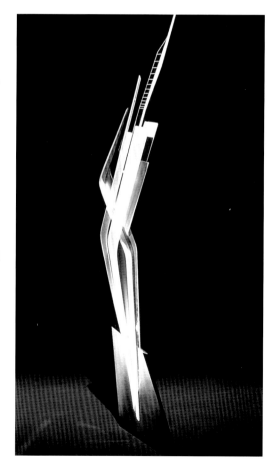

especially older ones, have become desirable collectors' objects. Frank Gehry has only recently begun to understand the value of his models, which were previously considered workaday ephemera of the office process. The fact that Gehry Partners has "everyone in the world beating down their door to exhibit their models" (as one employee, Keith Mendenhall, put it)—people are willing to pay millions of dollars to purchase them—has forced some architects to reconsider their worth.[31]

The collectors of these objects are principally museums; the space taken up by models makes them less attractive to private collectors. Before the 1980s, there were scattered collections at the Museum of Modern Art in New York, the Royal Institute of British Architects in London, and a number of city and national collections in both the U.S. and Europe. But more vigorous collecting began at about this time. Several new museums entered the fray, including the Canadian Centre for Architecture, the Netherlands Architecture Institute, the FRAC Centre (Fonds Régional d'Art Contemporain) in Orléans, France, and the Deutsches Architektur Museum in Frankfurt. MOMA intensified its interest, and other institutions like the San Francisco Museum of Modern Art began to include models in their scope.[32] Collecting policies became more sharply defined.

The setting up of the new architecture museums of the 1980s coincided with growing academic attention to the architectural process, to architectural practice, and to the representation of architecture, a trend that ran parallel to the focus on process in the fine arts. The 1975 "École des Beaux-Arts" exhibition at the Museum of Modern Art, which displayed the exquisite drawings of that school, was an early, visible contributor to this trend.[33] Throughout the 1980s, a scholarly interest in models swept across Europe, demonstrated in museum exhibitions and in numerous articles in art and architectural periodicals.[34] Entire issues of journals were devoted to models: in France, the *Revue de l'Art*, in 1982–83; in

Britain, the *Architects' Journal*, December 1985; in Italy, *Rassegna*, December 1987; and in Germany, *Der Architekt*, April 1989. In 1990, in the U.S., *Architecture New Jersey* devoted an issue to the subject of architectural representation.[35] These were accompanied by a barrage of one-off articles that significantly increased the total accumulation of literature on the subject. Finally, 1991 saw the first effort to investigate the modern model in book form: *The Art of the Architectural Model*, by Akiko Busch.[36]

Some architects responded directly to the dialogue on models in their work. In Odile Decq and Benoît Cornette's exhibitions "Maquettes Invraisemblables: The Model Is the Message" (1989) and "Hyper-Tension" (1995), the importance of the model as medium was underlined, and issues of model representation were directly addressed.[37] The almost frenzied attention that models received in the late 1980s was due to a convergence of factors. Not least among them was the economic downturn resulting from the oil crisis of the 1970s, which depressed the building industry and reduced many architects' opportunities to gain commissions, making models a focus of creative activity for them.[38]

The broad-based attention paid to models during this period only increased their value in architects' eyes. And those who use models need little encouragement in this respect. For many architects, the attachment to their models goes beyond an affection for the symbol of their achievement. The model is the means for them to realize their idea, but it also represents their idea in its original purity of conception—as the completed building, often a compromise for reasons of structure, client conflict, or cost, may not. It preserves the unsullied ideal, an image often more beautiful than reality, where weather does not stain the finish and where trees "do not shed their leaves, [and] dogs . . . cannot foul the pavement," as writer Alastair Best eloquently described.[39] If a project is abandoned, the model, which may be the only physical presence to survive, can become a lasting memorial of a cherished dream. Like the Renaissance images that show donors

Odile Decq Benoît Cornette (France). Social Housing, Rue Manin, Paris, France, 1987–89. Model.

Exhibited in "Maquettes Invraisemblables: The Model Is the Message" in 1989, this model disregards the conventional approach to representation and instead shows the layering of the building's wall planes in exaggerated perspective.

TIME

JANUARY 8, 1979 $1.25

IRAN
Violence and
Chaos

U.S.
Architects
Doing
Their Own
Thing

Philip Johnson

0 02
724404

OPPOSITE
Sir Edwin Lutyens (U.K.).
Dollhouse for Queen
Mary. Maker: J. Parnell &
Son, Rugby, England.

The dollhouse was sent
from the drawing room in
Lutyens's house to Windsor
in about 1921. The archi-
tect was admonished by
one of his clients for giving it more of his attention
than his project for
the headquarters for the
Persian Oil Company.

Philip Johnson and his
AT&T Building model on
the cover of *Time*,
January 8, 1979.

clasping models of their buildings (diminutive replicas, symbolizing their efforts and aspirations), contemporary images of architects with their models abound. The message is primarily one of identification, but like an image of a proud parent with a baby, or a satisfied owner with a gleaming new car, it communicates a sense of pride and ownership.[40]

Models hold further attractions for architects. They free them from the pressures of reality, the need for practicality or even realism. They embody, as Toyo Ito holds, "a labyrinth of reality and fiction."[41] Models can be singularly functional working tools, but they also offer an opportunity to experiment with imaginary ideas, impractical or unbuildable. They offer creation without responsibility, a release from the real world. There are parallels with the play of childhood: Frank Lloyd Wright was not alone in his youthful appreciation of building toys. Often, architects experience the first stirrings of their vocation in this encounter, and they can retain an enthusiasm

for playing with architectural form in the same way that many people like to tinker with their (or their children's) dollhouses or miniature railways.[42]

Dollhouses themselves offer an obvious opportunity for unencumbered play. The great Edwardian architect Sir Edwin Lutyens was delighted at the chance to design a dollhouse for Queen Mary, with every detail of the interior and exterior created by a leading contemporary craftsman and perfectly reduced to scale. Competitions on dollhouse design can prove hugely attractive to architects. Associated with the modeling mania of the 1980s was one organized by Andreas Papadakis in London, which

> turned out to be a massive undertaking: No one had any idea at the time just to what extent the competition would seize the imaginations of architects, designers, and students around the world, and how overwhelming the response would be . . . A total of 260 entries were received from twenty-seven countries.[43]

Animal houses, Larchill, County Kildare, Ireland.

Reducing the normal scale of a building changes the customary relationship between viewer and building. Alongside several follies on the grounds of Larchill house stands part of an ornamental farm built in the eighteenth century; the local architect performed his architectural experiments for the benefit of the pigs.

Other forms, such as follies, are equally tempting. The Victorian architects William Burges and Richard Norman Shaw both produced fantastical furniture articulated with miniature Gothic finials and towers. In his article "Micro-Architecture as the 'Idea' of Gothic Theory and Style," François Bucher describes how, in the same way, architects of the thirteenth and fourteenth centuries used small sacred works as a "laboratory for stylistic refinement," developing stylistic innovations in reliquaries, stalls, fonts, pulpits, and tombs that "allowed them to perform sophisticated model experiments" on their architectural ideas.[44] More recently, Michael Graves and others created "Tea and Coffee Piazzi" for the Italian firm Alessi, the architectural terminology for the project (piazza, or town square) reflecting the architectural nature of the designs. Like other contemporary architects, Graves has used product design as an alternative format for modeling architectural ideas.[45]

Models encourage a special intimacy. Rashid of Asymptote describes them as "something very close to my heart."[46] John Hejduk was known to carry small models fondly in his pocket. Michele Saee recounts the intense relationship developed during the process of building his Golzari Guest House model (see page 92):

The reason it took that long to build was because it almost became like an extension of me. [It was as though] you could tell the moods I was in, you could tell the things I was thinking, through the model. And it was very bizarre, I had a friend visiting me in that period, and he could just come in, and basically, by the way the model looked, would say how I felt.[47]

Michael Graves (U.S.). Tea and Coffee Piazza for Alessi, 1983.

Alessi's publication on the series describes the Piazza as "three-dimensional volumes placed upon the polished enclosure of a tray like the meaningful elements of some bizarre architectural planimetry . . . [Graves] designs coffee-pots and milk-jugs as if they were the portals and monuments of a scenic urban perspective."

Models have extraordinary power. They have a way of augmenting meaning, both for their creators and their owners. Witness Adolf Hitler (who combined the characteristics of failed architect and megalomaniac) lingering over his models for the new Reich capital in David Welch's analysis of the regime *Nazi Propaganda: The Power and the Limitations:*

> not even the *Wehrmacht*'s imminent Operation Norway and the grueling preparations for the forthcoming French campaign could keep Hitler from his favorite occupation. Time and again during the war he was drawn to the model rooms to be informed of the progress being made.[48]

In the same way, Louis XV's vast collection of models of fortified towns (such models had been built for strategic purposes since the seventeenth century) became for him "objects of prestige," which he showed off to foreign diplomats and visiting military men, intending to impress them with the power and wealth of his kingdom. In this context, they have been appropriately described as "princely toys."[49]

It is not just for the architect or client that models symbolize ownership and achievement. Models representing captured cities, the spoils of war, featured in Roman triumphal processions.[50] British comedian and writer Ben Elton mercilessly lampoons today's stereotypical politician and would-be urban planner. In this excerpt from *Gridlock*, Digby

Adolf Hitler with the architect Albert Speer viewing a model of the German pavilion for the Paris World's Fair of 1937.

OPPOSITE
French collection of strategic models. Drawing: Vigneux.

The relief map gallery was installed in the Louvre in Paris in 1749.

Parkhurst, minister for transport, was preparing to depart for a conference in Brighton:

> He was a little sad because he was going to have to leave his beloved models, mounted on trestle tables all through his department . . . Digby wandered like a dreamer from one pristine model to another, touching them gently, stroking their contours. In this exquisite private moment he even knelt down and pressed his cheek against the cool surface of a miniature flyover. As he stood up, a faraway look crossed his features. He could see clearly in his mind's eye a sunny day, a crowd of dignitaries standing on the spotless concrete, a long, blue ribbon of delicate silk stretched across the ten proud lanes, he himself sternly holding the golden scissors. "I, Digby Parkhurst, Her Britannic Majesty's Minister for Transport, do hereby declare the UK orbital ring road open."[51]

What emerges from a closer look at models is the complex tangle of levels at which they operate, the concentration of meaning they can carry, and the wonder they inspire far beyond the office door. It would be foolish to ignore such receptacles of magnetism and power.

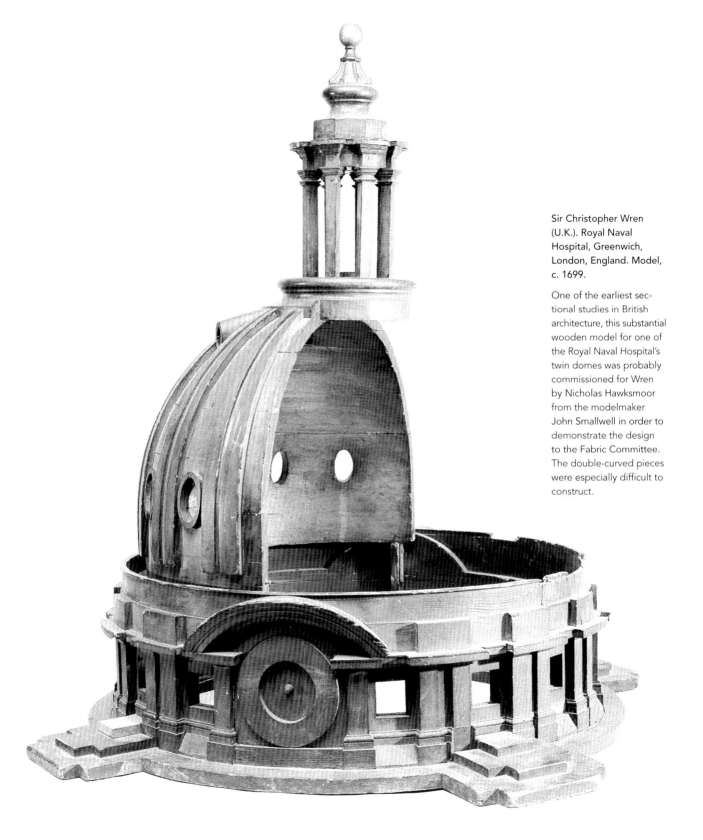

Sir Christopher Wren (U.K.). Royal Naval Hospital, Greenwich, London, England. Model, c. 1699.

One of the earliest sectional studies in British architecture, this substantial wooden model for one of the Royal Naval Hospital's twin domes was probably commissioned for Wren by Nicholas Hawksmoor from the modelmaker John Smallwell in order to demonstrate the design to the Fabric Committee. The double-curved pieces were especially difficult to construct.

CHAPTER 2

A Common Thread

Architects have used models to develop their ideas and communicate their intentions to others since antiquity. Despite some swings in popularity, and minor fluctuations in purpose, these functions, and the employment of models in general, have remained constant over time.

Models are created by architects to ensure the validity of their designs and to test technical performance. Any innovative architectural feature requires evaluation. However certain the calculations, however detailed the drawings, a model verifies the concept in a physical and substantive way. When American architect-engineer General M. C. Meigs was working on the design for the dome of the U.S. Capitol in the late 1850s, there was "a good deal of controversy over whether or not the dome would stand if built according to the plans." His great-granddaughter records that Meigs had a metal model made to test the structure "for his own satisfaction."[1] Similarly, Steven Holl had a half-size model of his design for the new Helsinki Museum of Contemporary Art constructed to gain approval for innovative aspects of the structure's engineering, which were held in doubt by the project's builders.[2]

In earlier eras, when two-dimensional means of representation were less developed, calculations to estimate the materials and cost of construction were often made on the basis of the model. Alberti noted that models "provide a surer indication of the likely costs . . . by allowing one to calculate the width and the height of individual elements, their thickness, [and] number."[3] In 1567 the French architect Philibert de l'Orme advised that during a building's design stage, a series of models should be made, of details as well as the whole, so that "the expenses can be precisely calculated to spare the principle [*sic*] surprises."[4] The model has not been altogether superseded in this role. Today, Frank Gehry traces

Foster and Partners (U.K.). Reichstag (New German Parliament), Berlin, Germany, 1993–99. Model, 1:20, medium-density fiberboard, acrylics, foamex, brass, and steel: Atelier 36, 1996.

This model of the plenary chamber, dome, and light cone suspended within was hoisted onto the roof of the Reichstag to test the lighting in February 1996.

his models with a digital scanner, and the information is transferred to a computer program through which the estimating is done (see page 202).

As models have been vital for the architect's own study and design development, so they have persistently acted as a line of communication between the architect and others. In this capacity, the model serves primarily as mediator between the architect and client, filling the combined roles of informant, translator, and advocate. But models can also form part of the dialogue between the design and construction teams. For example, the Greeks used "specimen models," created for construction workers to copy.[5] Vasari described Brunelleschi's use of models as a pragmatic on-site tool: "He carefully examined the stones of the stonecutters to see that they were hard or if they contained any flaws, and showed them the way to make the joints by models made of wood and wax, or even of turnips, and doing the like with the ironwork for the smiths."[6] Though rather more finely conceived than the last, Sir John Soane's model of the construction of a masonry niche for the rotunda of the Bank of

England was almost certainly built for the same purpose.[7] Sir Christopher Wren produced detail models for the builders throughout the construction of St. Paul's; indeed, the workmen's needs were anticipated early in the project's chronology. In his report to the cathedral's commissioners of 1666, he urged,

> And for the Encouragement and Satisfaction of Benefactors that comprehend not readily Designs and Draughts on Paper, as well as for the inferior Artificers clearer intelligence of their business; it will be requisite that a large and Exact Model be made.[8]

Models were evidently still employed in this way as a matter of course in architect George B. Post's New York office in the late nineteenth century. There, "contractors [were] received in the general office to transact their business, and in the office of the foreman of the draughting room to examine drawings, models, etc."[9] And this practical function persists. In contemporary practice at Foster and Partners, they are "still used to give contractors a general overview of a project, and sometimes specific models are commissioned to demonstrate special problems that need to be addressed."[10]

While there are broad similarities between past and present model use, there are some differences. Before the nineteenth century, models often formed part of the legal contract between architect and client, but this is no longer the case.[11] Construction drawings and materials specifications have taken over this function and remain the standard documentation for construction today.

The model was also seen by architects of the past as the guardian of their intention in a direct and practical sense. Some models were meant to preserve the definitive design in case, as Sir Christopher Wren explained, "the work should be interrupted or retarded. Posterity may [then] proceed where the work was left off, pursuing still the same design."[12] Even were construction to proceed as slowly as it did then, it is not likely that models would be seen as the primary documentation in such a case today.

Sir John Soane (U.K.). Bank of England, London, 1794. Model, mahogany: Henry Provis.

Made in fourteen pieces, Soane's mahogany model of a niche in the rotunda was most probably made to demonstrate the construction system to the masons on the job. This delightful model can be taken apart and reassembled like a child's toy.

A COMMON THREAD 35

Certain minor functions of the model may now be obsolete, but newer, stronger ones have come forward. At least two factors emerged during the sixteenth and seventeenth centuries to contribute to the establishment of the site model as a form: the production of military and strategic models (which in many cases encompassed entire towns and their environs) and an increased interest in garden planning.[13] However, the advantages of this new model type were not fully appreciated until well into the twentieth century, when issues of context and urban planning came to the fore.

And it is only since the second half of the nineteenth century that, through the invention of the camera, models have been used to create two-dimensional images. The insertion of a model photograph into a site photograph, the superreal eye-level view, the art photos of models produced for architectural monographs, and the moving images of model films and videos have all provided new avenues of employment for the medium.

Throughout, models have remained in continuous use. They have contributed to the practice of architecture in cultures as disparate as ancient Egypt, Ottoman Turkey, India, Russia, and Japan. In Egypt there is evidence that models were created especially to aid construction.[14] The Ottomans found them essential for design development, and for communicating their ideas to clients and convincing them to

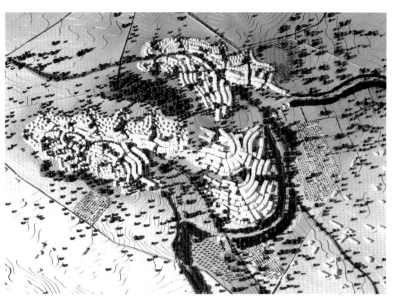

Richard Rogers Partnership (U.K.). Parcbit Urban Ideas Competition, Mallorca, Spain, 1994. Model, CNC-milled styrofoam block and Rohacell foam.

This site model was presented to the government of the Balearics. While site models have been constructed by architects since at least 1600, they have become commonplace only from the late 1940s.

RIGHT
Military model under construction, from Alain Manesson-Mallet's *Les Travaux de Mars, ou l'Art de la Guerre*, Paris, 1691.

build. In one recorded incident, a model was lowered into an emptied pool in the sultan's palace. The grand vizier descended alongside in order to explain the design, while the sultan watched from a royal seat overlooking the scene. On the basis of this presentation, the form of the projected building was resolved.[15]

The reliance on models often runs in architectural "families." The preference for models of

Miniature showing a model of the Süleymaniye Mosque being carried during a festival in 1582, from the Ottoman manuscript *Sūrnāme* by Intizami, illustrated by an artist working under the guidance of Baba Nakkas (Nakkas Osman).

particular influential architects, educational systems, or schools is passed down to a new generation of young practitioners and students. Harvey Wiley Corbett, one of the architects of Rockefeller Center, was unusual for his time in his regular use of models as part of the design process (see page 43); Wallace K. Harrison, who studied under him, also used models extensively.[16] Eero Saarinen, who worked routinely with models during the 1950s, passed along his enthusiasm to many young architects in his office, including Cesar Pelli and Kevin Roche, both of whom still use the medium today. Similarly, Mies van der Rohe influenced the architects with whom he worked. Peter Pran remembers: "I came to Chicago and worked for Mies van der Rohe, whose model shop was of enormous importance." Pran's mother was also a modelmaker. Here, the legacy of a real as well as an architectural family was passed on.[17]

The impact of formal architectural education has been equally significant, particularly at schools such as Columbia University, the Cooper Union, and SCI-Arc in the U.S. and the Architectural Association in Britain, where an emphasis on models has a decisive influence on the students' chosen media for design development. But architectural training and the influence of peers can also have a negative effect on the use of models. This was true, for instance, in the period of Beaux-Arts supremacy, when great importance was placed on drawing and the reliance on models was reduced. This led to a lack of interest in models in a number of regions during the nineteenth century.

General perceptions of design and architectural style carried over centuries have also been influential. While model use has never really ceased, there has been a good deal of fluctuation, making the story complicated. With a few exceptions, the earliest surviving models made by architects in the course of their work come from the Italian Renaissance. From that period until today, factors affecting the model's use have included building booms and depressions, labor costs, the availability of craftsmen, the introduction of new materials for modelmaking and new techniques in architectural representation, developments in building technology and architectural style, and the level of recourse to public opinion considered appropriate. Contemporary comments are often a useful aid to understanding the model's vicissitudes and certainly illuminate the perceived reasons for change current at the time.

Eero Saarinen (right) and Kevin Roche considering the model for Morse and Stiles Colleges at Yale University in the studio of Eero Saarinen and Associates, Bloomfield Hills, Michigan, c. 1957.

Michelangelo Presents to Pope Paul IV the Model for the Completion of the Fabric and Cupola of St. Peter's. Oil on canvas: Domenico Cresti di Passignano, 1619.

The model's importance in the Renaissance period is elegantly summarized in this famous painting.

During the Renaissance, the surge of building, accompanied by the introduction of new, non-Gothic forms, prompted an increase in the making of models as a means to demonstrate the architect's intention to the client, as well as for design development.[18] Undoubtedly the frequent employment of competitions during this period (in which, to ensure equality, all architects were required to make models) encouraged this modelmaking trend, as did the more open nature of the architectural process: submission of the scheme to committees or even to the public for approval was common.

Sixteenth-century architects began to rely more on two-dimensional forms of representation. Measured drawings were refined as a system of architectural communication, and there was greater dependence on perspective.[19] But the use of models continued. The earliest surviving models from both France and Germany date from the first quarter of the sixteenth century.[20] Models were again pivotal in the Baroque period, when the focus was on the very qualities of architecture that the model most uniquely illuminates: space, the effects of light and shade, and complex, sculptural form.

In the later eighteenth century, in reaction to the Baroque, architects sought a more severe and simplified form of design. Neoclassicism, which concentrated on proportion, the classical orders, and composition of the elevation, provided less fertile ground for the model. Along with the rising cost of labor and increased reliance on drawings, this era saw a decline in model use, apparent by the end of the eighteenth century across Europe as well as North America. Thus Soane lamented in his early-nineteenth-century lecture series, "Formerly, models were considered as essentially requisite in Civil, as in Military Architecture, and no building was begun without a Model having been previously made."[21]

Further pressures contributed to the model's decline during the nineteenth century. Referring to a detailed and accurately made model of a London mansion, the work of a professional modelmaker, one writer commented in 1848:

> In this age of casting, electrotyping, and otherwise reproducing, a hundred pounds, which would, perhaps, little more than pay for the time and talent spent on the model before us, would seem a large sum, and be willingly paid only by a very few.[22]

The blueprinting process introduced in the last quarter of the nineteenth century reduced drafting costs and further exacerbated the problem. The expense of skilled labor continued to rise, and by the end of the nineteenth century, especially where the influence of Beaux-Arts training was prevalent, models came to be considered an expensive luxury.[23] This appears to have been particularly true in America, which, unlike Europe, had no extended model tradition. Those makers whose superior skill in their craft won them major commissions, like the models for the U.S. Capitol or buildings for the World's Columbian Exposition (see pages 143 and 151), were relatively secure, since such jobs could occupy a team of modelmakers for several consecutive years, but others were vulnerable.

So small in number, diversely spread, and little known are the examples that remain from this period in Britain that it was formerly assumed that models had played little part there, too, in nineteenth-century architectural design. Without question, the model's role was diminished. However, research for the exhibition "Marble Halls: Drawings and Models for Victorian Secular Buildings," which opened in London in 1973, revealed that models were used throughout the nineteenth century in the production of important public buildings and monuments, churches, and engineering projects such as bridges.[24] More than seventy models were submitted to the 1839 competition for the Nelson Monument in Trafalgar Square. Competitions also brought about the construction of a fourteen-foot-long model of

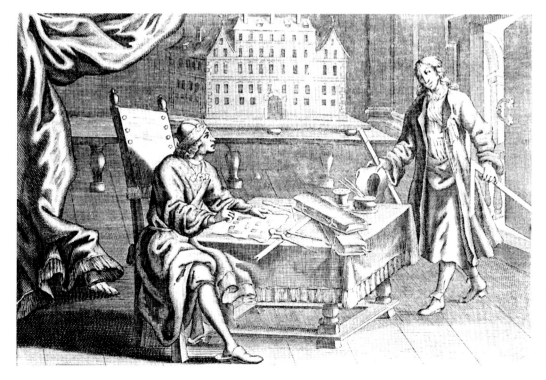

Architects in their studio with a model, from Franciscus Philippus Florinus's *Oeconomus prudens et Legalis*, Nürnberg, Germany, 1722.

John Pollard Seddon
(U.K.). Law Courts
Competition, London,
England, 1866. Model.

St. Mary's Pro-Cathedral in Dublin in about 1814 (see page 65) as well as more modest examples by George Edmund Street and John Pollard Seddon for the competition for the Law Courts in London in 1866.[25] In America also, even when the use of models was at its lowest ebb, they were still considered necessary for important and elaborate buildings regardless of the price.[26] The large 1904 plaster model of the U.S. Capitol cost $2,139.25 and took more than two years to build. But models were little used in general practice; they were thought to be "too expensive to be practical and . . . really only for a fad or for very important projects which will justify a large outlay in the study of their design."[27]

Toward the end of the nineteenth century and in the early years of the twentieth—particularly in the United States, where the use of models was most limited—it became recognized that the Beaux-Arts infatuation with virtuoso drawings, at the expense of three-dimensional study, was having an adverse effect on the quality of design. This concern would be raised with growing frequency between 1900 and 1920. One early critic feared that too much emphasis on plans and elevations had made architects "lose the capacity to think in the solid."[28] Another, an educator, pointed out that "the end and aim of architectural instruction is to teach the students to build good buildings rather than to make beautiful drawings"; he was referring to what he saw as the failure of "the French school," whose "wonderfully facile drawing . . . does not give a correct idea of the building when built."[29]

The cost of modelmaking had increased during the nineteenth century, along with the scale of the projects for which the practice was employed and the level of skill required for working in plaster. On the occasions when models were made, "complete miniatures" of the final structure were generally demanded, and they were "usually elaborate and meticulously finished, entailing weeks of work by

Smithmeyer and Pelz (U.S.). Library of Congress, Washington, D.C. Model: James Parrington Earley, architectural sculptor, c. 1889.

This section model shows the reading room and stack areas of the Library of Congress. During the nineteenth century, models of whole buildings—as opposed to models of ornamental details—were generally restricted to large public projects.

Hornblower & Marshall (U.S.). Baltimore Customs House, corner pavilion, Maryland. Model: James Parrington Earley, architectural sculptor.

skilled craftsmen."[30] So specialized and expensive
had modelmaking become that studios could be run
only in larger urban areas, as one writer explained:

> The services of the architectural sculptor who
> makes the casts, contribute, of course, [an]
> expensive item . . . Every town does not boast
> of an architectural sculptor, to be sure, and
> in the absence of such a man it would be
> difficult to carry out the making of the models
> as described.[31]

As a result, in the early part of the twentieth
century, the impression was that architectural models
were "difficult and expensive to make." But as
Frederic C. Hirons argued in the American architectural journal *Pencil Points* in 1920, the difficulties of
making models did not have to be significant, nor
did the model have to be expensive to construct.[32] A
search for alternative materials began, as well as for
methods of making that were suitable for in-house
construction (thereby avoiding the cost of professional craftsmen). Dozens of articles extolling the
virtues of cardboard arrived on the editorial desks of
American architectural periodicals between 1918 and
1926, but the return to models was already in
progress.[33] In 1915, the offices of Charles A. Platt,
McKim, Mead & White, Horace Trumbauer, and
Frank J. Helme were among those to be seen availing
themselves of the advantages of models in *American
Architect*, which remarked, "many prominent architects are fully realizing the vast range and value of
the model and are placing more and more importance
on its use."[34] One West Coast writer of 1919 declared,

> Five years ago a scale model was something
> of a novelty, but today it is recognized as one
> of the necessary adjuncts to the architectural
> profession. This is proven by the fact that
> scale models are very rapidly supplanting per-
> spectives and rendered sketches as a means of
> portrayal and presentation.[35]

In 1921, Alwyn T. Covell summarized the
change in American practice in this way: "For many
years past the scale model has been used in showing

Harvey Wiley Corbett
(U.S.). Bush Building (Bush
Terminal International
Exhibition Building), New
York, New York, c. 1916.
Model.

Corbett promoted card-
board models of this kind
in a series of articles in
Pencil Points in 1922. The
staggered outlines of
the architect's skyscrapers
(partly molded by New
York City zoning regula-
tions) lent themselves to
dramatic presentations.

Frank Lloyd Wright,
Baroness Hilla Rebay, and
Solomon R. Guggenheim
with a model of the
Solomon R. Guggenheim
Museum, New York, New
York, 1947.

Wright presented to his
client one of the newer
architectural forms. Such
forms contributed to the
resurgence of models dur-
ing and after World War II.

BELOW
Le Corbusier with a model
of Villa Savoie, Poissy,
France, 1935.

the design of large public and semi-public buildings,
but it is only recently that the same method has been
used either in the architect's own study of a house,
or in his presentation of the completed design to
his client."[36] By 1925 it was being said that "the
weaknesses and limitations of the usual method of
portrayal by means of rendered drawings and perspectives, are too self-evident to mention."[37]

The twentieth-century revival of models had
begun, and not only in America. Examples survive
from the pre–World War II period by architects
as varied as Gerrit Rietveld, Eric Mendelsohn,
Le Corbusier, and Frank Lloyd Wright. But cost,
and the scarcity of professional makers, continued
to restrict the wider use of models for some time,
according to one Canadian commentary from 1948:
"the cost factor, for the most part, is the villain
which heretofore has limited the use of accurate
scale models . . . In prewar times, architects received
little or no help from professional model-makers
largely because professional model-makers were
extremely few and far between."[38] In fact, World
War II gave models a boost in North America,
where "accurate models of all types were urgently
required for military purposes."[39]

But by this time another factor was having a positive impact on the model's adoption. *Pencil Points* explained,

> Particularly since the development of the newer and less familiar contemporary architectural forms has there come about a need for three-dimensional visualization through models . . . now with the freer plan solutions and the resulting combinations of asymmetrically arranged masses that go to make up our modern architecture, the model has become almost a necessity for both architect and client.[40]

A British article supported this theory in 1942:

> models are almost a necessity in the processes of present day architectural practice. The directness and simplicity of contemporary architectural expression tends to be deceptively stark, almost arid, and in the normal conventional presentation of elevation, section and plan, so much so as . . . to mislead the uninitiated . . . drawings cannot convincingly convey to clients unaccustomed to them the effects which modern architecture is designed to produce.[41]

As had been the case in the later eighteenth century, changes in architectural style were influencing the model's fortunes.

The postwar building boom contributed to an upsurge in modelmaking activity on both sides of the Atlantic. A decade or so later, British commentators would characterize the phenomenon as a "revolution" or "renaissance" in modelmaking and struggled to understand its origin. One identified the chief influencing factor as the "explosion of commercial and local authority redevelopment which erupted during the 'fifties."[42] American observers credited the change in architectural style as an equal cause, also citing the "war-born advances" in construction techniques, which had helped to reduce costs.[43] British critics agreed that "the revival in the use of models during recent years is undoubtedly related to the revival in the importance of form in

Richard Rogers Partnership (U.K.). Tribunal de Grande Instance, Bordeaux, France, 1992–98. Model, styrene, acrylic, and Rohacell foam.

Models continue to play an important role in elucidating the complex, unconventional forms of modern architecture, such as those of this design-development model for the Bordeaux Law Courts.

British architecture."[44] Buildings, insisted Stanley Abercrombie in one 1978 article, with their "eccentric profiles, romantic excesses, curving surfaces and giant interior atria" were now "so extravagantly complex . . . that drawings tell almost nothing about [them]." Models had become "indispensable."[45]

There was more in store. Even the oil crisis and subsequent building slump of the 1980s failed to halt the model's by now meteoric rise: half-starved for building opportunities, architects nevertheless "[kept] their spirits up with the surrogate building experience of the finely tuned model."[46] In addition, the model was popular in this period in Russia, Australia, New Zealand, and Japan.[47] Neither has

the subsequent introduction of three-dimensional computer modeling had a significant impact on the model's use, though its long-term effect on the medium is more difficult to predict.[48]

The influences bearing on the model over time have been diverse, and this complicated picture disrupts any simple notion of a continuous pattern of use. Yet however fluctuating the constancy of architects, it is impossible to pinpoint a single period in which the model was completely abandoned.

Any analyst of the model's history must heed one general warning: the surviving evidence may not be honest. The differing verdicts reached by historians of the Victorian period serve to highlight this

Lev Vladimirovich Rudnev with a model for Moscow State University, Russia, c. 1950–52.

There has been a long and distinguished history of model use in Russia. The design for the university by Rudnev and his team received a Stalin Prize.

problem. The extant remains present a confusing picture; the story they tell is unclear. The problem of model history is a result of the model's vulnerability.

A modelmaker once described, in somewhat ironic tones, the life of a competition model. As the closing date nears, everyone's attention is centered on the model. The architect frets and hovers around the workshop. The modelmakers are intent. Everything depends on the model. On the day of judgment, in the quiet of anonymous assessment, it will be the architect's voice. When the competition is won, the architect is magnanimous. The model and its maker bask in glory. But now, slowly, the interest moves to construction. The focus on the model fades. It begins its gentle journey to oblivion.[49]

Time is not on the model's side, particularly when the model is part of design development. When that process is complete, its value to the designer, and to the client, diminishes. The larger the model, the more difficult it is to keep; the smaller, the more easily lost; the more refined, the more liable it is to damage; the more crudely made, the more likely to be discarded. (It is difficult to imagine Brunelleschi's turnip models lasting long.) Even when models remain in the architect's hands, their fate is by no means certain. Only designers particularly attached to their models, consciously dedicated to preserving them, and possessing sufficient resources to do so succeed in preserving their collection of models from past projects. The innumerable models that Hugh Hurland, master carpenter to Richard II, made for the Westminster Hall roof "occupied so much space that rooms in the King's palace had to be reserved for them."[50] Few present-day practices can hope for such options to emerge; few can afford the luxury of an archivist or a specially designated storage area. Visitors to the Hôtel des Invalides in Paris, with its historic collection, or to the model store of Richard Meier can appreciate the space that models require.

Models, too, are extraordinarily fragile and expensive to repair. There are endless stories of

Carrère & Hastings (U.S.). U.S. Capitol, Washington, D.C. Model, 1/5" scale, plaster: Emile Garet, 1904.

This plaster model was made after Meigs's metal model of the dome. The damage recorded in the photograph was probably incurred when the model (see page 151) was shipped to Spain for the 1929 International Exposition in Seville.

damage in transit. Often they are insufficiently insured, and the cost of repair can seem disproportionate to their usefulness as a project nears completion. Others expire from neglect or mishandling; the most sturdy are vulnerable. Even General Meigs's robust metal model of the U.S. Capitol dome, which stood "a yard or more high," is unlikely to have survived the treatment to which it was subjected when its moment of glory had passed. His great-granddaughter remembered:

> My mother . . . lived in the house of Gen. Meigs, her grandfather . . . [She] said the model was built of strips . . . which fitted tightly together. She remembered how she & her sister & 3 brothers used to play with the model in the backyard. It was great fun, she said, when you kicked the model at exactly the right place, & then the dome collapsed into all its separate pieces![51]

Like the buildings they represent, models can fall on hard times when their initial purpose is obsolete. And when, like buildings, they are appropriated for reuse, the change in function takes its toll. Hawksmoor's model of the Radcliffe Camera was reincarnated as a dollhouse after its value for the project was past. It was later retrieved from this role in "battered" condition—gentle treatment compared to the fate of many models, since the vast majority,

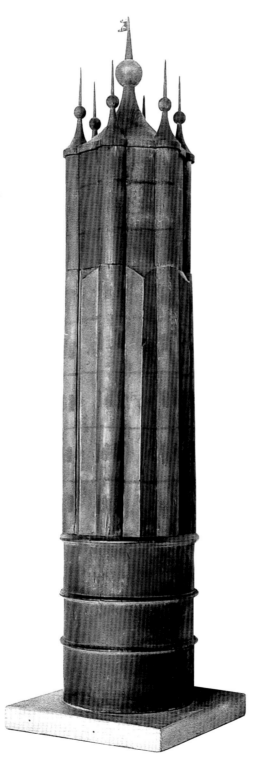

Wooden model for the Luginsland Tower, 1515, from the collection of the Augsburg City Museum.

at all levels of finish and cost, simply disappear, are cannibalized, or destroyed.[52] Some obsolete buildings have their materials pillaged for use in other structures; in the same way, models can suffer. The great 1930s model of Sir Edwin Lutyens's design for Liverpool Cathedral (see page 94) was partly broken up for wartime firewood.[53] Most of the huge number of models made by the office of Cesar Pelli perish ignominiously. "We once figured a while ago," he says, "that we build an average of about six hundred models per project of all kinds. Many of those models last only a few minutes or an hour. I look at them, I change them, I cut them apart, or if we make ten variations or something, I choose one, and we throw the other nine away."[54] These sad facts of model life distort our understanding of its history.

In what circumstances do models endure? Collections have sometimes been accumulated for particular reasons. One of the earliest assemblies, mainly from the sixteenth century, is found in the Augsburg City Museum, a result of the forward-looking policy of the city authorities during that period. Architects were required to submit models when new work was done, and these were retained by the authorities. Sometimes large architectural projects, which develop over many years or centuries, amass significant collections in crypts and attics. Among these are St. Paul's in London, St. Peter's in Rome, and Barcelona's Sagrada Familia. A small number of individual collectors, like Sir John Soane, were motivated by educational objectives but also collected for pleasure; interestingly, Soane's collection combined his own models with historic examples. Other model collections of different types have been gathered. Schools of architecture, especially during the nineteenth century, assembled large groups of models, mostly replicas of famous buildings and their details, for teaching purposes. Eighteenth- and nineteenth-century Grand Tourists collected replicas of their favorite buildings as souvenirs, in the same way contemporary travelers collect T-shirts. (Today's architects still number

Antoni Gaudí (Spain). Church of Colonia Güell, Barcelona, Spain, 1898/1908–15. Model, 1898–1908.

The architect's celebrated twenty-by-thirteen-foot "hanging" or catenary model (at 1:10), made from strings and weighted sacks, survives only in photographs, though a carefully researched replica was made in 1982–83.

among compulsive model collectors, whether collections of their own models, like Richard Meier's, or of antique examples, like those of Washington, D.C., architect Leo Daly.) More commonly, the survival of models is haphazard: they linger longest in places untouched by time—forgotten storerooms, churches, the distant, undisturbed corners of public buildings, and country retreats.

Other kinds of evidence fill out the historical picture. Information may be held in building records, which sometimes refer to the payment of model-makers or the cost of the materials used. Models are also mentioned in texts or recorded in photographs. While the survivors seem like a motley crew, they are not a random sample: the evidence is skewed. Study models in particular are habitually discarded, despite the key information they might hold. Frequently made from nondurable materials, and without the attraction of polished surfaces and refinements of craft, they have been valued less, at least until recently. Ultimately, the predominance of finished models among those that remain is unrepresentative; all that is certain is that the model's full story will never be known.

CHAPTER 3

A Question of Scale

The choice of scale is a significant decision. According to Scot Walls, of the practice NBBJ, it is the first thing a modelmaker must consider when designing a model: "It's the first big issue—there's a wrong scale, there's a right scale, there's a balance. And there are a lot of outside influences that determine the scale, and that you don't really *want* to determine the scale, but that's one of the issues."[1] Here are just some of the questions the maker must ask:

Will the model be easy to transport? An elaborate wooden model made in 1599–1600 for the architect Giacomo della Porta had to be sent by boat from Rome to Florence to be viewed by the client, Grand Duke Ferdinando I de' Medici.[2]

Will it fit through the door? Until 2000, models made in the small upstairs workshop of A Models, in Clerkenwell, London, could not exceed thirty-six inches in one, or seventy-eight in any other, dimension if they were to be conveyed beyond the workshop walls.

Can we see the spaces within? Antonio da Sangallo's model of St. Peter's in Rome weighs about six tons, is more than twenty-four feet long, and is big enough for four people to sit inside.[3]

Can we judge the suitability of the proposal in relation to its site? Foster and Partners' 1:5000 model of Stansted Airport includes representation of the motorway link two miles away.

Different scales enable the model to fulfill a variety of functions. Most typically, the model is reduced in scale from the size of the envisioned building, which facilitates the assessment of overall

massing and provides visual access to otherwise out-of-reach parts. Yet while a reduction of scale can assist analysis and open avenues of exploration, it can also close doors. Reducing the scale impedes access to the interior and may cause apparent distortion by presenting an impossible viewpoint. And it can have other, stranger effects on the viewer's psyche, arousing associations otherwise unsought.

A separate decision on scale must be made for every model constructed. Particular scales have their

Architects in the office of Foster and Partners with a model of the Nîmes master plan, Avenue Jean Jaurès, France, 1990.

Many models portray relatively large geographical areas surrounding the project site. Foster and Partners' 1:2000 model was made to study the road links and to explain the design strategy to the client, with potential later use in public consultation.

OPPOSITE
Richard Meier with a model of the Getty Center, Los Angeles, California, 1994.

This huge wooden model, made at a scale of 1/4" to the foot (or 1:50) and measuring 37 feet 6 inches by 21 feet by 5 feet 6 inches, is comprised of seventeen separate pieces. It was produced for coordinating and finalizing the construction documents; for site study; and for presentation. Viewers can "walk into" unbuilt areas to study different vistas.

own advantages in relation to specific projects. Emile Garet, a French modelmaker working in Washington, D.C., at the beginning of the twentieth century, recommended ¼″ scale (one-quarter inch to the foot, or 1:50) for his model of the U.S. Capitol "so that the new working drawing may correspond. Also to show off to better advantage. The carved details will then show perfectly."[4] The choice of scale influences the model's impact, the amount of detail that can be shown, and the question of whether such things as the texture of materials can be appreciated. In the past, when drawings were meticulously inscribed by hand, as Garet's comment indicates, the availability of existing drawings in a suitable scale was a relevant consideration.

The type of project is another significant factor contributing to the choice of scale. While Garet may have found ¼″ scale the most serviceable for a building of the magnitude of the U.S. Capitol, it might be inappropriate for a building of more modest proportions—evidently the case with a model illustrated in *Architectural Forum* in 1919, for which the same scale was deemed unsuitable:

The scale at which the model is to be made is very important. If the scale is large, one-half inch, for instance, the details are easy to cut and handle, though their size and increased number greatly increase the cost. If the scale is small, say one-eighth inch, most of the details can be left out. But in between is dangerous ground, for the details must be shown and are yet so small that they are difficult to work with, taking much time to make and assemble.[5]

Some scales may seem more appropriate than others for specific building types, especially when presentation is in mind. Ross Wimer, who has been involved in a number of skyscraper projects at Skidmore, Owings & Merrill, says, "I think the scale of the model that you present has a lot to do with how the design comes off. Obviously, when you do a tower, if you do a tiny little unthreatening model, it has much less visual impact than one that's six feet tall. So we try to manipulate the scale to its best effect."[6] Even for skyscrapers, bigger is not always better. The "right" scale for a particular model is

OPPOSITE
Architect Minoru Yamasaki with his ¹⁄₁₆″-scale model of the World Trade Center, c. 1969.

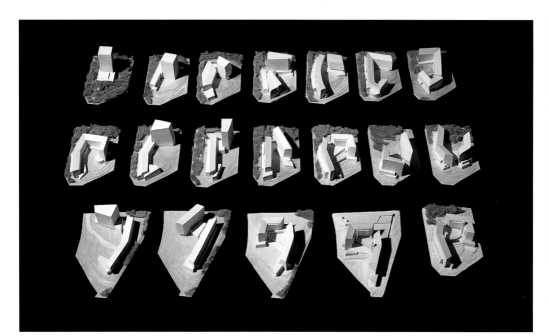

Kohn Pedersen Fox Associates (U.S.). Gannett/USA Today Corporate Headquarters, McLean, Virginia, 1997–2001. Models, 1997–98.

These development models in wood and clay were made at a small scale to examine the basic volumes of the design. They depict the progression of the design concept from a single tower (back left) to the final scheme (front right).

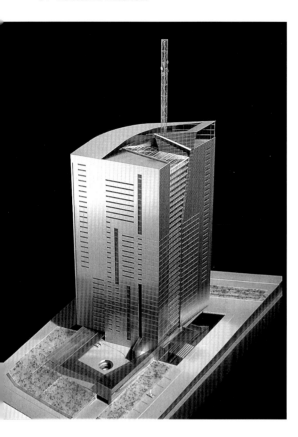

also affected by the materials chosen, the techniques available, and the tastes of the individual client. On another occasion, a quite different approach may be equally successful. Wimer continues,

> We have cut some models from the laser or we've had the pieces made out of house, etched out of metal; you can get an exquisite sort of jewel-like quality that is often much more convincing. It depends a little bit on where you're presenting it, and who you're presenting it to as well.[7]

Sometimes the choice of scale is influenced by factors beyond the specific circumstances of the project. British modelmaker Ray Pfaendler noted in the mid-1960s: "There has been a growing inevitable tendency to work to smaller scales in recent years, due to the general rise in costs and the greater complexity and size of the schemes

required."[8] Earlier in the twentieth century, models had been small in scale, becoming gradually larger in the 1940s and 1950s, after which time they began shrinking once again. One factor probably responsible for the increase in size was the change in materials from cardboard to plastics and metal. Cost is necessarily an important consideration, but its impact on the model's size is not as straightforward as Pfaendler's comment implies. A larger model uses more materials, but a smaller, detailed model can be tricky to make and may require a great deal more time to construct.

Usually the choice of scale for a model will be determined by the overall size of the project and the portion of it that is to be shown. But the scale can also be affected by the amount of information available, which relates to the stage reached in the development of the design. "Quite often," explains Ross Wimer, "the scale is limited to the amount of time we have to design it. The bigger the scale gets, the more detail you have to have, and the more you have to understand the design to make the model look convincing. So it takes a while to get up to a big scale."[9] Models made during the project's development, then, tend to get larger as the design progresses from initial concept to the resolution of finer details.

The models most often seen by today's public are the finished, presentation-style models made for the client or building committee, large enough to show some detail, yet of an easily transportable size. But models are made throughout the design process in every conceivable size and scale. The range can

Skidmore, Owings & Merrill (U.S.). Abu Dhabi Investment Authority Headquarters, United Arab Emirates. Model, 1:200, acrylic, mahogany, and acid-etched stainless steel with fluorescent and incandescent lighting, 1997.

This competition model for a skyscraper is about three feet high.

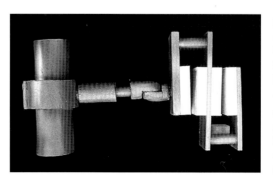

Eric Owen Moss Architects (U.S.). The Umbrella, Culver City, California, 1996–2000. Model, 1999.

The firm built a full-scale model of a glass clip to study the detailing and to facilitate review of the design by the structural engineer.

sometimes seem bewildering. The smallest models can be held in the hand, while the largest may be the same size as the building. Yet a large model can be of a single component, like a glass-panel clip, while a much smaller model may study the entire urban area surrounding a single structure.

Architects make regular use of both extremes of scale. Full-size models are often made, though they typically represent only a portion of the building. In 1922, a professor at Columbia University's School of Architecture remarked that it was "common practice to have the cornice erected in model [at full scale] and studied from the street level before the actual cornice is built."[10] At that time, as in the previous century, detail models most commonly focused on ornamental or sculptural elements and projections, like cornices and capitals, which are difficult to appreciate in drawings. These were made at full scale, during the development of a design, and might be supplemented by a reduced-scale model of perhaps ¼″ (1:50) or ⅛″ to the foot (1:100) of the entire scheme.

Precedents for this type of study are found in ancient Greece. Classical archaeologist J. J. Coulton, in *Greek Architects at Work*, concludes that reliance on full-size models is likely to have been normal building practice in the fourth century B.C.E. "Specimen" models, known as *paradeigma*, were produced in wood, stucco, or clay as guides for workmen. The practice probably went back at least as far as the sixth century B.C.E., and there is no evidence of Greek architects working at reduced scale.[11]

In the Baroque period, full-scale models were again prevalent. According to George C. Bauer's article "From Architecture to Scenography: The Full-Scale Model in the Baroque Tradition," Michelangelo was the first artist of the period for whom sculptural and architectural models at actual size can be documented. He constructed the famous wooden model for the cornice of the Farnese Palace in Rome, as noted by Vasari, and other full-scale models in stone for the Capella dell'Imperatore at

St. Peter's.[12] From the later sixteenth century on, records of full-size models become more frequent. Borromini's mid-seventeenth-century design for the lantern on the dome of Sant'Agnese in Piazza Navona was constructed in "perishable materials" and set in mortar in its intended position "so that its proportions might be judged from afar."[13] Many subsequent examples are more universal in scope. In perhaps the most celebrated instance in Italy, Bernini had a considerable portion of the colonnade of St. Peter's erected in situ at full size. Yet this was only part of his program of design development for the

Smithmeyer and Pelz (U.S.). Lamp standard similar to those in front of the Library of Congress, Washington, D.C., c. 1893–94. Model, full size: James Parrington Earley, architectural sculptor.

OPPOSITE

Raubin, Kellogg and Crane (U.S.). Department of Agriculture Building, Washington, D.C., 1905. Model: James Parrington Earley, architectural sculptor.

Full-size test pieces were not uncommon in the development of large public buildings in the early twentieth century. The row of houses in the background indicates the model's actual size.

Ceremony of the Laying of the First Stone of the New Church of Sainte-Geneviève, September 6, 1764–65. Oil on canvas: Pierre-Antoine Demachy.

The church was designed by Jacques-Germain Soufflot, and the painting shows the full-size canvas model made for the ceremony.

piazza of St. Peter's, for "insofar as it was possible, every stage of the design, from planning to the execution of details, was tried out and considered in place before being cut in stone or laid in mortar."[14] No expense was spared in the visual detailing of such operations:

> the full-scale model was carefully crafted to imitate the form and substance of the intended material. Sculptors made figures in stucco or papier-mâché; wood-carvers reproduced architectural details; and . . . painters were called upon to provide substitutes for either or both, as well as to give the models the appearance of real materials.[15]

A similar attachment to the full-size model was apparent in France. The minutes of a meeting at the French Academy of Architecture in the early eighteenth century recorded: "This society is . . . convinced that construction becomes more perfect and complies more with the salient rules of architecture the closer the models come to the project in size."[16] Like Bernini's colonnade, French examples were

often ambitious in their attempt to make a strong impression of the whole building or, failing that, a large part thereof. Pierre Lescot fabricated a full-size model of one of the pavilions in the large courtyard of the old Louvre (1546–51), François Mansart had almost the entire facade of the Chateau de Maisons (1642–51) constructed in stucco, and Jacques-Germain Soufflot had his design for the facade of Monsieur de Marigny's house of around 1769 drawn in full size on a plaster surface constructed especially for the purpose in front of the buildings to be replaced.[17] These must have been remarkable events to witness. When Soufflot, a few years earlier, had constructed a representation of the Sainte-Geneviève Church facade on canvas screens (if we are to believe the painting of the occasion by Pierre-Antoine Demachy), several townsfolk imperiled their lives by mounting the nearby rooftops to view the spectacle— an object of wonder for all, at the same time both real and illusory.[18]

It is not easy to determine why this ambitious approach faltered in the nineteenth century, when the full-size model began to be relegated chiefly to details. Whether it was due to cost, to the improvement in graphic forms of representation, or to the more cognitive conception of design that replaced the visual drama of the Baroque is unclear. Sir John Soane indicated the beginnings of nineteenth-century usage when, referring to the period after Wren, he noted that a "general model" of the whole building at reduced scale would commonly be made and "likewise many of all the cornices and other enrichments, of their full size."[19] This remained the normal pattern of use until the end of the first quarter of the twentieth century.[20]

In the early twentieth century, there were brief indications of a revival of the more holistic full-scale tradition. (One writer put this down to the introduction of "slabs," presumably concrete, "an excellent vehicle for cheap experimentation.")[21] Several examples of partial reconstructions have been recorded. The architects Raubin, Kellogg and Crane had a full-size model of one and a half bays of the Department of Agriculture Building erected on-site in 1905 on the Mall in Washington, D.C.; Carrère and Hastings carried out a similar operation in New York to assess the firm's design for the Public Library in 1902; and Charles McKim had a significant part of the corner of the Public Library in Boston erected at full scale as an on-site model.[22] In Devon, England, around 1916, Sir Edwin Lutyens produced a full-scale timber mock-up at Castle Drogo in an apparently fruitless attempt to persuade his client to approve a range of additional buildings; in 1912, Mies van der Rohe had another constructed, of the Kröller-Müller House in Wassenaar, the Netherlands, of canvas stretched over a wooden frame.[23]

An impressionistic, pictorial approach to the portrayal of buildings at full-size is apparent in some of these early examples, especially those in France, where at times the objects produced were closer to large-size canvas paintings than to three-dimensional models as such. From the second half of the twentieth century on, large-scale models have increasingly

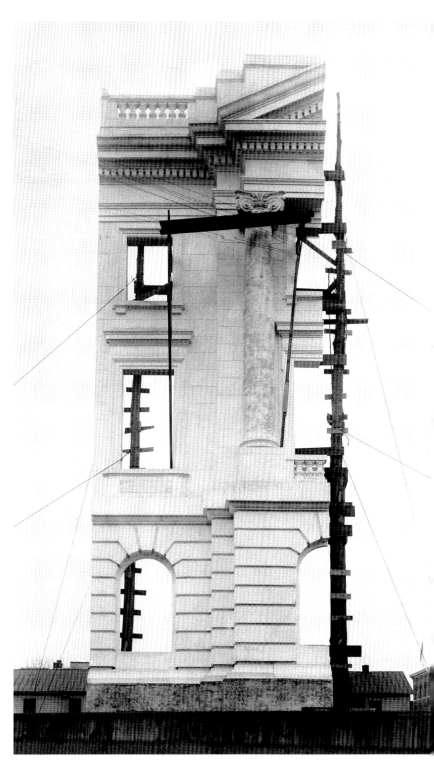

Eero Saarinen testing his
design for the stairway to
the St. Louis Gateway
Arch on a full-size model,
c. 1958–59.

been used with differing intentions. As might be
expected of a modern architectural approach, there
is more concern with formal arrangement and massing, as well as the effects on these of light, and with
a return to the earlier practice of testing structural
elements of the design. Eero Saarinen employed
models to test a range of issues. In one case, he constructed a portion of the facade of his John Deere
Building, largely of wood, to assess the articulation
of the design (see page 69). In another, he fabricated
a plywood replica of the access stairway to the St.
Louis Gateway Arch to see if the lengthening of

each successive step would pose a problem for
walking.[24] Foster and Partners performed a similar
exercise to test a step ramp for the 1997–2000
Daewoo Electronics Headquarters. Other full-scale
mock-ups by Foster and Partners have included the
handrail design for the Millennium Bridge and the
concrete panel system, seating, and signage for the
Bilbao Metro. Eric Owen Moss created a full-size
mock-up to test his idea for an irregularly shaped
roof section in his Umbrella project in Culver City,
California. Full-size models of complete buildings
have occasionally been made in recent years, though

rarely, and not often in much detail. I. M. Pei's model for the extension to the Louvre was sketched out in situ with a simple metal frame.

Many contemporary practices draw a distinction between full-size "models," which simulate the design, and "mock-ups," which are constructed with actual building materials. The latter can be visual in intent, but more often are for analysis of particular functional considerations. Mock-ups of one kind or another are used for almost all the projects at Gehry Partners. For the 1990–93 Weisman Art Museum at the University of Minnesota, the firm built part of the gallery in a Los Angeles warehouse, complete with artworks and lighting fixtures, to check illumination levels. Full-size fragments of the interiors were constructed on the university campus to investigate the effect of lighting shifts caused by changing weather, seasons, and times of day.[25] However, the most simple and regularly occurring example of the use of full-scale mock-ups by the firm involves the construction of walls: a particularly complicated wall section may be built to

test component fabrication and overall construction methods and materials.[26]

From the twentieth century on, since the emergence of the Modern Movement and the growing acceptance of Adolf Loos's dictum "ornament is crime," model studies of ornamental elements have become less necessary. But intriguingly, the venerable tradition of full-size detail models has been modified. To some extent, the ornamental function has been replaced by the deliberate exposure of structural and service assemblies. Such models are now used instead in the visual resolution of, for instance, a girder support.

Many architects today make models of their buildings and parts of their buildings that are large in scale but less than full size, like the half-size model Steven Holl had made for the Helsinki Museum of Contemporary Art, both to win over engineers and to "demonstrate the quality of light and the economy of surfaces and textures."[27] Both Sir Norman Foster and Frank Gehry (the latter claims to "think in full-scale much earlier than most architects")

I. M. Pei with a diagrammatic model of the Louvre extension made from cables, c. 1982.

The architect had difficulty winning the confidence of the French people with his unusual proposal for a glass pyramid for the Louvre until a full-size model was set up on-site.

Roomful of models made by Cesar Pelli & Associates during the development of the Crile Building at the Cleveland Clinic, Ohio, c. 1981.

make studies in a range of larger scales—1:2, 1:5, 1:10, 1:20—according to their need.[28]

While large-scale models are helpful for design purposes, and continue to be made, it is in fact small-scale models that are used in the greatest numbers. Usually these are made at the outset of a project—dozens of nutshell impressions are created as architects brainstorm ideas. These diminutive studies, modeled in a plastic medium like clay or plasticine, carved from blocks of foam, or built from sheets of paper or cardboard, are used for developing formal ideas, exploring massing possibilities, and investigating concept. A smaller scale facilitates rapid fabrication and broad appraisal of the project idea. Small scales are also employed for context models, in which the project building is visually related to its surrounding site. In exceptional cases enormous models at small scales have been made to explore large urban sites for a variety of purposes, architectural and other. The Panorama of New York City, a model of heroic dimensions (encompassing 9,335 square feet) built for the 1964–65 World's Fair, remains on display at the Queens Museum.[29]

Occasionally, architects produce tiny miniatures of a successful building late in the project. These may be retained by the architect like a trophy or given to the client as a gift or to a friend as a memento. Like the cork souvenir models of Greek and Roman ruins collected by eighteenth-century travelers, these miniatures have meaning beyond immediate replication. They preside on a mantelpiece or an office desk for all to see, a reminder of accomplishment. For a friend, the display confers prestige by the association it implies with the project's architect. Unlike the tourist's acquisition, however, these souvenir models are produced by the building's designer.

As a representation is reduced in scale, design details must be successively shed. First to go are door handles and the finer moldings; then the texture of materials, light fittings, railing details, and signage; and finally the larger moldings, projections, and window recesses. Rather than trivializing the resulting object, this process often reveals a fascinating distillation of the architect's own priorities. The building is instantly recognizable, despite the depletion of details and the most sparing indication

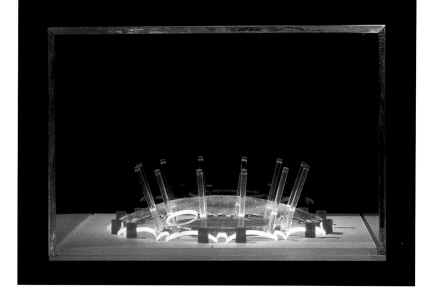

Richard Rogers Partnership (U.K.). Millennium Experience, Greenwich, London, England, 1996–99. Minimodel, Plexiglas ELiT, 1999.

The buildings in the table-centerpiece models (see also page 183) are instantly recognizable, despite the tiny size of the models.

of form. Spencer de Grey of Foster and Partners comments,

> All modelmaking, even full-size, to some extent or another is an abstraction— there is no way you can reproduce at 1:100 what the real building, the full-size construction, is going to be. So you have to read into any model. There is a sort of translation system converting an abstraction into reality.[30]

At 1:1000 (the scale of a minimodel by the Richard Rogers Partnership of its Lloyd's of London Building), it seems that the model's relationship to the building would necessarily be quite distant. Yet surprisingly, even at such small scale, a model can still represent the idea's essential force. Rogers's practice has produced a number of minimodels over the years. Mike Fairbrass, model shop manager at RRP, remembers: "We gave [the client] a little model of Strasbourg. We made pepper pots

Designers viewing the interior of the model for the Office of Metropolitan Architecture's Jussieu University Campus Libraries project in Paris, France, c. 1992.

out of the Bordeaux boardroom." The firm also created a decorative table centerpiece from a series of miniatures of its best-known projects, each set in a four-inch transparent cube. This sort of scale "shows the basic mass of the building broken down," explains Fairbrass, who remarked of the earlier Lloyd's minimodel:

> To keep it simple, yet visually complex, the makers used only Perspex and etched metal. The Perspex fills the volumes, and the etched metal represents the cladding and the way the cores stack up. I think it's purely a sculptural choice—pared down to just two materials— to show something that definitely represents the building but is very sculptural.[31]

The reduced scale of most models gives rise to a perennial problem: they are too small to enter. Too often the viewer's experience is restricted to the proposed building's external form. Only with the imagination (or a little peeping through the window) can we access the interior. This characteristic exteriority of the model—a result of its smallness—has perhaps meant that the users of buildings, who inhabit the interior, in general lose out to casual passersby. While there are other, two-dimensional, means through which the interior may be successfully studied, this difficulty with models has long been considered by architects and over time has been partly resolved.

Various stratagems have been adopted over the centuries to combat the model's reduced scale and facilitate comparable attention to the inside of a building, the most conventional being the removal of part of the model's exterior (walls or roof). This involves a process of depletion curiously reminiscent of that required in the reduction of scale—only this time large chunks of the building are discarded in succession as we move further inside. In the second half of the seventeenth century, Sir Roger Pratt recommended the following system of dismemberment: "but that the inward parts may so clearly appear to us, the sides of the model are so to be ordered, that the four corners of it remaining always firm, as to the rest they may be pulled up as occasion shall require."[32]

In some cases, with models of single interior spaces, nothing is left of the building's exterior at all. Logically, a model of the interior needs no representation of external form, a point not lost on Luigi Vanvitelli, whose model for the grand staircase for the Royal Palace of Caserta abandoned any attempt to represent the outer portions of the building.

Built for King Charles II of Bourbon and completed in 1760, the model comprises a highly detailed and realistic portrayal of an interior stairway hall, the walls of which form the model's external casing. Viewed from the outside, the model appears to be a crudely made wooden box, parts of which have been cut away and fitted with "doors" with rough exposed hinges. Great is the contrast as the doors swing open to reveal the hidden glories within.[33]

The Baroque interest in interiors encouraged a view of the model that worked from the inside out; in many models of the period, depicting the interior was clearly the principal purpose. The production of such models continues. In the mid-twentieth century, Eero Saarinen produced many models solely for the study of interiors. Some of these illustrated central supports or stairway structures with only the barest attention to detail in the walls surrounding the space.

Other devices for revealing the interior were already current in the earliest surviving architects' models of the Renaissance period. Giuliano da Sangallo's 1489–90 model of the Palazzo Strozzi was made in three detachable stories that can be lifted up to show the rooms within.[34] Michelangelo tried an alternative method, still commonly used, for the Church of San Giovanni dei Fiorentini: he represented only half the structure, slicing through the most important interior space.[35] Tommaso Guisti's elaborate model of the Clemenskirke in Hannover, constructed in 1713, "can be dismantled into twenty-four parts so that the internal wall decorations can be easily seen."[36]

When resources were available to build a model of sufficient size, the floors were made to be removable to allow the entrance of the spectator. In his Great Model of St. Paul's (see page 142), Wren removed the floor beneath the dome so that the viewer could enter and, standing waist high,

experience the dynamics of the space.[37] Further enlargement makes envisioning the interior even easier. A model created for the Versailles Opera (1761–68) appears to have been "a real 'room' in which one could stroll about."[38] A large model of St. Mary's Pro-Cathedral in Dublin, approximately ten by fourteen feet in plan, was also "large enough to enter and move about inside."[39] On smaller models, a hole cut in the floor to accommodate the viewer's head produces a similar effect. Kevin Roche, among other contemporary architects, still creates models of this type.

Franz Alois Mayr, an eighteenth-century German architect, may have been the first to make use of an optical device to avoid either disassembling or enlarging the model. By fitting a mirror into the model's floor, he enabled his client, Abbot Emmanuel II of Raitenhaslach, to view the colorful ceiling frescoes of his new Church of Mariae Himmelfahrt in a reflection through the model's door.[40]

Disegno d'un Modello non messe in Opera fatto per San Gioáni [...] de i Fiorentini in Roma la reduttione del quale e di doi palmi per oncie la longhezza et larghezza e di [...] Pal'9 [...] et l'altezza di Pal'7

Michel'Angelo Bonarota Inuentore

Iacobus Mercier Gallus fecit Romæ Año 1607.

Model for Michelangelo's San Giovanni dei Fiorentini in Rome, made by Tiberio Calcagni. Copperplate engraving: Jacques Le Mercier, 1607.

St. Mary's Pro-Cathedral, Dublin, Ireland. Wooden model: A. Rosborough, c. 1814.

The model rests on stilts so that viewers can see the model from the inside.

While the same old tricks for accessing the interior remain decidedly current (though the removal of parts is now often powered automatically), some modern approaches take different directions. Transparent materials like acrylic have made it possible to see inside the model without dispensing with exterior parts. See-through walls, ceilings, and floors can reveal selected internal features—pedestrian routes, room arrangements, structural elements, heating and cooling services, or partially decorated rooms—while maintaining in outline an image of the building's external form. The wireframe models made by Zaha Hadid and Peter Eisenman simultaneously indicate the outer form and the basic pattern of internal arrangements. Like Michelangelo's amputated sanctuary, these models retain their three-dimensionality, but at some expense: there is an exchange of accessibility for realism. Penetration or disassembly of the exterior may elucidate, but only through the acceptance of a different level of reality.

The model's normally contracted scale has other fundamental drawbacks besides restricting the interior view. However precisely the model represents the intended building, it remains a reduction, failing miserably when it comes to transmitting a sense of the building's size. Again, various methods have been adopted to counter this problem, aiming for the most part to suppress a consciousness of the model's immediate surroundings. An initial step is the placement of in-scale accessories of any type on the model (people, trees, cars). While this decor aids the imagination, these items cannot in themselves dispel awareness of the model's true size.

One simple solution has been to encourage viewing from the correct eye level, which gives an impression of the building as it would appear to a real-life spectator, bringing it into the foreground so that it dominates the field of view. *The Builder* devoted an article to this subject in 1843; the introduction of photography around this time had probably drawn architects' attention to such matters of visual perception.[41]

Eisenman Architects (U.S.). Hotel am Spree, Dreieck, Berlin, Germany. Model, 1999.

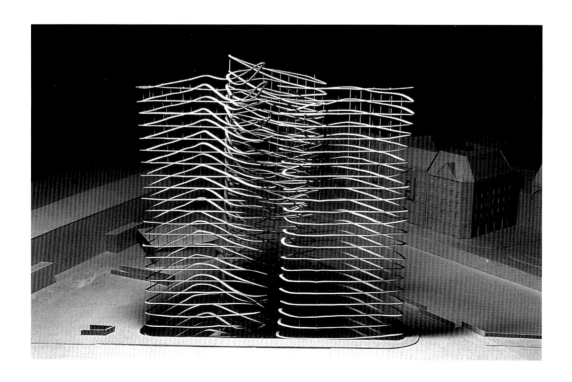

"How to Study a Model," from Edward W. Hobbs's *Pictorial House Modelling*, 1926.

Viewing a model at true eye level "corrects" its unnatural scale and makes the proposal seem real.

The path that Mayr had marked out with a mirror proved useful in countering other limitations of the model. It was pursued with new zeal as the use of models increased in the 1920s: attention was again turned toward the possibilities offered by optical devices. Viewing through a restricted opening was found to be helpful, since it limits the observer's view, and thus consciousness, of the model's surroundings. As Professor Alciphron Boring of Columbia University's School of Architecture noted in 1922, "If a completed model is observed with the eye at the correct level, particularly if viewed through a small hole in a card, the simulation of the completed building in natural size is convincing."[42] Other systems were suggested. The viewer "receives a vivid and realistic impression of the finished building," wrote Jean Hetherington (a rare female commentator of the period), again in 1922, "if he does so at a distance, through the medium of a pair of opera glasses."[43] Both these methods involve distracting the viewer's attention from surrounding full-size objects to trick the brain into losing a sense of the model's scale.

Photography of models was taken up by architects at an early stage. John Physick and Michael Darby relate in *Marble Halls: Drawings and Models for Victorian Secular Buildings*, that

> Charles Garnier used photos of a model composed of interchangeable parts to study his design for the Paris Opera in 1861, and five years later Owen Jones superimposed a photograph of a model of his competition design for the National Gallery over photographs of the site.[44]

Harvey Wiley Corbett (U.S.). Metropolitan Life North Building, New York, New York. Site model showing an unbuilt scheme, c. 1929.

OPPOSITE
Eero Saarinen and Associates (U.S.). John Deere and Company Administration Building, Moline, Illinois, 1957–63. Model, c. 1959.

The facade was modeled at full scale.

Photography of this kind, which placed the model in a convincing setting, was ideal for addressing the problems of scale, but again, it was not until the 1920s that the medium was energetically applied to this end. Early efforts were impeded by technical inadequacies: photographic lenses and equipment were insufficiently developed to cope with the combined difficulties of close-up work, inaccessible viewpoints, and the considerable depth of field presented by the model's diminutive proportions. It was sometimes necessary to resort to a pinhole in a metal plate rather than a lens in order to create a realistic view. "The camera lens fails us," complained Harvey Wiley Corbett, who nevertheless managed to create convincing images of his projects through model photography before they were built.[45]

After World War II, the application of model photography expanded. Offices using models intensively for design were among the first to take up model photography. In Eero Saarinen's office, Balthazar Korab created convincing interior and exterior images with models made by the in-house modelmaker Jim Smith.[46]

The Modelscope—basically a tube fitted to a camera at one end, with an angled mirror at the other—was invented around this time. It worked like a periscope, increasing accessibility to the model's interior and making possible eye-level views from most points of the model's surface. Now "the false viewpoint and irrelevant pleasure that [come] from miniature replicas" could be minimized, as British modelmaker Ray Pfaendler remarked in 1966.[47] Soon after, a similar adaptation of film and video cameras, known as the "snorkel camera," would provide the additional advantage of movement.[48]

A real-life, correct-scale context for the model, without photography, is also useful in this respect. Some measure of success can be achieved by standing the model in front of a painted landscape or photographic enlargement. But the incorporation of a landscape within the model photograph is much more effective, and this is possible in the technique of photomontage. Model shots, cut and pasted into site photographs (as tested by Owen Jones), counterfeit reality and disguise the model's nature as an object of reduced scale. So effortlessly and successfully does photomontage achieve these ends that it has become one of the principal modern solutions to the problems of both exteriority and miniaturization. While older methods remain in use, new means to deal with these drawbacks are now rarely sought. But again there is a trade-off, this time between images of reality and objects of three-dimensionality.

The realism of the photograph—as indeed of the model—is heavily dependent on the accuracy of the model's scale. The slightest error of proportion can be devastating to an otherwise persuasive image. Our sensitivity to scale is acute. Out-of-scale

figures, furniture, or roof tiles belong to the child's dollhouse or toy, which allow for a more casual attention to such detail. For the model, though, they will not do—or it may also become an object of amusement.

An investigation of this innate sensitivity to scale uncovers a fascinating layer of the unconscious. It is a quest in which the dollhouse, that object strongly favored by architects, is again encountered. Our sensitivity to scale is instilled throughout the years of childhood, when most things within our experience are either too big (knives and forks, the heights of chair seats, door handles, or windows) or unnaturally small (toys that are miniature replicas of adult effects). Our relationship with these objects continuously changes as we grow. Some authors of children's books cleverly employ the child's confusion to enter his or her world. In a series of encounters in *Alice's Adventures in Wonderland*, Alice longs to change her physical scale to gain control in an unfamiliar environment: one minute she is too big to go through the door into the garden, and in another she has grown too small to reach its key, left on the tabletop. Later, in the White Rabbit's house, a sudden and disorienting increase in her size imprisons and threatens her. An obsession with scale runs throughout children's literature, from traditional stories of giants, like *Jack and the Beanstalk*, to the adventures of Omri in *The Indian in the Cupboard* and to the characters of the more contemporary *Toy Story*. In Beatrix Potter's *Tale of Two Bad Mice*, the mice in question are delighted to discover the children's dollhouse to be in perfect scale with themselves ("All *so* convenient," they cry), though the "real" incumbents—the dolls—still see them as intruders.[49]

Indeed, so attentive are we to the minutest details of scale that deliberate enlargements or inaccuracies of proportion throw us off guard and appear instinctively diverting. But the reduction of large objects to manageable proportions most commonly provokes what Pfaendler termed the "irrelevant pleasure" of scale, and again, the child-

hood experience informs the adult response. That which was once beyond us can be grasped, comprehended, possessed, controlled—at last (apparently) understood.[50] The miniature battlefield figures of children's armies promise an opportunity for dominion, the desire every childish frustration prompts. Battlefields and model railways have traditionally been the male counterparts of the dollhouse generally preferred by girls, and neither loses its charm for the adult. One industry analyst quotes the proprietor of an American model railway business (which, typically, "has no clients that are women"), "Guys want their trains. They can go into their train rooms and close the door, and the world is under their control. It is now predominantly an adult's hobby, a fact the industry is recognizing."[51]

The often alarming character of the juvenile experience of scale (large and threatening dogs or adults, or even foreign and formidable rooms) and the associated feelings of vulnerability can apparently be forgotten by the adult. Yet most adults retain the child's delight in the miniature. Because of their reduced size, miniatures attract, hold memories, and invite play. The model's diminution of buildings—though in reality they come in ever larger and more awe-inspiring sizes—has a similar effect. Reduced to the dimensions of a dollhouse, the building loses the power to overwhelm. It captivates, just like a dollhouse, because of the satisfyingly perfect and complete world it presents the viewer: a world that allows absolute manipulation and control of an environment closely parallel to life.

Few who write about architectural models have failed to mention this mysterious appeal. Architects' models, after all, are miniatures and have been favorites at shows and expositions for centuries. In the early nineteenth century, Du Bourg's in London was among many popular establishments that put on shows featuring models, including miniature replicas of architectural (and other) forms "with every decay of time and tint of colour as the Originals, with greatest nicety."[52] A large plaster model of the U.S.

Capitol, built during development of the project under the superintendence of Elliott Woods in 1904, was in perpetual demand for exhibits and traveled extensively. By 1956, it had appeared at the 1904 Louisiana Purchase Exposition in St. Louis, the 1915 Panama-Pacific International Exposition in San Francisco, the 1926 Sesquicentennial Exposition in Philadelphia, the 1929 International Exposition in Seville, and the 1937 Great Lakes Exposition in Cleveland.[53] Similarly, the magnificent model of the Cathedral of St. John the Divine (see page 112), built for architects Cram and Ferguson, was requested for the 1939 New York World's Fair, where other spectacular models—Consolidated Edison's City of Light diorama and the Panorama of New York

City—would compete for attention.[54] Mies van der Rohe's model of the Seagram Building was exhibited at the Brussels World's Fair in 1958 and the Paris Cultural Centre in 1959.[55] Model exhibits of all sorts are equally enjoyed today.

In the architectural sphere, the charm of models has not gone unnoticed. As they began to appear with more frequency in the exhibits of the Architectural League of New York around 1914, one critic noted, "it is significant of the interest they create that visitors tarry longer in their examination of models than in the other architectural exhibits."[56] C. N. Godfrey of Cram and Ferguson complained bitterly of this magnetism and its physical effects on his model to the cathedral authorities on the

Alice trapped in the White Rabbit's house, illustration by Sir John Tenniel from Lewis Carroll's *Alice's Adventures in Wonderland*, c. 1865.

Scale is the stuff of dreams and nightmares. Carroll probes our mysterious sensitivity to scale in his celebrated children's story.

City of Light, Consolidated Edison's exhibit at the 1939 New York World's Fair in Flushing Meadow, receiving its finishing touches.

occasion of its celebrated display at Grand Central Station in 1934. Spectators, he claimed, had

> broken off small sections of the model of the cathedral; in fact, there are indications that souvenirs of various kinds, even sections of the masonry, interest the visitors. You doubtless are aware that the small human figures that were placed around the cathedral model to give it scale, were taken off in the first few days of the exhibition, but now they have begun to break off sections, especially in the more elaborate detail of the West Front.[57]

The most recent example of miniature mania occurred in the 1970s and 1980s. Modelmaking and -collecting as a hobby experienced a huge rise in popularity, with a "so-called miniatures industry" developing, represented by more than four thousand retail shops specializing in dollhouses and miniatures and thirty thousand subscribers to America's *Nutshell News* ("for the hard-core miniaturist") by 1989.[58] The craze for model railways, which accelerated after World War II, still attracts 350,000 followers, who spend $400 million annually in the United States alone.[59]

Models, like miniatures, intrigue. Part of their mystery is the element of craftsmanship: how is such miniaturization possible, and how is it achieved? An important attraction at a 1789 exhibition of a model of the city of Bath was the sight of craftsmen working on unfinished parts.[60] No doubt some of the visitors rushed home to experiment themselves: in the eighteenth century the making of model buildings was a favorite hobby of the idle rich, "the male equivalent of netting purses or embroidering firescreens," explains Helen Buttery. "Booklets of instruction were even published for enthusiasts, giving tips on techniques."[61]

There is also the experiential aspect. The miniature is an object of wonder, but even more so if it comes apart. Such revelations enchant the child, especially the indefatigable juvenile scientist eager for discovery or (even better) dissection. This is not

a passion that abates with maturity. The drama of pushing a button and seeing a model open holds continual fascination.

Monique Mosser, in her article "Models of French Architecture in the Age of Enlightenment," refers to the "symbolic—relatively magic— implications of the reducing process": "It creates, as it were, a concentrated picture, the quintessence of the monument in a small format."[62] This is the power that the model, tightly embraced (both literally and metaphorically) by Philip Johnson, holds. It safeguards memories. Its significance is more than the sum of its parts. "The innate power of the reduced model," as Claude Lévi-Strauss has explained, "lies in the way it makes up for a lack of sensual dimensions by an increase in intellectual dimensions."[63]

The full-size model may be of great practical service, but it holds less charm. When portraying an entire building, it may amaze, but its presence is remote from any sense of possession: it is not held within us. Reducing the scale has the unaccountable effect of concentrating and intensifying the model's significance. By the same count, it also increases its value. "Jewel-like" is a term commonly applied to models of fine craftsmanship and miniature elegance, and it is not an idle choice of word. Behind the secret, glinting surfaces of precious stones lie concealed ambitions and the memory of primeval desire. The jewel, like the model, holds value disproportionate to its size. Considerable amounts of money are spent on both—the Great Model of St. Paul's, for instance, cost as much as a three-story house.[64] Sir Roger Pratt admitted "the charge [to] be great which is expended about [them]" and thought it worthwhile:

> Nor ought we at all to wonder at it, for that the model being often well considered and examined as it ought, it will not only prevent all future alteration in the building, a thing of most vast expense, but will likewise avoid all complaint of the master, and abuse of the

Illustration from Johann Friedrich Penther's *Einer Ausführlichen Anleitung zur bürgerlichen Bau- Kunst*, Augsburg, 1746.

contriver, being that this will ever remain a justification of the invention of the one, and a most plain conviction of the consent of the other.[65]

Today, models can cost hundreds of thousands of dollars, but the additional "intellectual" value has never been easy to tally. After all, a peep at the staircase model of Caserta filled King Charles II with an emotion "fit to tear his heart from his breast."[66] For architects, working familiarly with models day by day, the model's evocations are less than conscious. Yet the fascination with scale is difficult to relinquish, as Hani Rashid of Asymptote suggests:

> What's happened now is that, in our built work, we are trying to build things that actually have the ambiguity of scale that the model had; whereas at the beginning I used to think modeling was putting people in at a certain scale, what I'm beginning to realize is that it's the scalelessness of the model, at any scale, that's so compelling, architecturally or artifactually. And now we get to building the real thing. It's very powerful if you can maintain that kind of ambiguity. You could almost say that in our practice we're trying now to build full-scale models.[67]

Asymptote (U.S.).
Yokohama International
Passenger Ship Terminal,
Japan, 1994.

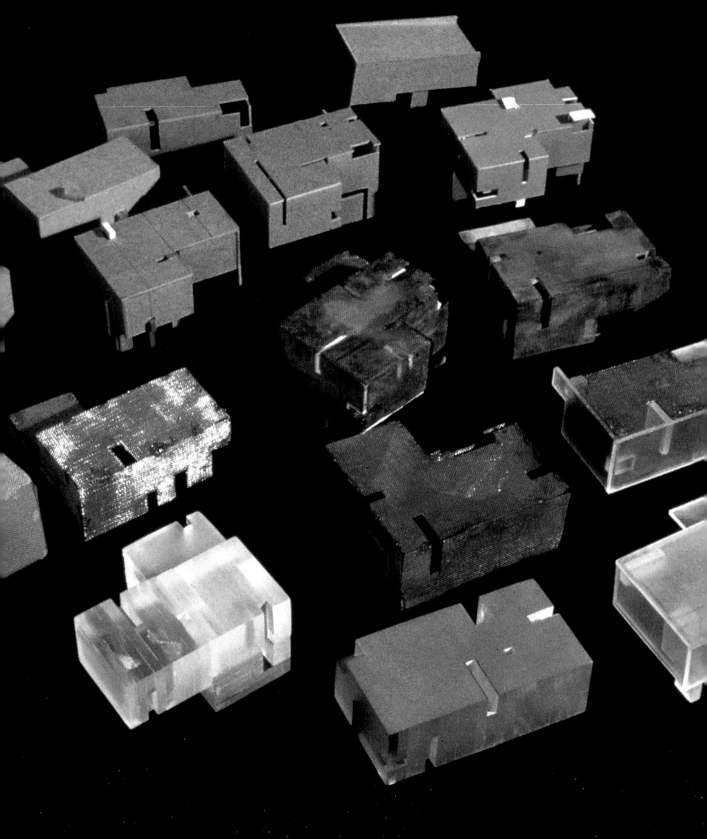

CHAPTER 4

Vision

The connection between the artifact and the imagination has grown since the beginning of the twentieth century. Models have become more intimately integrated into the activity of design. Additionally, the trend toward abstraction has positioned the model at an increasingly elemental level in the creation of architecture, allowing it to convey the architect's underlying vision in all its primal power. It is the study, or process, model, created during design development (often, but not always, in-house), in which these characteristics of the contemporary model are most obvious, and to which the architect's imagination is so closely bound.

The process model is now such a familiar feature of architectural practice that it is difficult to imagine it has ever been otherwise, though of course it has been. Design-development models, which came to renewed prominence during the twentieth century, are now employed more widely, and produced in larger numbers, than in any previous period. Many of the most celebrated architects of the last hundred years relied on models for design development. Antoni Gaudí worked constantly with models, developing both formal and structural concerns in model form. Mies van der Rohe's model workshop took up a quarter of his office.[1] Eero Saarinen studied his TWA Terminal from every angle, through models of every conceivable scale. In recent years, architects have become even more dependent on models for design development. Today, few with an interest in architecture are unaware of the weight Frank Gehry gives to study models in his design process. Renzo Piano's workshop, too, is renowned.

Foster and Partners has a fully equipped, professionally staffed workshop in a prominent position on the office's main floor.

Before the twentieth century, the model's usefulness was not unappreciated; indeed, its ability to help clarify, analyze, and test design ideas made it invaluable. In fourteenth-century England, Hugh Hurland created "innumerable models" while designing the Westminster Hall roof, and found that making his trusses first in model form anticipated the problems of both structure and erection.[2] Texts as well as models survive from the Renaissance to underline the prominent role of process models throughout the period. Alberti devoted several pages of his Renaissance treatise to promote their use, arguing for the contemplation of the design through models over a length of time. This, he stressed, would prevent rash and foolish mistakes, which afterward would be a "source of continual grievance."[3] Sir Henry Wotton, writing in 1624, considered study models essential: "Let no man that intendeth to build," he warned, "setle his fancie upon a drought of the works in paper, how exactly sower measured or neatly set off in perspective; and much lesse upon a bare Plant therof, as they call the Sciographia or Ground lines; without a Modell or type of the whole structure, and every parcel and Partition in Pasteboard or Wood."[4]

Many other architects and commentators have pressed for the study model, and emphasized its importance. Sir John Soane used models to investigate such matters as the effect of alternative fenestration arrangements or unusual structural designs

Steven Holl Architects (U.S.). Sarphatistraat Offices, Amsterdam, Netherlands, 1996–99. Process models.

Sir John Soane (U.K.). Bank of England Stock Office, London, 1791–93. Model, painted wood, copper, and yellow glass: Joseph Parkins, 1793.

A design model of the Stock Office was made to assess the hall's proportions, stability, and lighting effects. Soane's approach to architecture, involving both structural and technological innovation, increased the necessity for such models.

on the lighting of his interior spaces, and argued for their wider use:

> Many of the most serious disappointments, that attend those who build, would be avoided if Models were previously made of the Edifices proposed to be raised. No building, at least none of considerable size or consequence, should be begun until a correct and detailed Model of all its parts has been made . . . wherever the Model has been dispensed with, I am afraid the building has suffered in consequence thereof, either in solidity or convenience, and perhaps in both.[5]

In 1710, the French Academy of Architecture was constrained to admit, "After considerable deliberation concerning the difficulty, indeed the occasional impossibility of hitting upon everything with drawings and doing all that is necessary for the construction of a large building, this society has reached the conclusion that for the complete realization of the project, drawings as well as models cannot be dispensed with."[6] The eighteenth-century Russian architect Vasily Ivanovich Bazhenov held:

> In order to understand how beautiful and excellent the building will really be [the architect] must inevitably imagine it in perspective; and in order to be even more convinced of it, he must make a model for it. Indeed the making of the model is considered to be half the work.[7]

The practice of using models as tools for understanding the design and working out details of construction was common from the sixteenth to the eighteenth centuries but subsequently declined. In the nineteenth century, it was the study model that suffered most, despite its proven efficacy. In

America, it was retained primarily for the study of ornament. Elsewhere its use as a design tool was also affected, as this comment in a British journal of 1942 indicates: "during the last century or so model making for practical purposes was rare. Models were not considered necessary by architects, though clients might occasionally commission them."[8]

The rough sketch model so familiar today was regarded as unusual in American architectural periodicals of the early twentieth century, which bombarded readers with articles that focused mainly on the neglected merits of models for studying the design.[9] As architects awoke to the study model's utility in office practice, schools of architecture also contributed to its reinstatement. The answer to the failure of "the French School," as the Beaux-Arts was familiarly termed, was not just the model, but the study model applied as a tool of design. Architectural instructors urged their students to visualize their conceptions in three dimensions instead of thinking of them as drawings.[10] The idea of including modelmaking in architectural training

was first mooted in 1914: "It is very desirable that all students in the architectural schools all over the country should be taught architectural miniature work in the elementary stages at least."[11]

The Columbia University School of Architecture was one of the first institutions to introduce modelmaking to the curriculum, around 1921, and thereafter models increasingly became an integral part of architectural education.[12] In America, by 1939, one journal noted that "Even the architectural schools are installing well-equipped model shops these days and including instruction in making models along with their courses in drawing as comprising an essential part of the equipment of the well-trained designer."[13]

In Britain too, observed another writer in 1942, "most schools of architecture now regard scale model making as an essential part of training."[14] This was the same period in which modelmaking in the architect's office was becoming more broadly accepted, and references to the use of study models more frequently recorded. Mies van der Rohe's

Odile Decq Benoît Cornette (France). "Hyper-Tension," installation for CNAC, Le Magasin, Grenoble, France, 1993. Model.

A rapidly produced, rough sketch model attached to a line drawing contributed to the formation of ideas during the design process.

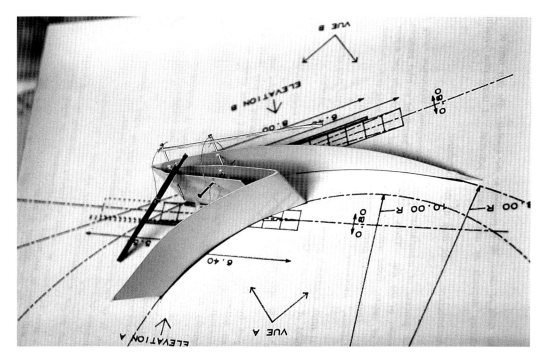

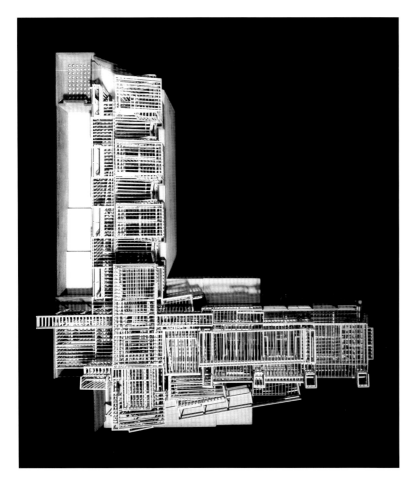

RoTo (U.S.). Teiger Residence, Bernardsville, New Jersey, 1994. Framing model.

In contrast to Odile Decq Benoît Cornette's sketch model, this carefully constructed framing model studies one aspect of the architects' design in considerable detail.

through drawings or on a computer and, when a satisfactory formulation is reached, reproduce the design in model form as a "reality check"—to ensure that it works in three dimensions. In some practices, models of this type might be made periodically to test the idea as the design progresses. However, these models are created to validate the concept rather than contribute directly to its formation in a dynamic, experiential way. They are supplemental rather than core in character.

The model's integration into the design process can be understood as a scale of involvement that moves from the passive, or contemplative, model at one end to the active, or experiential, at the other. Henry Millon noted this distinction between active and passive in his study of Renaissance usage: "The model, then, for Alberti, was . . . a means to study and realize an idea. For Brunelleschi and later for Michelangelo, on the contrary, the model was apparently the representation of an idea already formed in the mind to serve as a guide for workmen in construction."[16] At Alberti's end of the scale, models are fully integrated in the process, engaged at every point in developing the proposal and in analyzing the ideas behind the design. The model itself is the vehicle of discovery: it is instrumental in realizing and fixing those evanescent, conceptual ideas that dart about in the architect's head during the early stages of project development; it contributes to the evolution of the emerging design, stimulating ideas as the material is formed; it continues as the basis for change and development throughout the design process.

Even as models are more closely engaged in the process, a subtle distinction can still be made between direct and indirect involvement in envisioning the design. Models can be introduced with increasing frequency to check the development of ideas. They may be used to assess nonvisual aspects of the design, including acoustic qualities, wind resistance, and underlying structure. Yet until they are grasped and manipulated, their commentary remains passive. Only when the model is engaged as

practice took up models with full force from 1944 on, "model making [replacing] perspectival drawings as the dominant tool of research into space and volume."[15]

As the twentieth century progressed, the employment of models as an exploratory tool in design development became ever more widespread. Previously, when models of a full building were made, they were produced toward the end of the project for overall assessment by architect and client, or occasionally during the development of the design in a larger project. This continues to be true in practices where models play a minimal role and are not considered central to the process. Many architects today establish form and overall concept

Chermayeff, among others) was already describing the active manipulation of "sketch models . . . introduced very early into the conception of a building" and their impact on design development:

> In this way faults and weaknesses that never reveal themselves on paper become instantly apparent, and these can be rapidly studied by altering the model or by adding and taking away pieces as desired, until the best solution is found, providing true "manipulation of space." All the elements of the design, from the largest to the smallest, can be worked out in this way.[17]

In the second half of the twentieth century this experiential use of models grew stronger. A 1958 article in America's *Architectural Forum* drew attention to the crucial role of models in Eero Saarinen's design of the TWA Terminal.[18] Although such architects as Le Corbusier and Mies van der Rohe had relied on study models for their projects of the 1930s and 1940s, the intensive way Saarinen worked with

Antoine Predock working on a plasticine model for the Recreation and Physical Activity Center at Ohio State University, Columbus, en route to a project presentation, 2001.

a creative tool of expression is it fully utilized, becoming, like two-dimensional sketching, an intrinsic part of the architect's thinking about the design.

This active, exploratory use of models for the three-dimensional study of a building is characteristic of today's design process—an approach that burgeoned over the twentieth century. Physical manipulation in the nineteenth century was largely limited to the development of ornamental details and was carried out mostly by specialists (architectural sculptors), rather than by architects themselves. The twentieth century brought the manipulation of models back into the process in a way that had been little used since the Baroque era. Early instances can be seen in the 1890s, when the traditional materials of the sculptor (clay and plaster) were used in conjunction with the fluid lines of Art Nouveau, and later by the Expressionists. Gaudí, Rudolph Steiner, Herman Obrist, Hans Poelzig, and Eric Mendelsohn all worked with models of this type. But even as less malleable materials like cardboard and sheet plastic were adopted, the medium continued to be taken on more broadly as an exploratory tool. Concurrently, the International Style was beginning to dominate architectural design. In an *Architects' Journal* article of 1936, illustrating early British Modern Movement architecture, a modelmaker (whose clients included Connell, Ward and Lucas, and Mendelsohn and

Eric Mendelsohn (Germany). Einstein Tower, Potsdam, Germany, 1919–21. Plaster model.

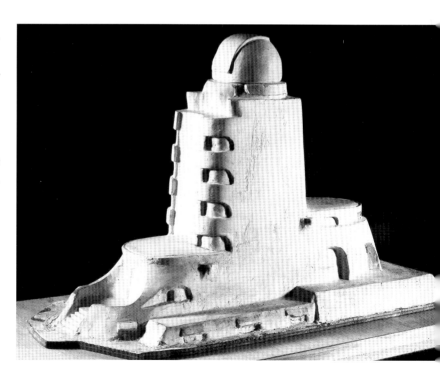

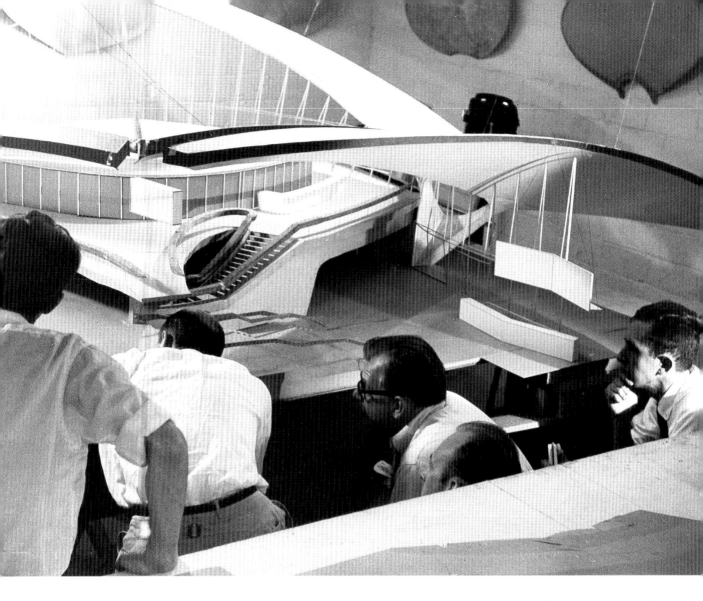

models to develop the building's complex forms and his designers' total reliance on model manipulation for some parts of the design were clearly novel. The article described how Saarinen and his team, including Kevin Roche, used models to arrive at the overall shape of the concrete shell. These early models revealed structural problems, and to find a more logical form, "scores of rough cardboard models" were subsequently made. The models became the active focus of team meetings ("models allowed the team to cut and try, test and discuss") and were at the hub of a vigorous physical dialogue ("during conferences, models were torn apart and rebuilt on the spot"). A caption more familiar to road repairs bore the warning: "Designers at Work." Throughout, the writer stressed the physicality of the process: "At one meeting . . . the idea was suggested of breaking the long axis of the roof to match the curve of the street. Codesigner Roche performed the operation directly—with a saw."[19]

By the 1970s this would have seemed a much less remarkable practice. In the opinion of some commentators, sketch models had already "largely replaced drawings as basic tools for design."[20] Several larger as well as smaller offices in Europe and America, notably Skidmore, Owings & Merrill, I. M. Pei & Partners (now Pei Cobb Freed & Partners), Perkins & Will, Foster and Partners, Arup Associates, and Philip Johnson, Architect, had by this time established substantial, well-equipped, in-house workshops where models became a vital force in resolving the design. This practice grew internationally. At the turn of the twenty-first century, the rapid fabrication of multiple sketch and study models in the manner of Saarinen is a much more pervasive practice, and current discussion of model use in the architectural press is usually initiated by a broad-based interest in process, or a noting of extremes, rather than by any surprise at the use of the medium. Frank Gehry's employment of "hundreds" of models per project merited a write-up in 1992, for example, while Perkins & Will's use of only six or seven had been enough to prompt an article in 1967.[21] Gehry's description of the part played by models in the development of his Nationale-Nederlanden Building design in Prague is now quite typical:

> I was struggling with the window breakup in the adjacent nineteenth-century buildings . . . so I thought, how can I make blurry edges so you don't realize that there are more floors? I started making the model, and I started to push the windows up and down. I pushed one up to the top of the ceiling and one down to the floor . . . I built it on the model, and the texture of it fit in, so I knew it was all right.[22]

These twentieth-century developments made clear that bringing models into architectural training, and establishing them in-house as a central medium for design development, encourages three-dimensional understanding. They have also drawn architects into a more physical involvement with resolving design problems. No longer purely a "drawing board" matter, design involves actual fabrication. The nature of

the architectural activity has subtly changed. NBBJ's office in Seattle has recently installed a model shop staffed by professionals. Its mission: to encourage the integration of models in the design process from the earliest stage. The firm is now persuaded that models actually stimulate architects to think differently. At a recent discussion between NBBJ architects and modelmakers on the influence of the model shop, one participant noted, "The more senses you can engage, the better the learning opportunity; it affects an individual's thinking process, which becomes more active. There is something significantly different about a tactile experience—you will understand things that you cannot understand just with your eyes." One of the modelmakers added,

> You take some architects and get them on a saw or sander manipulating shapes . . . It takes a period of time to manipulate a shape right, and that amount of time to reflect on what you're doing. For instance, it may be a six-sided box—they come away with just so much more understanding of that cube, and the volume it represents.

Architects working with one of the many models created by Eero Saarinen and Associates during the design of the TWA Terminal for John F. Kennedy International Airport, c. 1958, including Saarinen (with glasses), Cesar Pelli (right), and Kevin Roche (second from left).

Such models were also used by the designers as a basis for photographic studies taken to aid analysis of the proposed spaces. These studies, with the use of mirrors, smoke, and some airbrushing of the resulting prints, extended earlier photographic experiments.

Architects and modelmakers considering a model of the Millennium Tower, Tokyo, made in Foster and Partners' in-house workshop, 1990.

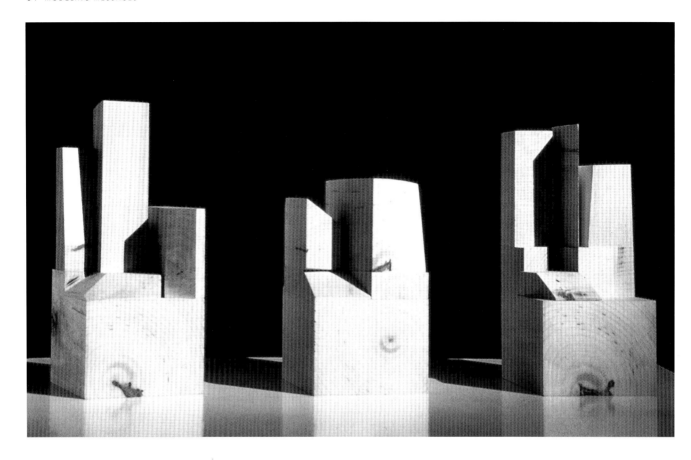

He went on to list some of the many practical factors illuminated when models replace two-dimensional sketches: "beam clearances, placement, juxtaposition, and the effect of light."[23] But above all, as another of the modelmakers explains, "these are thinking tools."[24]

Today the manipulation of materials in a more plastic way has become widespread. The contemporary activity of modelmaking includes molding materials like plasticine and clay, cutting and bending card, machine-working wood, and carving blocks of plastic foam. The twentieth century's focus on form (as opposed to the nineteenth century's focus on ornament) encouraged the need for three-dimensional exploration; a wider availability of materials suitable for office use must also have contributed. If the architect of the nineteenth cen-

tury could be characterized primarily as a draftsman, then the architect of the twentieth century might more readily be described as a sculptor.

The experiential use of models generates fascinating artifacts that emerge from the imaginative process at different points and in different forms. These models are more likely to be sketchy, yet the more essential they are to the process, the more fascinating they become as objects. The sense of excitement and inspiration, which often accompanies the architect's initial response to a project brief, is present in the earliest artifacts created. Far less constrained than later drawings or models, these embryonic objects express the architect's primary vision for a project and often record for the architect, and reveal to others, the inspirational concept, or architectural idea, in its "purest" form. As a writer in

NBBJ (U.S.). United States Federal Courthouse, Seattle, Washington, 2001–4. Small-scale wood models: Kay Compton, 1998.

American Architect noted in 1918, "Office models oftentimes are more fully imbued with the spirit of the designer and his ideal than the finished product."[25] Antoine Predock has called his earliest models and drawings "the first moves or gestures toward making the piece that becomes the building." He refers to the drawings as containing "a kind of encoding or DNA that will inform the making of a building."[26] This descriptive terminology is equally applicable to models and highlights the seminal character of such artifacts, which provide a reference point for anyone seeking to understand the nature of the building concept. These are objects of energy and imagination, which in themselves are symbols of intent, intensely meaningful to the architect. Often haphazard in construction, they reflect in their making the unrestrained but purposeful surge

of ideas. Such models can be entirely ephemeral: hung together with tape, pulled apart, remade, discarded—intimately tracking the process of thought. Or they can be fabricated more solidly and produced in series, each representing a finite stage in the development of the idea, moments frozen in time.

Models are introduced into the design process at various stages. Working with models first, before using other media, is not the most conventional practice, yet it comes naturally to those with a history of contact with materials and making things by hand. Hani Rashid grew up in a climate of craft activity based in the traditions of modern art. His father was a sculptor, ceramist, and painter. While he was at architecture school as an undergraduate, his model-centered process was viewed as unorthodox: "I remember driving my teachers crazy because

Coop Himmelb(l)au (Austria). Groninger Museum, East Pavilion, Groningen, Netherlands, 1993–94. Model.

This sketch model, held together with pins and created through the layering of two- and three-dimensional studies, was central to the project's development. The architects "attempted to capture the random liveliness of this sketch model and translate its sculptural details to the scale of the actual building."

I would always start my projects with a model, before I put pen to paper," he recalls. "They'd say, well, you haven't designed the building yet, or you haven't done a sketch, or you haven't done an analysis, or you don't know which way the windows face the sun." But because of his father and the way he was brought up, he explains, "I just had this attitude first and foremost toward the project, to form it in a three-dimensional way, and then begin to structure it as drawings."[27]

Others with a sculptural background have shared this outlook. Antoni Gaudí, for instance, plunged directly into physical models before he made designs on paper, filling his studios with an assortment of rapidly worked plaster sketches.[28] Yet however much some architects—Frank Gehry, for one—may insist that they find using models faster than drawing, the comparative convenience and accessibility of drawing (the back-of-an-envelope sketch at the dinner table, for instance) cannot be denied.[29] As a result, while some architects do experiment directly in model form, it is more common for the model to follow an initial sketch. The two-dimensional moment can be fleeting.

"We're very up front," declares Ivan Harbour of Richard Rogers Partnership in London. "After an initial scribble, the next thing the model is made. It's on the second day. It's a reflection of how we work. It's easier to look at a model to describe something than anything else."[30] Wolf Prix and Helmut Swiczinsky at Coop Himmelb(l)au in Austria also begin with a drawing, their "first emotional imprint," to initiate a process that quickly moves to models, then oscillates between drawings, models, and digitized model images.[31]

Another form of information transferal, typically two-dimensional, is yet more necessary when an architect depends largely on others to build the model. Frank Gehry experiments with rapidly executed line drawings, while simple blocks representing the program components are tried out by his team. As the process moves forward, the first expressive models of the exterior forms are based on these sketches.

A more unusual two-dimensional manner of conception characterizes the design method of both Zaha Hadid and Will Alsop. These two architects develop their ideas in semiabstract paintings and

Coop Himmelb(l)au (Austria). Rooftop remodeling, Falkestrasse, Vienna, Austria, 1983/1987–88. Model with superimposed drawing.

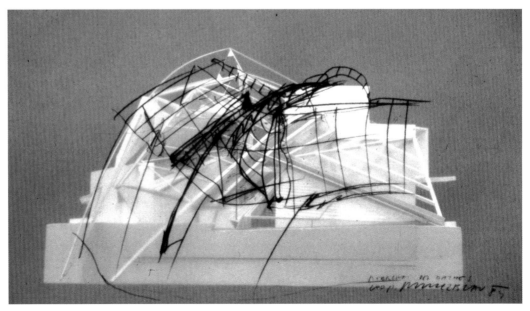

Alsop Architects (U.K.).
Blackfriars Station,
Thameslink rail service,
London, England, 2000.
Model: Unit 22.

The model was developed
through an alternating
series of color drawings
and physical models.

sketches, alongside studies of three-dimensional
form (see pages 11 and 16). Will Alsop's paintings
often precede and become a basis for the models.
Curiously, this idiosyncratic process can be seen by
participants as "quite straightforward," as Jonathan
Leah, associate director at Alsop Architects, explains:

> Will's approach is to do paintings, and then
> we try to take the painting straight into the
> model . . . The paintings suggest certain
> shapes and forms, and you can then go into
> the model shop and carve those . . . We have
> to make the leap between the painting and the
> model. The important thing about this is that
> when Will paints, he discovers new things,
> and when we make the models, other oppor-
> tunities are discovered. The process remains
> fluid and open to new interpretations.[32]

Some architects begin with diagrammatic for-
mulations of the project idea. Steven Holl creates
"concept diagrams" based on an "initial intuition"
that is more conceptual than visual. These inform
the making of a series of models, drawings, and
watercolor renderings, each continuing the development of the idea according to the qualities of the
medium. Here Holl describes part of the process
of design for his Museum of Contemporary Art
in Helsinki:

> From the beginning of the design process,
> the museum contained a perspectival series of
> spaces which are separate rooms connected
> through an unfolding perspective. We made
> plaster models to study this further, because
> the nature of the concept was volumetric
> rather than linear. So the process went from

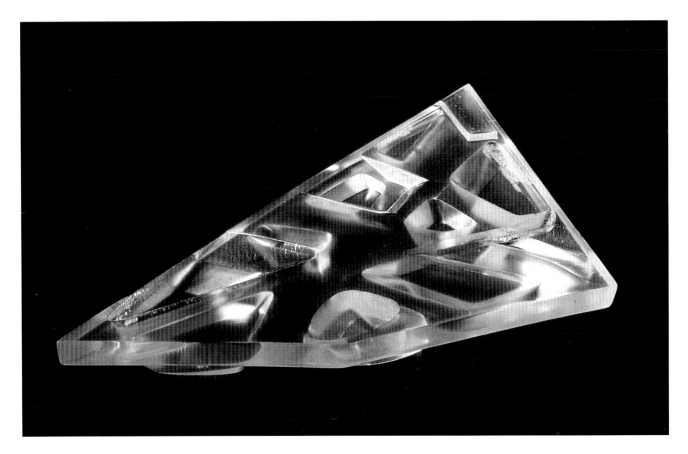

Zaha Hadid Architects
(U.K.). Science Center
Wolfsburg, Germany,
2000– . Acrylic block
model.

OPPOSITE
Foster and Partners
(U.K.). Carré d'Art,
Nîmes, France, 1984–93.
Models, foam, resin,
and acrylics, 1985.

Steven Holl Architects (U.S.). Simmons Hall, Massachusetts Institute of Technology, Cambridge, 1999–2003. Model, 1999.

This early study model of a student residence hall, built from sponge-printed layers, is suggestive of a watercolor rendering, one of the architect's favored two-dimensional forms of exploration.

those plaster models, where the conceptual strategy is vaguely set, to the development of all the internal aspects. I then drew water-color perspective drawings which I always do before the plan is set. Very often we build models based on these drawings and then try to make plans for the perspectival condition to take precedence over the plan."[33]

In most cases where architects begin with models, their use is continued throughout project development. The approach adopted can vary. Michael Sorkin explores formal relationships and solutions in an activity close to sculpture (see page 100). For him, the physical model is an essential medium of design. "There's no substitute," he insists, "for seeing the whole three dimensions as part of the working process. I know of no other representation that is as satisfying or comprehensible."[34]

For a broad spectrum of architects, modeling is a fundamental technique in the search for form. Kohn Pedersen Fox Associates' approach to a slab of clay parallels Michelangelo's to a block of marble. "Sculpting with clay," as John Koga explains, "particularly for skyscrapers, [is the] perfect medium for expressing the building's massing. It's inherently a subtractive rather than an additive process, i.e., you start with the neutral block and find the form within.

Multiple forms of a skyscraper can be found within the block."[35] Gehry Partners has developed an expressive and intuitive process in which models are continually modified by twisting and shaping card and by adding and removing balls of crinkled paper (see page 169).

Such formal searches can be driven by a number of preoccupations. The concern may be mainly visual, as in Koga's description, motivated by a desire to create a dynamic external or internal form. Alternatively, it may be more cognitive, involving the analysis of an abstract theoretical idea. Peter Eisenman's models are linked to preconceived mathematical and geometrical hypotheses; these are studied through a long series of exploratory models, which, in Luca Galofaro's words, "constitute the office's design system."[36] "I know what I'm trying to achieve theoretically," explains Eisenman, "and the models tell me whether or not I am getting there."[37]

Then again, the search for form may be program-driven, that is, dominated by the details of the building's usage as dictated in the project brief. Cesar Pelli outlines this course of action:

We start all projects by building a site model, with the right topography and with its adjacent structures, and then I start thinking about the design on the basis of the site models, by putting my building on the site. I start by just putting a couple of boxes that represent the correct volume, because I cannot think of form until I have an idea of the impact that the volume required by the program has on the site. Then the forms develop, and I start to study spaces, and relationships of forms.[38]

These various approaches are not necessarily separated in practice. Hani Rashid explains how they can interlink in the work of Asymptote, the firm he founded with Lise Ann Couture. "The formal strategies that we employ in the design process are not autonomous from other aspects of the architectural projects," he says. "Rather, the process of generating form cannot be seen as separate from the process of generating programs or responses to other, contextual issues."[39] In reality most models have multiple ends, weighted according to the architect's purpose. For instance, Predock uses cutout cardboard shapes to represent different parts

of the functional program. He then tests these against his clay forms, as he shapes and assembles them, to ensure that "the program is embedded from the start."[40]

While such processes provide an effective method of resolving questions of design, the practical activity of making has its own benefits. It offers a physical and sensory means of approaching the discipline of architecture, a discipline so preoccupied with abstract theoretical concerns (building codes, properties of materials, structural calculations, social issues, virtual imagery, and electronic communication systems) that the link with any physical reality sometimes seems tenuous. The attention paid by the writer in *Architectural Forum* to the physicality of Saarinen's process was not accidental. The tactile and physical contact inherent in modelmaking has contributed to its present importance. This preoccupation persists. Antoine Predock's description of his preliminary design endeavors is couched in active and physical terms, as the "first moves or gestures." Frank Gehry

Eisenman Architects (U.S.). City of Culture of Galicia, Santiago de Compostela, Spain, 1999– . Model.

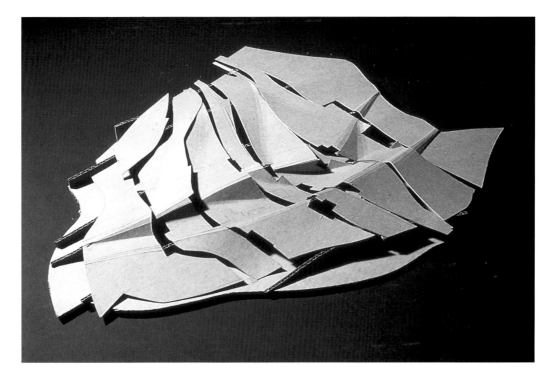

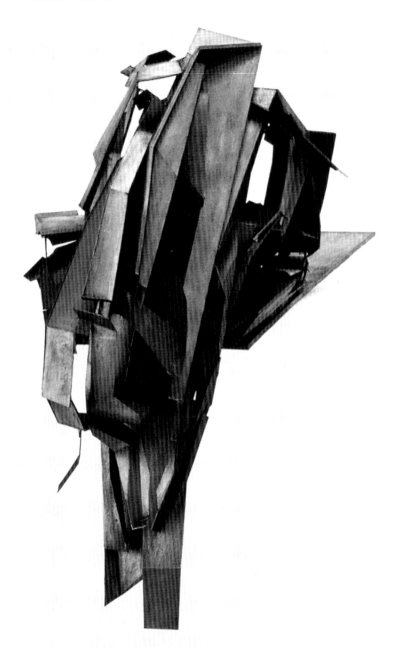

Michele Saee (U.S.).
Golzari Guest House,
Westlake, California,
1995–96. Model.

compares the process of "pulling and modeling" to a "sculptor's struggle" from which ideas emerge, his workshop exuding, according to one observer, "a strong sense of the violence of making things."[41]

Another West Coast architect, Michele Saee, creates large, dynamic objects that have the presence and physicality of sculpture. His nearly six-foot-high Golzari Guest House model, now in the collection of SFMOMA, is large enough to enter. "That model got disassembled and reassembled, and parts were discarded and added, literally five or ten times," he remembers. "And every time it would slightly change, the parts would get altered, but overall it would get closer to the final product. I'm five-eight, and basically the model is as big as my torso. It needed that scale."[42] Wolf Prix sees the process of design as emotive and expressionistic in character, a "very complex and dynamic act":

> We try to define the feeling, the emotion that the space is later to radiate. And then we have a drawing, sometimes on a sheet of paper, sometimes on the table, sometimes even on the wall or the floor, and at the same time a model evolves.[43]

For such architects there is a bond between conception and the physical act of making, indicated in the language and metaphors that they and others use to describe their activity. For them, this sensory experience, this confrontation with materiality, is essential to the creative act. The large number of contemporary architects actively involved in making process models suggests an underlying need for this experience. Architects are obliged to work with

representations of their designs and seem ever more separated from construction. Models engage architects with the real world in a vital physical encounter, in which the act of making forms the bond or link between idea and actuality.

Other forces, such as the rise of abstraction in the fine arts, strengthened the model's tie to the imagination during the twentieth century. Abstraction freed the model to engage directly in the imaginative process, enabling the architect to isolate theoretical ideas, as well as unformulated fragments of vision and imagery, from other aspects of the intended reality. Today, NBBJ's modelmaker Alec Vassiliadis can divide the models he works with into distinct categories: "There are two kinds of models: one is the models that are more or less representational of what we're trying to do, but the ones that I take most pleasure in making are those that represent our ideas."[44] Scot Walls, another of NBBJ's model professionals, explains further: "There are models that manifest themselves as a miniature of the building, but there are theories and concepts that can be modeled. There are thought processes that can be done in 3-D—I call it 4-D; I don't actually call models 3-D."[45]

A recent library project at NBBJ elucidates these comments. The design team used models to explore the "sense of place" associated with the idea of "a library." The architects attempted to represent the feelings relating to the activities of library use and the atmosphere of the place envisaged as a sculpture or other three-dimensional object. Although a seemingly arcane and entirely abstract exercise, the archi-

tects found it helpful in establishing a conceptual framework, a vision for the project.

More tangibly, models have always served as a record of the architect's original creative intention, while the buildings themselves, frequently altered through external influences (like building codes or late-stage economies), are a more complex source. It has often been recognized that Sir Christopher Wren's Great Model of St. Paul's records his ideal vision for that ultimate architectural expression of the Anglican faith. Wren's intentions were frustrated by the clergy, and the design was never realized, a very altered one taking its place. The model, testimony to his earlier, preferred design, has been considered "the supreme memorial to Wren's unfettered imagination."[46] Similarly, Lutyens's model for the proposed Roman Catholic cathedral in Liverpool has been described as the

NBBJ (U.S.). United States Federal Courthouse, Seattle, Washington, 2001–4. "Ideagram" concept model: Mike Mora, 1998.

Sir Edwin Lutyens (U.K.).
Metropolitan Cathedral of
Christ the King, Liverpool,
England, 1929–58. Model,
yellow pine and cork:
John B. Thorp, 1933.

"principal means of communicating Lutyens's great cathedral vision to the world."[47] Thomas Jefferson's model for the Virginia state capitol at Richmond, made for him by noted French modelmaker Jean-Pierre Fouquet and brought by Jefferson from France, is now accepted as a definitive reference for the architect's original intentions. Recent detailed research on the model unexpectedly revealed a two-color scheme, which is now likely to be instated on the building.[48] Models, too, have always had the capacity to reveal elements of conceptual design thinking that are not visible in the built architecture. An original Gothic model for the Church of St. Maclou in Rouen (1434–1521), discovered by an American architectural historian in 1907, was received with great excitement, not just because of its age, but because it revealed the structure's underlying geometry more clearly than had previously been distinguishable through a study of the building.[49]

Such models have been made from early times, but it is only since the twentieth century that architects have relinquished realism, aspiring to portray their conceptual ideas alone, without concern for context. This position has been reached through a progressive rethink of the model's design, techniques, materials, overall aesthetic, and above all, the level of realism chosen.

Paolo Soleri's Arcology models—his visionary ideas for vertical cities made at the end of the 1960s—are a case in point. Created in clear acrylic, they were not intended to represent the physical reality of the projected structures. Clear acrylic used on its own was not a conventional material for modelmaking, nor was its level of abstraction familiar in the representation of buildings. The medium was chosen by Soleri not for its realism but for its effect, and this effect was startling. The material's transparency and light-transmitting qualities harnessed the drama of the model's inner light source, creating

an otherworldly luminosity. The ultramodern associations of this relatively new material—suggesting
an all-glass (technologically futuristic) structure—
were compelling. Visitors to the Corcoran Gallery's
hugely popular 1970 exhibition of Soleri's models
were struck, and did not miss the allusions. "[We
might] view them prophetically as artificial planets
constructed on earth," enthused Donald Wall in the
accompanying catalog; for him they were charged
objects. Interior views of the models shown in the
catalog appear like the inside of a spaceship.[50]

While the pressures to make client models
highly realistic are many, models made during the
design process can be more expressive and personal.
Such models were the first to benefit from this new
way of seeing, and have continued as the primary
focus for abstract modes of thought: revealing the
intimacies of imagination and telling the inside story
of design development. Yet as time progressed,
these models began to straddle the architect's public

Paolo Soleri/Arcosanti
(U.S.). Hexahedron
Arcology. Model, acrylic,
42 by 48 by 12 inches,
c. 1970.

Soleri's Hexahedron
model in an evocative
landscape setting,
c. 1970.

Leibowitz/Ellerbe Beckett (U.S.). Consolidated American/Northwest Airlines Terminal, John F. Kennedy International Airport, New York, New York, 1989. Model, metal and acrylic.

and private zones of operation. Now, like diaries intended for publication, process models are purposely shown. They are sometimes self-consciously abstract and are often more complex in their intentions than they appear. Vision has moved from the private to the realm of public display.

It is not surprising that Soleri's models were espoused by an art museum. By discarding superfluous detail and realism and sharply defining its message, the model becomes a tool for conveying particular ideas about the design, not least the vision and poetry of inspiration. So Peter Pran's 1989 model for the Consolidated American/Northwest Airlines Terminal at JFK Airport in New York was created to emphasize his key design idea: "a long, curved, floating steel roof that seems to come out of the ground with no beginning or end."[51] The model showed the main planes of the design in a simplified

form, as if suspended in space. For Pran, this selective tailoring of the model enabled it to express "the tectonic feeling of the whole building. But it went beyond that: the model became a poetic statement of my whole vision for the project." Similarly, a later model he was involved with, for the Kwun Tong Town Centre, a project developed by the design team at NBBJ, completely caught the spirit of the idea, according to Pran (see page 140). His personal goal for the project was to attain the quality of a Brancusi sculpture—an aim that could be more clearly expressed in a model than in a building. For him, this inspiration, "the whole poetic essence of the design," was communicated in the model.[52]

Further examples show that architects have increasingly seized the more abstract model as a means for eloquent expression. Toyo Ito's model for the Shanghai Luijiazui Central Area urban design project powerfully conveys his vision. Ito is fascinated by the impermanence of our modern electronic world, where invisible objects (electronic impulses) are constantly flowing through space. Built of glass and perforated metal, his buildings appear light in weight, floating above the ground; below and around them stream cars, lights, and moving crowds, which for him take the place of water. Ito's model communicates this vision through its interwoven layers of colorful, transparent, and semitransparent materials, which flow between the high-rise buildings.[53]

Daniel Libeskind's model for Berlin's Potsdamer Platz reconstruction is built from distinct segment blocks, which represent his image of the city, splintered by disparate "muse lines" that traverse "the geography of Potsdamer Platz, as well as . . . the topology of Berlin's culture." The model's detachable mosaic pieces interlock as in a jigsaw, representing symbolic fragments of memory in a literal rendition of his concept of site-as-puzzle.[54] The physical form of this model, with its jagged broken outline, also conveys the fractured nature of his Deconstructivist vision. The sleek models of Zaha Hadid, also associated with the Deconstructivist movement, are in stark contrast. They relate closely to her paintings, which depict objects in collision—geometrical splinters flying through space with the exploding dynamism of shattered glass. Her early concept model for the Zollhof 3 Media Center reduced this vision to a simplified statement composed of emblematic, translucent, light-filtering solids. Models generated by the Los Angeles office Morphosis and its principal designer, Thom Mayne, express other concerns. They function as symbolic, monumental, sculptural objects preoccupied with materials and the qualities of surface (see page 23).

The first concern in these models is not for realism; something else is being conveyed. They articulate the architects' feelings and vision. Only secondarily do they address what the building will look like. The irony is that while the growing

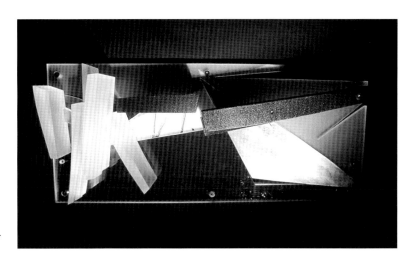

Zaha Hadid Architects (U.K.). Zollhof 3 Media Center, Düsseldorf, Germany, 1989–93. Concept model, acrylic.

BELOW
Toyo Ito & Associates (Japan). Shanghai Luijiazui Central Area, Japan, 1992. Model, acrylic.

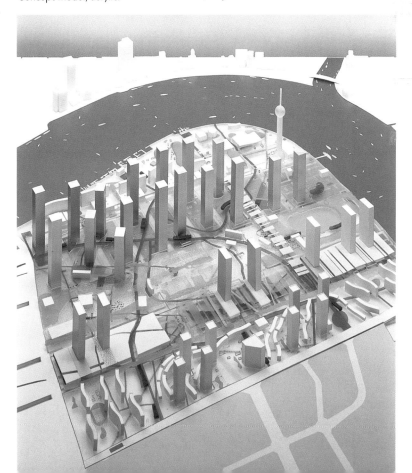

Studio Daniel Libeskind
(Germany/U.S.).
Potsdamer Platz project,
Berlin, Germany, 1991.
Model assembled (above)
and disassembled
(opposite).

Michael Sorkin Studio
(U.S.). Urbanagram,
Columbia University
design studio, New York,
New York, c. 1995.
Model, wood.

popularity of models in the twentieth century reflected the architect's need for contact with physical reality, it was not tied to the portrayal of physical realism. As architects seek to express their inner vision by exaggerating the principal underlying ideas, and by loading the model with meaning, their models have become less like buildings. This is not unintended. As Michael Graves explained in a commentary on models in 1978, "we're not making real buildings; we're making models of ideas." Libeskind's models have been described as "reproductions of concepts," and Michele Saee's approach has been called an "architecture of urgency, which does not distinguish between the idea and the building." Of his liberating, expressionistic process, Wolf Prix says, "we want to keep this design moment free of all material constraints."[55]

Michael Sorkin sees the level of realism chosen for a model as highly significant. In his Urbanagram studies, he employs flexible or "elastic" strategies of representation, using "abstracted versions of operative principles." Sorkin considers "the way in which one proceeds from the relatively abstract to the relatively concrete [to be a] big issue for model-making." It is easy, he continues, to fall into the trap of going at it too directly, by pursuing extremes—either the "pure appeal of abstraction, or the overly concretized reality." For Sorkin this has meant "a long study of trying to find techniques of modeling that dwell persuasively in that intermediate zone."[56] This is a common concern for many contemporary architects, and the intermediate zone has proved to be one of the most exciting and productive areas of contemporary architectural creativity.

Architects are prepared to defend their right to use models expressively and to choose the level of realism appropriate to their purpose. To criticism that his preliminary studies do not look like the buildings they precede, Michael Graves counters, "That's not the point." Why should a drawing or model mimic a building, he argues, "any more than a paper cutout or a collage of a Cubist guitar by

Picasso should look just like a guitar? I think probably the metaphors or the rituals or the ideas of a kind of a formal structure are more to the point than trying to imitate some sort of miniature reality."[57]

Architects demand that the model should allow them this freedom of expression, leaving room for the imagination and facilitating creativity. Jun Yanagisawa writes of Toyo Ito's models in very similar terms:

> they are not required to have the reality of the actual building which they represent. They constitute only an intermediate state of the building. In other words only a very blurred state before the start of the building construction can be depicted, still leaving much scope for the imagination . . . What needs attention when constructing these study models is not just to depict the rules of reality in miniature, but to detach oneself from these rules and to supplement the viewpoint and manner of handling, looking for what will arise beyond the rules to make the creation of the building possible. Models cannot become alive without achieving this.[58]

Toyo Ito & Associates (Japan). Yatsushiro Fire Station, Yatsushiro-shi, Kumamoto, Japan, 1995. Model, acrylic.

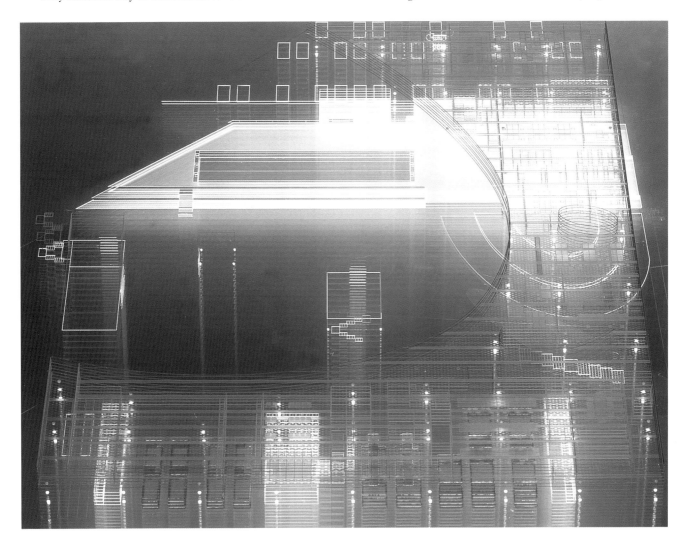

Kasimir Malevich. *Architekton*, c. 1918–21. Model, plaster.

The models that come alive express the dynamism of the creative process and look beyond the rules of reality into the realm of the imagination. For many architects, their vision, that irreducible primal visualization of the idea often more readily expressed in the model than in the building (like Pran's Brancusi inspiration), is more important than the end product. In the late 1990s, Zaha Hadid was described as operating "in a world of pure form"; reluctant to come to terms with construction, as one critic claimed, her work was all vision.[59] This vision, as manifested in the model, sometimes seems to govern her architecture. Intriguingly, her buildings have been criticized for being too much like the models: structures without details.[60] For Peter Eisenman, the *process* of architectural design is paramount. The steadfast attention he gives to this process, some have suggested, ultimately produces an "architecture devoid of meaning."[61]

It is almost as if some architects relate so strongly to the model that they wish to remain in its world. The model becomes part of the architect's personal journey, in itself the fundamental experience of architecture. Michele Saee's focused relationship with his Golzari Guest House model is relevant here as well: a model that shared his moods, that became "almost . . . an extension of me." He elaborates,

> Of course, I had to give up, because the model was removed from my hands, but it's something that I could have actually seen myself work on forever. I think I would like to build the actual building in the same way I built the model—you know, go to the site and maybe get a permit for parts and just keep adding to it.[62]

For some participants, architecture has become almost a branch of the fine arts in which the activity itself is self-justifying. Architects may or may not be operating in the "real world"—that is, they may or may not succeed in communicating their ideas to clients, or in seeing their buildings built. Yet ironically, this allows them the freedom to experiment, which leads to some of the most compelling models; and these individualistic experiments inject new life into architecture as much as they do into the media of its representation.

Architects' urge to represent the abstract development of ideas, and their struggle to resolve issues of realism and abstraction, cannot be isolated. These preoccupations have been present as well in the debates surrounding twentieth-century painting and sculpture, reflecting a longstanding connection between art and architecture. The pull of the fine arts is evident in Frank Gehry's admission, "Crossing the line between architecture and sculpture is something that's been difficult for me."[63] For the model, Kasimir Malevich's Suprematist explorations on volumetric and spatial forms were perhaps the decisive moment.[64] Recognizing that his abstract formal researches, carried out in three dimensions as well as two, addressed the problems of architecture as much as art, Malevich called his series of plaster studies, modeled from around 1918, *Architektons*. He made no claim for these compositions to be anything more than "idea," distinguishing between the "purely architectonic, devoid of purpose" and the "specifically architectural, the material expression of a stated purpose." (His *Architektons* belonged to the former category.) By representing nonrealistic, conceptual architectonic thinking in solid form, Malevich provided a new outlet for architectural expression. It is no coincidence that the earliest representations of abstract architectural thought correlate closely with the emergence of abstraction in the fine arts.

There is another interesting parallel with the fine arts. Just as the invention of photography in the nineteenth century made painters question the purpose of painting (the pursuit of imitative realism having become superfluous), the increasing technical ability of modelmakers to mimic reality, from the mid-twentieth century, has made architects question the purpose of models and what it is that they should convey. "Photographic" realism was never necessarily what architects wanted: for analytical models, perhaps; for clients, sometimes; for themselves, rather less so. In fact, from the 1970s, the more experimental and innovative the architect, the greater, it seems, his or her distaste for realism.

The link with twentieth-century art movements is plain in the work of Hadid, who explicitly acknowledges the influence of Malevich and others. Wolf Prix, too, who produces installations as well as buildings, concedes that the nature of his design process has "undoubtedly more to do with art."[65] Of Odile Decq and Benoît Cornette's 1995 exhibition "Hyper-Tension," Andreas Ruby writes, "In their models, the two architects seem to have realized one of the most essential insights of modern art: that it is unnecessary to simply double visual reality." Stretching an understanding of representation, he adds, their models "extrapolate certain realities of a building (i.e. its structural system, its primary space-forming elements or even a specific view) while neglecting others."[66]

This territory of abstraction, this intermediate or blurred zone in which such models—freed from realism—operate, is where Graves's "metaphors, rituals, and ideas" are explored. It is the place of abstract architectural research and artistic self-determination, the place to which contemporary progressive architects seem magnetically attracted. Models now offer a much richer medium of investigation, whether for research of a speculative nature or the study of visionary ideas. For Ito, as Yanagisawa explains, "The model is the link between the real existing building arising under the influence of numerous conditions, and the utopia existing inside the architect," a transitional region appropriately defined by Yanagisawa as "a utopia called model."[67]

Utopia is a significant word. Models, which do not need to function in the real world of construction, lend themselves particularly to the representation of the imaginary or ideal. They are the natural territory of vision, perfectly adapted for projecting futuristic, visionary proposals, however intrinsically unbuildable they may be. From Soleri's Arcologies to Archigram's "Living Pod" or Lebbeus Woods's nightmare cities, models contribute an important dimension of persuasion, making the fantasy seem more real than would two-dimensional counterparts, which often retain the detachment and romance of a compelling graphic style. Such use of the model, of course, has not been restricted to the present. From the Baroque, for instance, came models "giving a bird's-eye view of principal residences, usually including the gardens; these models followed ideal concepts based on architectural theory, . . . imaginative thoughts . . . frequently realized only in part if at all."[68]

Fractured from the universe of production, the model is indisputably autonomous and can stray into the field of "pure architectural art," as with Moscow's "paper architects" of the 1980s, whose disillusionment with the stagnation of architecture under Brezhnev gave them a distrust of the entire process of realization. Their drawings and models became an "act of liberation," "exercises in the survival of the imagination."[69]

Many architects who lose themselves in the model's dream world are those whose opportunities for building are slight. In 2000, Hani Rashid explained the significance of models in the early years of Asymptote. "We're only beginning now to build. We have really been a practice of making models as ideas for ten years because nobody would let us build anything; we had to make it as a model."[70] For an architecture student, the model is the first physical experience of architecture, and for the architect without commissions, the only physical, three-dimensional experience of architecture available. In both cases, the model is embraced as the place for fulfillment of frustrated desire, and gains proportionately in significance. Huge effort is often invested in models, which develop into a kind of substitute for the real thing, an end unto themselves. Hadid, who despite producing a series of award-winning designs, had had little built by the mid-1990s, gained a reputation as a paper architect by default. The constructability of her ideas may now be judged, with completed projects in Cincinnati and Innsbruck, Austria, and buildings on the rise in Rome, Salerno, Wolfsburg, and Leipzig, but her early designs survive physically only as models, giving these objects an unusual importance in the eyes of both the architect and others.[71]

The model's capacity for expression makes it one of the principal means by which the architect's imagination can be articulated and an invaluable source for understanding his or her conceptual intentions. Its importance is voiced by Rashid. On the borderline between architecture and sculpture, he comments,

> I think we as a studio moved in that direction from day one with modeling. It's part of that idea that they were these substitute/surrogate pieces of architecture, so the composition, and the materiality, and the making, were much more about that than it was about where the stairs are, or where the doors are. And secondly, we saw them as permanent pieces of work, almost pieces of art that would reside within our body of work.[72]

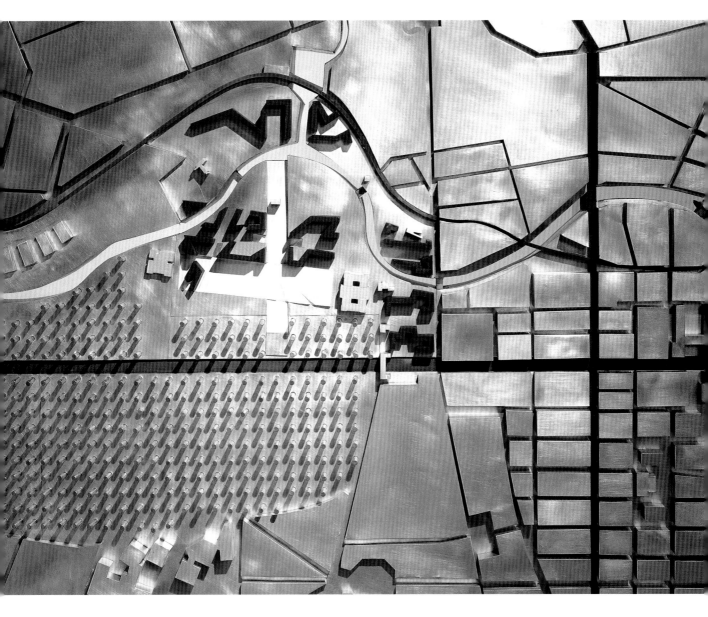

Asymptote (U.S.).
Parliamentary Precinct,
Spreebogen, Berlin,
Germany, 1992. Model.

CHAPTER 5

Communication: Idea and Identity

The model exists in both the mystic realm of vision and the more humdrum world of gaining commissions and constructing buildings. In this latter sphere, the model has proved to be essential for communicating the architect's idea beyond the office walls. The "presentation" or "client" model has evolved since the early twentieth century in response to a variety of influences, reaching a surprising level of sophistication—though it has been dogged by a parallel history of misunderstanding and misuse. A superficial glance instantly identifies the presentation model as a powerful medium, able to convey information with speed and clarity; closer scrutiny reveals a vehicle of remarkable subtlety. Public display of the model opens it to a host of external influences. At the same time, it exposes the architect, whom the model has come to represent, as much as the project idea. Challenged to respond, architects continually reconsider the model's design as their own concept of identity alters, and the model becomes a yet more enigmatic and layered object.

The physical immediacy of the model makes it an effective means of representation for conveying architectural ideas, particularly to the non-architect or layperson. Like any specialized discipline, architecture has its own language to facilitate internal communication. Orthographic drawings (plans and elevations) are the architect's shorthand. But this is a minority language, and there is no reason why those not working in construction, and a few other related fields, should know how to read it. The comparison between architectural drawings and musical notation is apposite. The ability to read and interpret both requires specialist training and personal aptitude.

The interests and experience of architects' clients vary widely. While some clients are perceptive interpreters of drawings, typically they have no formal training in reading plans or visualizing three-dimensional ideas from two-dimensional materials. Ask any modelmaker: even for the architect the process presents problems, and the first realization of his or her idea in model form may come as a surprise. At best, the client can hardly be expected to exceed the architect's ability. At worst, the drawings appear as "just a tissue of meticulous and inconsequent lines, conveying neither sense nor shape"—even to someone as broadly educated as the first duke of Newcastle, a contemporary of Sir Christopher Wren, about whom this comment was written.[1] It is with a "sense of surprise and disbelief," another commentator complained centuries later in America's *Architectural Forum*, "that the architect discovers that a drawing which to him obviously represents an object in three dimensions, is to his clients merely a series of lines, representing nothing."[2]

Wherever there is lack of training in the reading of drawings, or underdeveloped imagination, the material object has an advantage over the image. There is nothing more suitable than the model, observed Jacques-François Blondel in 1774, "for teaching those who are lacking in imagination."[3] As Alwyn T. Covell explained in 1914, the "proposition," or design concept, "has been brought just that much nearer . . . it has been taken off paper and put bodily into your thoughts."[4]

Foster and Partners (U.K.). Daewoo Electronics Headquarters, Seoul, South Korea, 1995–2000. Presentation model, acrylics, styrene, brass, and medium-density fiberboard, 1996.

For two-dimensional presentation, the quality of the photography contributes considerably to the impact of the model.

People today still find models more approach-able. B. J. Novitski described the nonarchitect's response to a model in *Architecture* in 1992: "they understand it, recognize it, and see relationships they might not see otherwise . . . the look and feel of a physical model are . . . important to clients."[5] Peter Pran believes that "the model is probably the thing the client responds most to."[6] Spencer de Grey at Foster and Partners holds that "if you have to choose one medium to explain a project to a lay-person, you would choose a model. I think models communicate to laypeople better than anything else."[7]

Models provide an instant snapshot of the idea, a complete and comprehensible picture, revealing the true nature of the design to the client—sometimes with such clarity that it may not always be to the architect's advantage. Sir Christopher Wren fully understood the impact this exposure can have only when his model of St. Paul's was rejected, though the drawings had been previously approved. (He

subsequently resolved to "make no more models . . . which, as he had found by Experience, did but loose time, and subjected his business many times, to incompetent judges.")[8] Sir Roger Pratt noticed a key difference between models and drawings in the sev-enteenth century: "Whereas all the other drafts aforesaid [orthographics and perspectives] do only superficially and disjointedly represent unto us the several parts of a building, a model does it jointly, according to all its dimensions."[9] Or as Diana Agrest and Mario Gandelsonas have expressed it more recently, "The traditional architectural draw-ing fragments the building to produce a knowledge of its parts and relationships. The traditional model verifies the building as an object."[10] Rendered per-spectives aid understanding of the proposal for the nonprofessional, yet as Richard Armiger of Network Modelmakers in London has noted, "for the client, a building on paper is still not real."[11] Three-dimensional computer images now also contribute to

Richard Rogers Partnership (U.K.). Rome Congress Centre, Italy, 1999. Competition model, acrylic and styrene.

The apparent simplicity of the photograph is decep-tive. The photographer created an image of the complete building, using a mirror and the computer program Photoshop, from a half-section model.

OPPOSITE
I. M. Pei presenting a project with the help of a detailed model of mid-town Manhattan, 1967.

concept presentation, but only the model has the unrivaled capacity to verify the building as an object, making it seem at once more concrete and, at the same time, subtly more feasible.

If this is the case for individual clients, it is even more so for larger presentations, whether to planning committees, neighborhood groups, or the public at large. This fact has been appreciated since Renaissance times. For the competition for Florence's cathedral dome in 1418, models were considered imperative for presentation to the Great Council, a group comprising the cathedral's thirteen wardens along with the consuls of the Wool Guild and various other consultants.[12] In the seventeenth century, Augsburg's master builder Elias Holl constructed a model ("meticulously executed and equipped with detachable floors") so that the assembled town councilors could "discuss the interior and organizational arrangements of the building without relying on complicated architectural drawings."[13] During the nineteenth century, the model's value in this respect was realized, even as its other functions had been largely dropped. This held especially true for the public—as one angry citizen maintained, "If the Government had shown the model of the British Museum barracks and stockade, or any of the monstrosities they had perpetuated, the public would have exercised their judgment before it was too late."[14]

In the 1920s and 1930s, as the use of models grew, a fresh awareness of their communicative capacity for both client and public began to stir. "A model demonstrates the architect's ability without the client's cooperation," mused one writer. "It creates a desire on the part of the client, who sees a beautiful creation without the exercise of imagination. He wants it. His mind is on the thing itself, *not the cost*."[15] A model further helps the architect to " 'sell' his design to the client, especially if the client happens to be a committee or group of people, or if the project needs the support of the public."[16] The tone of articles on models moved rapidly from an interest in their value to conviction of their worth.

Architects (including Louis Skidmore, far left) and amusement consultants meet in May 1930 to examine a clay model for the 1933 Chicago World's Fair.

By 1948, it was "doubtful whether any architect will cry out against the value of a colorful, accurate scale model in the presentation of ideas to builders and town or community planners."[17]

With the growth of urban planning and preservation initiatives, the role of models in presentations to the public increased.[18] "Concern for client and user involvement has led to a search for more open and accessible means of communication," explained one writer in the *Architects' Journal* in 1985. "Three-dimensional models are one such means."[19] Models became central to planning submissions and are still seen as key to successful approaches to the public, despite the introduction of electronic alternatives such as fly-bys and walk-throughs. Besides their universal legibility and their capacity for conveying the building as an object, models are more sympathetic to the psychology of a group meeting. It is more satisfactory for individuals to meet around a model for discussion than to orient themselves toward a screen or a graphic on the wall. Hani Rashid considers the physical presence of the three-dimensional model an important factor in group rapport:

> I put a model on the table, then someone sitting diagonally across from me sees something in the model that I can't see, and someone over here sees something, and then as we circulate around it so it creates discussion, I see the model as something that's conducive to a kind of multiple-points-of-view critique.[20]

If the model was recognized in previous centuries for its powers of persuasion, its genius had been only partially discovered. In the twentieth century, this propensity in particular would be developed; in the post-1950 period, the model's talent for manipulation was frankly and comprehensively exploited. This passage in the model's history is not a tale without interest or, indeed, entertainment; it is a story that must be chronicled if its implications are to be understood, for it has caused considerable tension in the present-day relationship between architect and model, as it has for its wider audience. It is a tale in which the model finally loses its virginity.

Our fascination with miniatures is instinctual, and not a recent phenomenon. In earlier centuries, at events less heavily promoted than world's fairs and international expositions, the model's charms have held sway. In eighteenth-century Bath, for instance, one enterprising carver and gilder set up two models of palaces and another of Wentworth House in Yorkshire to attract customers, and unwittingly started a trend. The following year, two separate modelmakers, Joseph Sheldon and Charles Harcourt Masters, exhibited their competing models of the city at different locations—each could be viewed, between the hours of 10 A.M. and 3 P.M., for a not inconsiderable charge.[21] More official showings proved equally enticing. In 1851, a model of Smithfield Market, displayed by the Corporation of London, drew enough attention to warrant the provision of a full-time lecturer to answer questions.[22] In New York, on a single day in 1902, seven hundred people pressed to view a model of the Cathedral of St. John the Divine.[23] Soleri's Arcology models broke attendance records in 1970 when exhibited at the Corcoran Gallery in Washington, D.C.[24]

Even models' makers are not impervious to their charms. In 1744, Thomas Eayre continued to marvel at his model of a Gothic bridge, declaring it "a prodigious curious and fine thing," even though he had made it himself.[25] Our patent fascination with models as miniatures combines with their directness and apparent clarity to make them powerful objects, able not only to convey ideas and carry messages but to convince and to persuade.

It is a quality that makes them invaluable for soliciting financial contributions. Again, architects in the past had some inkling of this appealing trait. In medieval France, models were sometimes made "to interest creditors in the plan, to awaken their desire to donate and to start the flow of alms, especially for building projects with financial or technical difficulties."[26] In 1924, as new work was planned at

the Cathedral of St. John the Divine, the cathedral staff noted, as Bishop William Manning divulged in a note to one of the architects, Ralph Adams Cram, that it was the "publicity people" who "seem[ed] to have their hearts set on our getting some sort of model."[27] So a model was commissioned to consider the design and also for exhibition to the public to promote the building of the cathedral. An article in Britain in the same period explicitly noted the model's ability to prompt donations:

> It is not until a model appears on the scene that the building begins to take on reality so far as the layman is concerned. This is fully understood by estate development and hospital committees, who know that subscriptions and donations come more freely when a model is at hand to give concrete shape to a projected scheme.[28]

Despite these precursory signals, the model was not fully exploited for fund-raising purposes until well after World War II. By 1985, its prominence in this role, particularly as a marketing tool to help raise development finance, was eliciting comment.[29] But by that time, the model was no longer considered demure.

The early days of the model boom were indeed marked by naïveté. Disenchantment with the deceptive potential of perspectives had led to an undiscriminating embrace of the model as the "innocent" alternative. Remarks made in *Architectural Forum* in 1914 illustrate this line of thought: "Perspectives may be more or less correct, but as a rule, are misleading, especially when beautifully colored and enhanced by the addition of affected surroundings, which only exist in the architect's brain." Other "artistic properties," the writer continued, "such as automobiles, street cars, and crowds of men and women, are introduced to make a taking picture. Such a picture is sometimes made to secure the approval of the design by the client, . . . who is, accordingly, unable to divest his eye of the glamour of the artist's cunning." On the other hand, a model,

the commentator assured his readers, "if properly made to scale . . . and carefully detailed in strict accordance with the architect's design, would make an honest statement of facts, which could not mislead anyone."[30] Another critic, in 1919, was convinced that, unlike the more wanton perspective, the model provides a means "of giving directly to the client a concrete idea of his future building" in a way that is "truth-telling" and "not dependent on cleverness of line and color," and concluded that "[the model] is honest, in that it can be seen for what it is, and is not falsely enhanced by a fairyland of landscape and sky."[31]

Over the next half-century the model industry was continuously developed, and by the 1980s these sentiments could no longer be sustained. Before, the perspective's honor had been suspect. Now exactly parallel expressions of discomfiture were made regarding the model. Doubts had already been expressed toward the end of the 1960s, by which time models were considered "relatively big business."[32] John Chisholm, a U.K. architect, objected in 1969: "For too long the apparently infallible honesty of the beautifully executed scale model has seduced planning committee, board of directors and general public."[33] In the U.S., too, it would become increasingly evident that "Architectural models can tell the truth, but they can also tell partial truths, and even lie."[34]

By the 1980s the seductive power of the model was irrevocably exposed. According to Jeff Bishop in the *Architects' Journal*, models, which could be remarkably effective with nondesigners, since they were less mysterious and easier to understand than drawings, could also be used by architects "to confuse clients, seduce them, and inhibit involvement"—though often by default, he added.[35] The clamor rose in Britain as the unscrupulous activities of some conspiratorial architect-client partnerships pushed inappropriate developments past planning committees to the detriment of town and city center alike. The defilement was complete: models had become "by and large vehicles for fraudulent seduc-

Cram and Ferguson's model of the Cathedral of St. John the Divine, New York, New York, under construction, c. 1924–26.

tion," and objections were raised at the consequences.[36] The situation was no different in America, if less colorfully described. There, even modelmakers were forced to admit, "sometimes I think we've gotten worse architecture along with this wonderful tool."[37]

Such knocks to the model's image are not new. Vincent Scamozzi, an early Italian writer, was doubtful of the model's intent. In 1615, he warned:

> Manie modells, being but inanimate and breathlesse things, have need of the Architect's, or some other worthy, & Knowing purson's speech, to expresse with words, and demonstrate with reasons, what they are, and to give them life, & motion. For thereby minds are excited, and inflamed, whereby resolutions may be taken in matters of moment . . . Yet modells are like young birds, mongst which one cannot discerne the males from ye females, but being growen bigger are Showen whither they be Eagles or

> Ravens: And therefore the owners of the workes may easily be deceaved by Modells.[38]

Sir John Soane quoted a contemporary's more forthright tone: "My late worthy and intelligent friend [James Peacock] . . . tells us, 'When the person who wishes to build is possessed of the Design, . . . his next step should be to cause to be made, not a gaudy eye trap, to dazzle and confound the ignorant and to take in the unwary, but a complete plain model shewing all the parts of the design he has approved.'"[39] In sixteenth-century France, Philibert de l'Orme complained, more particularly, of the elaborate cosmetics used to enhance a poor design: "A good architect who wants to represent a natural building must never produce a model which is 'made-up' or adorned with painting, gold-plating or colors. This is the manner of those who want to deceive."[40]

Tactics in the second half of the twentieth century were further advanced. Various strategies were devised to ease the project past unsympathetic eyes.

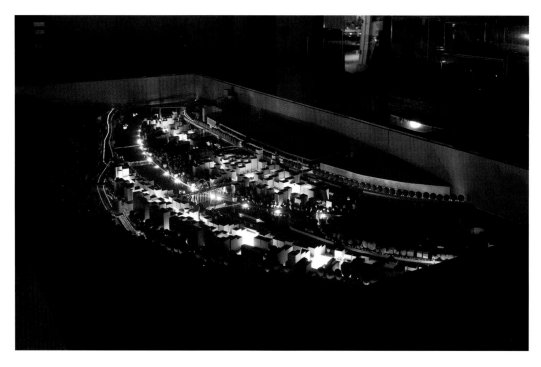

Richard Rogers Partnership (U.K.). Renault Competition, Ile Seguin, Paris, France, 1994. Model, timber, acrylic, and cork with fiber-optic and electrical lighting components.

Two and a half miles (four kilometers) of fiber optics, controlled by a small computer, were installed to light this model. At the press of a button, light pulses down the length of a specific route to show movement along transport links—road, rail, pedestrian, water, and so on. The photo is a long exposure showing all routes.

"There's room for artistic license, especially if the client wants to 'cheat' a bit," one 1980s modelmaker confided.[41] The main areas of influence in the sphere of model design were the project's context and the manner of representing the design itself.

The image produced by the model is readily manipulated. The project building can stand either on its own or in relation to its site. Presenting it as a freestanding object often takes best advantage of the building's form, despite the fact that, when constructed, it can never be viewed in that way. In a site model, on the other hand, the building can be made to stand out. The proposed structure may be carefully finished with internal lighting and other enticements, while surrounding buildings appear as monochrome blocks. Though few would deliberately change the project building's scale from that of surrounding buildings, its prominence and attraction can be emphasized by what is adjacent to it (and what is left out)—changing the size of trees or removing vegetation, disguising or omitting details that "spoil" the image (such as poor materials and finishes, nearby architectural eyesores, or rubbish heaps)—and more generally, by the overall choice of scale, height of presentation, and size and treatment of the base. Sir Roger Pratt appreciated the influence of appropriate display and advised for the presentation model: "Chiefly we must not forget to raise it somewhat from the earth, as well to avoid the inconvenience of water etc., as to give a grace and majesty to it."[42]

The traditional means of "prettying up" a perspective were now enlisted for the model: attractive color schemes, imaginative planting, delightful miniature figures populating the scene—in all, those very "artistic properties" and fairyland landscapes that had been repudiated by *Architectural Forum*'s writers in the 1910s. For a planning committee or lay audience, "The trees, people and street furniture help distract attention from a controversial building"; when the model is intended as a marketing device, the opposite strategy would apply: "instead of making the building disappear into its surroundings, the emphasis is on making it stand out. 'You've got to make it look different, better, so people will want to buy it.'"[43]

One useful ruse for planning presentations was to treat all buildings with the same finish and paint them in related colors, so that any conflict between the building and its context would be minimized. An immaculate picture of the design was also generally persuasive: "It's always spring and the cars are always clean," and (with regard to the planting), ". . . it's always forty years on."[44] But it was often human interest (bringing in tow associations with dollhouse and battlefield) that finally won out. The secret of one London modelmaker's success in the mid-1980s was the simple ploy of putting more cars, trees, and people in his models than anyone else.[45]

Moving parts, internal lighting operable by switches, working elevators, and motorized models that come apart have also been found to charm the viewer (not so long ago, perhaps, a juvenile scientist impatient to explore). The attraction of moving parts was not a new discovery. One of the details that gave Joseph Sheldon's model of Bath an edge over his competitor's was the "river in continuous flow."[46] In the 1970s and 1980s, the persistent and artful application of such devices was strengthened by the even greater opportunities for realism and success: techniques had advanced; models were no longer simply constructed, they were engineered. Large sums were spent on immaculately realistic detail. Motor power and artificial illumination contributed unending delights.

During the same period, model photography became an important source of additional impact for presentations. Charles Garnier and Owen Jones were among those who made early experiments in the mid-nineteenth century, and a few architects were using model photographs in lieu of sketches to present to clients in the 1890s.[47] But it was not until the model boom of the 1920s that, with regard to client presentation, anything substantial was

Kasimir Malevich, Project for a Suprematist Skyscraper for the City of New York, c. 1925–26.

Malevich's photomontage combines an *Architekton* and a site photograph.

RIGHT
Harvey Wiley Corbett's model of the Bush Building (Bush Terminal International Exhibition Building; see page 43), New York, New York, in a site photomontage, c. 1916.

Corbett designed the Bush Building in New York and Bush House in London for the same client.

reported in the press. A 1921 article in *Arts and Decoration* revealed the current state of play. It described in detail the New York architect Joseph Bodker's experiments, in which scale models of designs for country houses were "photographed into" imaginary landscape settings or combined with accurately aligned shots of the actual site. The article compared these and later photographs of the houses as built to underline the verisimilitude that could be achieved. Thus "the real effect of the house," Bodker triumphantly declared, "is conveyed by the model in a way that no drawing could accomplish."[48] *Pencil Points* joined the battle the following year with a four-part series of articles that covered Harvey Wiley Corbett's adventures with the medium. These again included composites with hand-painted landscapes, but in Corbett's case these were supplemented by photos of a model for Bush House in London incorporated into aerial shots of the site.[49]

Interest in model photography for presentation purposes surged over the next two decades, just as the model's own enlarged potential was becoming clear. Before the 1970s, model photography had been employed as much for the architect as for the client— for understanding and envisaging the design—but now new emphasis was placed on developing applications for presentation. The Modelscope also came into use, so the viewpoint could move inside. At the same time new techniques for photomontage emerged. The medium was currently enjoying considerable attention in the wider sphere of photography and among mixed-media artists. Architects were not slow to make use of the improvements. The montage technique, until recently the same cut-and-paste operation devised in photography's infancy, was revolutionized by the invention of emulsion stripping: portions of emulsion were removed from the film base in a photo lab and pieced together with other images and retouched, producing a result of much higher quality.[50]

The most convincing and sophisticated of these images were extremely expensive to produce, which

Model photographer's studio in the Hamden, Connecticut, office of Kevin Roche John Dinkeloo and Associates, with model for the office complex of the Royal Canada Bank, Toronto, c. 1971–72.

The firm has used model photography intensively over several decades. The elaborate model shop was built partly to stage photographic settings.

Photomontage of Minoru
Yamasaki's World Trade
Center model and its site
with adapted foreground,
c. 1969.

The photograph was
used for promotion even
after the buildings were
completed.

limited their deployment to the marketing of large
projects that would bring long-term financial rewards.
In one U.S. assessment of such cases in 1989, it was
estimated that a land developer could spend $100,000
to $400,000 in constructing the model, "add to that
the cost of photographing the model and physical site,
computer retouching, and the final sales brochure,
and the total usually tops $1 million."[51] Neither did
model films and videos come cheaply, but the impact
they had on clients was similarly gratifying.

After a long engagement, this bonding of model
and photography in the last quarter of the twentieth
century considerably augmented the model's ability
to communicate—and to deceive. Together, models
and photographic imagery enabled architects and
marketing personnel to produce convincing compos-
ite pictures of buildings as they would appear in real
life. Immaculate models incorporated "real" eye-
level views, which could imitate the experience of
seeing the building in its actual setting, of walking
around it, and of "touring" its interiors. So powerful
were the models that they were frequently left in the
building's foyer to remind inhabitants of the quality
of the building they were in—and to supplant any
untoward reality. So powerful were the images that
they sometimes remained in use after construction,
found preferable for publicity purposes to
photos of the finished structure. This enlarged arsenal of the architect further bypassed the need for
imagination on the client's part and presented the
project as already built.

One Italian writer, architect Piera Scuri, report-
ing advances of this nature at Kohn Pedersen Fox in
1985, compared the results to science fiction. It is no
longer necessary, she wrote,

> to wait for the skyscraper to be built. Business
> can already be negotiated on the basis of the
> model, further aided by photomontage. For in
> the attractively retouched photographic
> image, future is simulated in the most realistic
> possible way. Technology renders real what
> still belongs to a futurable world. Isn't that
> really what happens in science fiction films,
> where special effects contrive to render
> fantastic things so realistic as to make them
> "real"? Isn't it also the philosophy of Disney-
> land, where a highly refined and completely
> concealed technological apparatus manages to
> make the world of "fantasy" real?[52]

As the model's capabilities became more like science
fiction, the medium was also beginning to be
perceived as such. Scuri was aware of its "insidious"

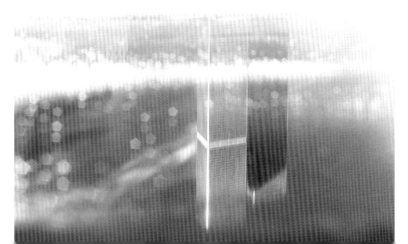

alter ego and drew attention to it in sections headed "Seduction" and "Deceptive Satisfactions." The model could no longer be regarded as the guileless provider of project information: its integrity had been shattered; its virtue was in tatters.

Thus is the story of the model's fall from grace. The new powers developed in the medium over this period made, and still make, its misuse severely tempting, especially when fund-raising models and their images enable clients to "raise half the money they [need] in two weeks."[53] Yet while this might seem attractive to developers and real-estate agents, in reality, for most architects, the short-term gains of winning a commission or getting the building past a planning committee do not weigh well against the longer-term losses to the individual's integrity and to public perception of the profession. If the merits of the design are misrepresented, the client and eventual users of the building will sooner or later make the discovery for themselves. Hence, while some architects have adopted these new strategies without scruple, manipulating their models to deceive and disguise, most take advantage of the new means on offer simply to present their proposals in the most effective way. Properly applied, the new

techniques make possible the clearest communication of design intent. Photography renders the benefits of the model more portable and enables informed assessment of the users' experiences, the building's impact on its surroundings, and the success of its proportions and internal spaces. Broadly speaking, it facilitates understanding. Neither architect nor client is naive any longer; the model is seen for what it is: just like the perspective, it is a representation, an interpretation. Further, perceptive architects and clients now recognize that realism does not equate with reality; instead, in many cases, the reverse can be true. Enhancing the realism of the model—with endless detail, naturalistic landscape, and accessories—actually creates a sense of unreality. (Scuri's reference to Disneyland was apt.) Both client and architect appreciate that to communicate clearly a model must be selective and concentrate on particular aspects of the design. The message must be identified, and decisions about aesthetics and content made in this light. Acceptance of the model's nature as a medium of representation frees the architect to choose between form and texture, between demonstrating the structural system and suggesting spatial effect, between addressing the

Richard Rogers Partnership (U.K.). Southbank, London, England, 1994. Competition model, wood and acrylic.

ideas behind the design and conveying its superficial visual character. Less often conveys more, and conveys it more clearly. Together, architects and clients have attained a more sophisticated grasp of the model's strengths, and models have benefited from the shared understanding.

Dangers remain, of course. The difference between intentional deception and creative interpretation can be subtle. It can be appropriate in different circumstances to portray the building alone or in relation to its site, or to focus on the most attractive aspect of the design. On one occasion, lopping off some part of a building might mislead; on another, it might reveal the underlying concept and aid comprehension. The validity of such embellishments as accessories and moving parts relates to the exact circumstances of their application. In an award-winning

representation by Kandor Models of Michael Hopkins's Basildon Town Square of 1983, the accessories help to convey a sense of activity and excitement appropriate to a project for a public space adjacent to a bustling shopping mall.[54] Some of Skidmore, Owings & Merrill's models, like the firm's competition model for Changi Rail Station in Singapore, also demonstrate that the use of eye-catching detail can be justified by the project. SOM's Ross Wimer explains,

> There are places, for instance, where there is advertising, where there are splashes of color that help highlight a retailer or something like that. In fact, there are a number of competition models we've done that were actually sort of tattooed with colored transparencies because the client was interested in an exciting retail

Foster and Partners (U.K.). City Hall (Greater London Authority Headquarters), Southwark, London, England, 1998–2002. Presentation model, 1:200, acrylic, timber, fiberboard, polyurethane-foam modeling board, and maple and lime veneer, 1999.

Richard Meier & Partners
(U.S.). Jubilee Church,
Rome, Italy, 1996–2004.
Model of the interior.

Technical improvements
have made it possible to
overcome the problems
with depth of field
encountered in early
model photography.

NATIONAL CONFERENCE CENTRE

environment and that was a good way to convey it.[55]

But this is dangerous ground, and such models are successful only when designed with considerable taste. While there will always be errors of judgment, ultimately the model's versatility is its merit, not its deficiency, and its "honesty" relates to the intention of its creator. The model speaks with its makers' voice, and the maker must take into account the sophistication and understanding of the audience when choosing the mode of representation.

The model's coming-of-age in the 1980s coincided, rather remarkably, with its newly acquired independence (spearheaded in the Conceptualist exhibition of 1976 "Idea as Model"). The model was now boosted to a new level of both public consciousness and self-consciousness. In its fresh incarnation, it was not universally welcomed. However, it was here to stay, and if it was regarded with more suspicion, it was also treated with more respect.

With the model to some extent unmasked, client and architect enter into a new partnership, one in which everyone is in on the secret. Clients recognize that, in a presentation, they are there to be persuaded. Instead of being duped by the imagery, they can enjoy the illusion. Somehow they have become joint conspirators, or accomplices in the crime. Today's participants, particularly in competitions and at major presentations, are more knowing and have greater expectations of the model, whether it be as

Kevin Roche John Dinkeloo and Associates (U.S.). Dublin National Conference Centre, Ireland. Model, c. 2000.

an object of art or of artifice. No one would want to disappoint the audience: all the stops are pulled out.

Presentation models have been described as the "show business of architecture," and this is not necessarily a negative assessment.[56] The circumstances of presentation often invite a dramatic approach, in which the most compelling devices can be justifiably employed. Early presentations involve a buildup of excitement for both architect and client. From the time of Brunelleschi, architects have taken this as an opportunity for a moment of theater, with all the trimmings of a special occasion. Brunelleschi's brick model of the dome for Florence's cathedral was built very publicly, in 1418, in the courtyard of the office of works. Eventually standing twelve feet tall, it was embellished by the finest craftsmen, including the sculptor Donatello, over a period of ninety days. After this time, the wardens and various consultants, plied with light refreshment, were invited to inspect. The model, big enough to walk inside, was an intriguing prospect and caused a considerable stir.[57] Evidently, Brunelleschi had a feeling for presentations and understood the power of anticipation. Vasari illustrates his method:

> Filippo also made a model for the lantern with eight sides, which is very beautiful for its originality, variety and decoration. He made a ladder up to the ball, which was a marvel, but as he had stopped it up with a little wood at the point of entrance, no one but himself suspected its existence.

When the time came for the model's display,

> Praise was lavished upon Filippo's work by all, but as they did not see any steps to ascend to the ball they concluded that it was defective . . . Filippo then removed the piece of wood at the base of the model and showed the ascent in a pillar in the form in which it exists to-day, of a vaulted cylinder, and on one side a channel with bronze rings, where, by placing one foot after another, one may ascend to the top.[58]

Similar exploitation of the element of surprise may have been used by Sir John Soane around 1793, when he presented his beautifully crafted model of Tyringham House to the Fleet Street banker William Praed. Already impressive as an object, it came apart in three layers, disclosing to the client the layout of the interior domestic arrangements.[59]

Like Brunelleschi, the twentieth-century architect Harvey Wiley Corbett was also a showman. At a memorial dinner in Corbett's honor in 1955, Hugh Ferriss recalled the architect's exploits, citing an incident that took place in Corbett's drafting room on the top floor of the Bush Building (see pages 43 and 116), which he had recently designed on Forty-second Street in New York:

> He was working on what appeared to be a model of a twenty-story structure. Actually,

Sir John Soane (U.K.). Tyringham House, Buckinghamshire, England, 1792–1800. Model, mahogany, 12 by 21 by 19 inches: Joseph Parkins, c. 1793–94.

this was a box, about two feet square, four feet high, with indication on the sides of twenty stories of fenestration. But this box was a surprise package; when secret strings were pulled, a second box inside the first came up, and you had the impression of a twenty-story building mounting before your eyes into a forty-story building. I got the point a little later when the clients came in: they were duly impressed when the twenty stories turned into forty stories, but the cream of the jest was when a third box, inside the second, shot up to eighty stories and hit the ceiling. This made a hit on the clients, too; they were so delighted by the performance that, later on, they built a real building considerably higher than the one originally intended.[60]

While such occurrences seem to have been relatively isolated historically, today they are a more familiar feature of presentations. Many architects will, from time to time, use some element of surprise. For his proposal for the Union Carbide Corporation in the 1970s, Kevin Roche created a full-size mock-up of an office interior that included real furniture; a projection of the surrounding wooded landscape was visible through the "windows." The model was made to demonstrate the merits of a more costly proposal, which employed an internal car park to prevent the view from being spoiled by a parking lot encircling the building. Being able to walk into the full-size office space and

Gehry Partners, Samsung Museum of Modern Art, Seoul, South Korea, 1995. Model in a cloud of dry ice.

"see" the landscape immediately "through the window" was a powerful way of communicating the idea, one that succeeded in convincing the client.[61] Frank Gehry revealed his preliminary model for Seoul's Samsung Museum of Modern Art in a cloud of dry ice, evoking the ethereal image of mountains, waterfalls, and clouds common to traditional Korean art while helping to convey a sense of the preliminary, hazy nature of the proposal at this early stage.[62] Another time, asked to make a presentation for the Lewis Residence project at a party, Gehry staged a dramatic entertainment, making "a big theatrical [foam] model that filled the room."[63]

Sometimes models have been disguised, or partially hidden, to heighten the moment of revelation for the client (and here the parallel with a child's anticipatory delight at the prospect of a new toy is especially pertinent). At NBBJ's presentation for the Daewoo Tower, the architect arrived carrying a small box, five by five by three and a half inches, the lid of which was tantalizingly flipped open and shut during the discussion. It was finally shown to contain a tiny sketch model of the preliminary proposal, to the delight of all.[64] On another occasion, in Germany, the architects Sauerbruch and Hutton entered a meeting room for the presentation of their Block 109 competition proposal, carrying what appeared to be a plank of wood, which they left on the table while introducing their scheme. Later the mysterious "plank" was opened: it consisted of two pieces with a removable lid. The lower portion was a site model of six blocks of the city, which included the project building. The lid was reversed to form the model's base. Frank Gehry has recalled another presentation coup, this time for the One Times Square project in New York, which intimates the model's wider potential: "We set it up theatrically. We made the building smoke. Superman came out. We showed [the clients] the whole thing. They were ecstatic. They danced around the model and told us what geniuses we were."[65] But architects must walk a fine line here: they can rarely afford to appear tongue in cheek.

The relationships between architect, model, and client are not simple or fixed; they evolve. The architect's awareness of client expectations, for instance, influences the model's design in all types of presentation. The general conception among architects, as German architect Michael Schumacher comments, is that, "Of course you can convince a client easier with a very realistic model with a lot of small people in it." Yet this is too simple an analysis; as he goes on to say, "Usually our clients don't pay for this kind of model, and we are not interested in them."[66] Some clients may respond to overrealistic models; others do not. The model's designer must be flexible—sensitive to the type of client and project at hand. What is the client looking for: a visionary building or a quick sell? And what is he or she impressed by: a piece of sculpture or a technological tour de force? In general, the client for an art museum may have different expectations of the model than the client for an office block or factory—but this is not always the case. Some clients will accept more freedom in the model's presentation, whereas others will see the architect's input purely as a professional service—a contribution to commerce, not to art. The architect is at liberty to accept or reject a commission, to enter or pass over a competition; but once the decision is made, the nature of the client is ignored at the architect's peril.

It is possible that an architect can become so sought after that he or she can afford to ignore the client's needs, and then the client must take the fact that the idea will "work" on faith. Frank Gehry has achieved this status. His rough, semiabstract study models, created in-house during development of the design, do not communicate his project ideas in any detail, although they are shown to his clients as the design progresses. (At first they can be shocked by this, he finds, but they soon become intrigued. Since the unfinished character of the model makes it more approachable, it becomes part of the dialogue, even encouraging the client to be physically involved, to suggest changes and move around the parts.)[67] However, even Gehry makes use of conventionally "finished" presentation models when circumstances require.

The presentation model is constrained by a profusion of demands and expectations, and its complexity has grown. Those for competitions are perhaps the most impressive and arcane. Competitions often call for some extra glamour in the model above and beyond the strict purposes of communication, but at the same time models are formed under a unique set of constraints. Briefs are sometimes short and the time allocation limited, so there is little opportunity to develop detail in the design and less information available for inclusion in the model. Cost poses a particular difficulty. Some competitions provide an allowance to a selected group of architects to cover their costs, but others are open, so that the contest becomes a gamble for the architect, who cannot afford to disregard expense. Competition rules, too, can pose limitations on the model's

design. Often the scale is stipulated, and sometimes even the color is restricted. The insistence on white models is a tradition in France: it "is very conventional," comments Odile Decq, "and it doesn't express everything about the idea." For her, white models fail to portray, for example, the material qualities of wood, metal, and glass, which are important elements in her designs.[68]

As a result of such pressures, competition models pose a more considerable challenge to the architect. They are very precisely designed. For in addition to all other requirements, the model must be dynamic, distinguishing the proposal and making the presentation as a whole stand out. Each office develops its own strategy for competition models. Modelmaker Mike Fairbrass and architect Ivan Harbour, who work together at Richard Rogers Partnership, explained theirs in a joint interview. The former notes, "We approach them as 'the model as object.' It has to convey the basic idea, the basic

Alsop Architects (U.K.). Puddle Dock Office Development, Blackfriars, London, England, 1998– . Model: Network Modelmakers, 1999.

intent of the design, and look great as an object as well." Significantly, neither thinks that realism is necessary or essential. Harbour says, "Definitely they're nonrealistic for us. We're only going to get across a concept for a competition. We're not anywhere near a reality at that point." Fairbrass continues, "So it would be kind of absurd to try and show it, because it would all change anyway."[69]

These are just some of the elements in a complex matrix of factors that affect the presentation model's design. Another is influenced by one of the fundamental divisions in architects' views on the model: whether they accept that it functions as an object in its own right. The model may be seen either as a means to an end—a discardable part of a process in which architecture is the only valid objective—or as an artifact worthy of being judged, in itself, as part of the architect's creative output. This long-standing split of opinion has been brought into sharper focus since the 1970s.

While concessions are generally made for presentation (in making the model more attractive), for a significant number of architects, models are not conceived as objects but as a practical means of communicating information about the design. Architects in this camp, like the fifteenth-century Alberti, see any focus on the model per se as unnecessary, distracting, and ultimately vain: the mark of a conceited architect who "[strives] to divert . . . attention from a proper examination of the parts to be considered, toward admiration of himself."[70] For the twentieth-century British architect Sir Denys Lasdun, too, the model was "a means of visualizing rather than a finished object to be gloated over in a glass case."[71] Cesar Pelli considers his models process objects, which are unsentimentally discarded after use. Gehry's statement "Drawing is a tool, the model is a tool, the only thing that matters is the building—the finished building" could not be more clear.[72]

Those who, on the other hand, value the model as an object are concerned with the overall impact of its design, and the particular messages it carries, in

addition to its basic communicative purpose. These are the architects who load their models with meaning, for like their buildings, the model is part of their oeuvre—a meticulously designed object. For these architects, the workmanship and materials of the model contribute significantly to their cause. Their models vary greatly in design and often have a recognizable personal style.

Any model, however purely practical it is deemed to be, will bear traces of the architect's personality, betraying something of his or her own outlook and interests. Just as an individual's manner of dress

Sir Denys Lasdun (U.K.). National Theatre, London, England. Models, c. 1964–65.

An occasional lack of concern for the model as an object has not had a negative influence on the number of models produced.

Michael Sorkin Studio (U.S.). Weed, near Yuma, Arizona (unsolicited master plan), 1994. Model, wood and metal, 6 by 15 feet (detail).

creates an image but also gives clues to his or her character and individual formation, so with the model. Such strands of personal meaning and vision carry into this presentation object that goes before them to promote their cause.

Hani Rashid's and Michael Sorkin's models are very physical, crafted objects. Their nature flows from factors in their makers' personal experience. For Rashid, Daniel Libeskind's approach has been influential, as have his artist father's activities. From his student days at Cranbrook, he remembers that Libeskind's

> pedagogy depended, really bordered on, medieval artisanship. So we spent a lot of time with materials, metals, . . . using technology that was four or five hundred years old or

earlier. I remember him priding himself on the fact that he made students work under candlelight, with a chisel—which wasn't really true, but it sounded great in a lecture. This reflected the kind of attitude that he had, and I think that a lot of that came down through a kind of craft tradition of modeling.[73]

Michael Sorkin has also expressed how, "coming from a kind of crafts prejudice" in the making of objects, he finds "something satisfying about smelling the linseed oil and working with the hands."[74] Frank Gehry's models are different. These are casually assembled, serviceable objects, like the man himself: "His hair is messy and appearing wind-blown, he wears simple, strong, humble khaki pants and button down shirts. He wears these clothes always . . . Everything we do here, the nature of the space, the way we work, the way things are placed, comes directly from Frank and his personality."[75] Richard Meier's office is immaculate, pristine, organized—as are his models. It is often difficult to separate, in any model, what is devised and what is not. Nevertheless, it is true that nothing about the model is arbitrary.

More than other types of model, presentation models are conscious objects. They are the architect's face, and have an ambassadorial role. They embody the architect's highest intentions and aspirations: the model's failure will be his or her own.

There has been a growing tendency, in recent years, for architects to identify themselves in the model—to create an image of themselves and an image of their work. The model's design is now often used to convey messages about the architect's artistic and intellectual frame of reference—a strategy that may be individual or shared among a group of architects aligned in a common cause. In 1990, Thomas Fisher noted, "How and why we make a drawing or model . . . are directly related to our philosophy of architecture. Is design a process or a product, an image or an idea, an art or a service?"[76] Thus, while the form of the model communicates the architect's vision for a particular project, it may also, in a more general way, be intended to identify the architect in relation to his or her peers. This enlargement of the model's agenda has contributed to greater diversity in its design.

Richard Meier and Daniel Libeskind may be taken as examples. Though the character of Meier's models has been developed specifically for their presentation tasks, their design also indicates his broader intentions. Meier's models, simplified and white, do not indicate materials or finishes. Detail is suppressed; the models are often unpopulated and without vegetation. Clearly the fundamental intention is a focus on form. Yet white models also have a history, of which Meier is well aware. Many plaster models in the nineteenth century were left white. In the twentieth century, early modernists, notably Le Corbusier, found the format sympathetic to their aims. While working in materials other than plaster, they continued to finish their models in white, finding the abstraction compatible with their formally motivated architectural approach (after all,

Richard Meier & Partners (U.S.). United States Courthouse and Federal Building, Central Islip, New York, 1993–2000. Model.

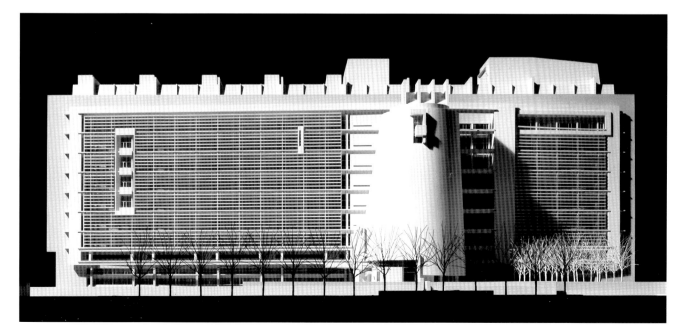

many of the buildings were in reality intended to be white). And so, solidly linked with modernism, the white model has become almost a badge of architects working in this tradition. In Meier's models this chosen association is clear. Libeskind's models reflect another frame of reference—his link to Deconstructivism. The jarring conjunction of disparate materials combines with his angular formal concept to undermine any sense of stability, fragmenting the overall view.

The approach to materials is often particularly indicative of the architect's wider meaning. Some architects are eager to celebrate the skills of craftsmanship and the quality of materials in their models, following a general preoccupation in their work. Modelmakers are keenly aware of the impact of such choices: "Lots of what we do in three-dimensional modeling has to do with subconscious triggers," Alec Vassiliadis explains.[77] Materials have all sorts of subtle associations. Metals and reflective materials can suggest high-tech leanings. Natural materials may associate the architect with environmental awareness. Richly patinated wood makes historical

allusions, linking the work to long-standing architectural traditions, museum objects, and the concept of hand-crafting rather than machine-making.

Many architects develop such a "trademark" style in their work. The choices of color (or the lack of it), method of construction, materials, and level of abstraction are personal, yet they may also be linked to passing fashions. Spencer de Grey has outlined trends in model style that have been evident across the international scene. Interestingly, white (which Meier has used consistently throughout this period) is returning. "White models in this office," notes de Grey, "are coming back into fashion. Whereas if you had come here five or six years ago, all the models would have been pastel colors, toned-down realistic colors. We had a white period before that, so it does go in waves. When I first joined the office, the idea of doing a wooden model was an absolute anathema. You wouldn't touch wood, never mind what material you used. It had to be Perspex or foam or whatever."[78] Foster and Partners' pastels of the 1990s were imitated widely, becoming known as "Foster colors" in the modelmaking trade. From the

Michael Graves & Associates (U.S.). Bass Museum, Miami Beach, Florida, 1993. Competition model.

As with the use of color by Foster and Partners, the playful approach to details and characteristic coloration in Michael Graves's models give them a recognizable style.

Morphosis (U.S.). Blades Residence, Santa Barbara, California, 1992–96. Model, 1996.

Landscape elements provide a particular opportunity for expression. In this model, the tree and land forms are deliberately nonrealistic. Through their sympathy with the geometric lines of the building, they also reflect the architects' intentions for the project: "Breaking out of the singular gesture of the main volume, [a] set of more intimate spaces fractures, tilts, and opens to the natural landscape beyond . . . the house moves from the order of the street to the freedom of the natural landscape, with the indoor/outdoor living/landscape space as the mediator between the two conditions."

1960s on, architects found other methods of distinguishing their models, including the stylized, hand-colored elevations created by Pelli.

Underlying these disparate choices and motivations is a lurking unease about the question of realism. This is not unique to models but extends across all the architect's representational media, including model photography. It is worth underlining the two main sources of this anxiety in presentation models: one familiar and one less so.

First, an overexact approach to realism is often equated with a lack of imagination and aesthetic sensitivity. In a widely held concept of the imagination, creativity ranks higher than reproduction. In 1914 in *Architectural Record*, Alwyn T. Covell explains why naturalistically detailed models have had uneven press among architects for hundreds of years: "they do not make imagination necessary, and for the same reason they are not works of art."[79] In

any case, "literal exactness and a multiplicity of details often befog the expression of truth rather than assist it," observed LeRoy Grumbine in *American Architect*. "Art, in order to be real art, must express a beautiful, noble, or truthful idea, or an experience of life, in a harmonious manner, and he who can do this in the simplest, clearest, most direct way, is the greatest artist. Therefore the modeler must know how to select, what to show and what to leave out, and how to combine."[80]

The second source of anxiety is the set of unwelcome associations prompted by realism, chiefly in connection with the childhood or hobby miniature and the manipulative "developer's model." These have become much more obtrusive since the 1970s: the miniature because of its growth in the hobby industry and its adoption for models of seductive appeal; the developer's model because of its tendency to deceive and its distressing prominence.

Together these have combined to cause an antipathy among architects for anything that appears too conventionally realistic. The strength of architects' reaction to realism is usually in direct proportion to their conception of themselves as artists.

It is almost impossible to make the model completely convincing as an exercise in realism when surrounding roads or vegetation are included, and the attempt can sometimes seem foolish. (Visions of toy town are immediately aroused.) The British term "model-railway model" or "train-set model" explains all. The railway enthusiasts–cum–amateur modelers who engage in the construction of elaborate landscapes for their railway networks discover that landscape is the most difficult part of the model to treat realistically, and they typically take a disproportionate amount of time to produce less than convincing results. Many such models are conspicuously lacking in artistic merit. For architects, "model-railway model" is not an endearing term. "Developer's model" and "corporate model" are similarly disparaging, implying at best that the architect is pandering to the client's lack of artistic sense and at worst that the model is dishonest.

The tainted history of the presentation model has engendered embarrassment for architects. High levels of realism and detail have become inextricably linked with the "selling" models of commercial architectural development, designed to manipulate and seduce; though not intending deception themselves, most architects working for corporate clients see themselves as under pressure. As Wimer of SOM notes,

> Quite often we have to produce very factual-looking, very realistic models for certain developers because they want to see people with pink faces or whatever—you know, bright clothes and cars that look like cars, and that sort of thing. I prefer models that are more abstract, that convey the idea of the building rather than exactly what it is going to look like. I prefer models that are much more abstract than perhaps a lot of the clients want.[81]

Architects really began to move away from realism at the end of the 1960s—at the same time the use of abstraction to communicate vision became more widely explored. In Britain, Sir Philip Dowson freed himself from the increasingly realistic, professionally built model by setting up an in-house workshop at Arup Associates to pursue the abstraction of wood. (Concurrently, Paolo Soleri was experimenting with abstraction for different purposes in his visionary Arcology models and model photographs.) As the manipulative exploits and technical triumphs of the 1970s and 1980s accumulated, the strength of feeling among architects mounted. The more an individual wished to dissociate him- or herself from "commercial" architecture, the less acceptable realism became. The antipathy to realism invoked in this period has left a twenty-first-century legacy that shows no sign of being dispelled. Many still see any capitulation whatsoever to realism in terms of compromise. Rashid's comments on the conventional, "finished" presentation model exemplify these feelings and express the sentiments of his peers. He calls them "slick . . . kind of bloodless," "nothing from the creative, or from the generative point of view." Asymptote's own, more abstract models are "where the ideas are," their professionally made realistic counterpart "just a bad fake."[82]

Some aspects of the model are more open to abstraction than others. For the building itself, it is difficult to evade the obligation to convey some "hard" information in the presentation model. The model landscape provides an opportunity for greater freedom. James C. Rose marked out the way for a new approach in his article "Landscape Models" in *Pencil Points* in 1939, recommending that for the representation of plant forms, "the more abstract the better for purposes of study." In his view, for study models "to attempt an exact reproduction of nature is the same laborious futility which possessed the early Dutch masters to paint with a single-hair brush every leaf on a tree or every hair on a Madonna's head."[83] His trees, made from blotting-paper discs

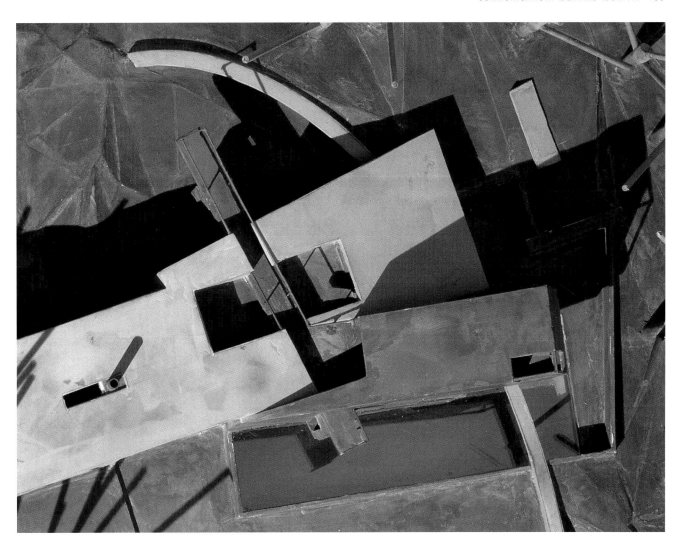

Morphosis (U.S.). Blades
Residence, Santa Barbara,
California, 1992–96.
Model, card, foam core,
paste, and wood,
1995–96.

supported on matchsticks, provided sufficient realism without running the risk of being labeled
"twee." From the 1960s, this approach was explored
more widely and began to influence presentation
models. Now the model's site and surrounding landscape have become a primary focus for artistic
experimentation, a place where architects identify
their position with regard to realism and make their
allegiances known.

There are additional opportunities for
establishing identity. The lighting of a model can
be treated in a variety of ways, from the accurate
reproduction of every illumination point to the
suggestive imagery of a general glow of abstract
blocks of light. And depiction of the building itself
is not excluded. Will Alsop, Zaha Hadid, Decq,
Morphosis, Libeskind, Toyo Ito, Sorkin, Peter
Eisenman, and Rem Koolhaas, for instance, all push
the limits of abstraction possible in a building's
representation, occasionally producing objects so
close to abstract sculpture that in some settings they
would not be readily distinguished as architecture.
Again, the more abstract the approach, the more
the architect is associating him- or herself with the
fine arts.

Zaha Hadid Architects (U.K.). Forty-second Street Hotel, New York, New York, 1995. Model, 1:240: Network Modelmakers.

Architects are attentive to the level of abstraction in the presentation of all aspects of their work. The monograph, where model photography contributes significantly to the intended effect, is the quintessential example. The architect's attitude to realism can be read in the direction of the view (from true eye level to apparently random points of observation), in the framing or fusing of images, and in the general concern with representation of the design (which sometimes appears to be considered dispensable). The monograph, particularly for architects with little built work to display, becomes an art book of carefully constructed imagery, a visual compendium of the architect's personal credo, in the creation of which the model photograph often plays a substantive part.

In the present climate, the options of more realistic representation may be too easily overlooked. Recent modelmaking activity shows that realism and creativity may be united. Models like Alsop's Palestra, London (see page 167), and Hadid's Forty-second Street Hotel, New York, aid visualization of the design concept with a subtlety in which art and integrity are combined, and in which knowledge of the model's audience is key. The creators of these models have perceived that realism is a tool of communication and that its use must be considered in relation to the model's purpose; they do not shun realism as such. After all, it cannot be denied that the virtuous-seeming abstract model exudes its own seduction and charm. To achieve a crafted balance between legibility for the layman and aesthetic acceptability for the architect and his or her peers, between conveying information and establishing identity, is possibly the greatest challenge in presentation models, requiring skill and sensitivity in both design and manufacture.

The contemporary presentation model is intensely sophisticated: full of messages that can be analyzed and read, layered with meaning. The model of today is an instrument so adaptable and acute in application that it requires the most exacting control. After almost a century of renewed attention, is it possible that the model may one day become too complex—too clever for its own good? If its twentieth-century journey brought about a dent of confidence in this "curious and fine" object (to borrow from Thomas Eayre's eighteenth-century description), it may not, in the end, be altogether a bad thing.

Eisenman Architects (U.S.). Church for the Year 2000, Rome, Italy, 1996. Model.

Peter Eisenman and other members of the office team reviewing a model for the Neues Fussball Stadion in Munich, Germany, 2001.

CHAPTER 6

Makers

Models are often the highlight of a presentation in contemporary practice. Their brilliance is vital to the success of the project. The current dependence on models, and their level of sophistication, has increased the need for competent makers. Yet despite the limelight bestowed on their creations, these makers remain shadowy figures. Who they are, and how they are trained, is something of a mystery, but crucial to understanding their productions.

The maker may be the architect, certainly the source of many a striking model. However, the ability to produce a satisfactory model is not necessarily one of the architect's set of skills. The success of a model is dependent on its maker's control and understanding of the medium, that is, his or her ability to convey the intended messages and necessary information in model form combined with a sufficient level of technical skill. Naturally, an equal facility with making and designing sometimes occurs. The clay models of both Michelangelo and Brunelleschi (who trained as a goldsmith and apparently made models of most of his major works "with his own hand") might be expected to communicate their purpose accurately.[1] But in order to transmit the multiple messages of today's presentations and to be in command of cutting-edge techniques, more than a practical facility with materials is required. Further, the demands of a thriving contemporary practice have eroded the architect's time. Though many younger architects and smaller practices make their own models, as soon as commissions begin to flow, regular personal involvement is often hindered. Even in the smallest offices, the burden of

making may be shared. More common among flourishing practices is the principal designer's dependence on the skills of others for all but the most basic three-dimensional sketches.

When the model is made by someone other than the architect, rapport between the architect and the maker is essential if the model is to carry the architect's idea convincingly. An effective model presents selected messages, and choices must be made through deliberation with the architect. "Modelmaking is editing," one professional explained.[2] But it is also more. Peter Eisenman works closely with young architects in his practice who make models as his ideas are evolving. In 2000, he described the relationship that develops in evocative terms. Of one of

Rem Koolhaas works on a model for the Office of Metropolitan Architecture's CCTV Headquarters, Beijing, China, c. 2002.

Leslie Thorp, son of John B. Thorp, working on model of St. Paul's Cathedral, c. 1949.

The modelmaker must be familiar with architectural design and the general principles and terminology of the discipline to discuss a project meaningfully with an architect and to accurately represent his or her ideas.

his staff, Selim Vural, Eisenman remarked, "He's my dancing partner . . . The modelmaker understands how I dance. To make a model, he and I have to dance together in a certain way, and when he gets out of range I have to say, 'Wait a minute, come back.'"[3]

Dancing with a partner requires responsiveness and artistic sympathy. Recognition of these requirements for modelmaking is not new, though they became of increasing importance in the twentieth century. Early in the modelmaking revival of the last hundred years, LeRoy Grumbine described the modelmaker's work as a form of artistic interpreta-

tion, the "relation to the architect similar to that between a pianist and composer."[4] Present-day modelmaking, like other artistic relationships, requires empathy, creativity, and a capacity for expression.

Not all modelmakers operate at this level. Some produce models that are repetitive and uninspired. Others make acceptable models, providing an essential service for architects who do not have such complex skills, on some occasions without even meeting the architect. Some modelmakers have different aims, specializing in high levels of accuracy and technical virtuosity: for them, creativity may still be central to the task, but it is channeled into problem-solving and ingenious construction rather than into the artistic nature of the design.

A first-rate modelmaker, however, can be all these things and more: creative, skillful, a master craftsperson, involved in realizing but also interpreting the idea; in many ways, like Eisenman's dancer, partnering the architect. Modelmakers often draw words of appreciation from the architects with whom they work. Though not regularly listed in project credits, their contribution is often warmly acknowledged off the record; sometimes the architect's sense of awe at the modelmaker's ability to translate sketchy ideas into a convincing design proposal or an electrifying object is more than implicit.

Both architects and modelmakers recognize that a combination of skills and attributes creates an effective relationship. Most such talents are long-term standards in modelmaking practice. An understanding of architecture is vital. "The modelmaker should be familiar with the fundamental principles of architectural design, with drafting-room practice, and with architectural details, so that he can interpret the architect's ideas with a minimum of effort and supervision,"[5] charged one adviser to the profession in 1925. In 1939, a commentator insisted,

> It is essential that the work be done by one with considerable knowledge and long experience in architectural design . . . It is in no sense a job for the ordinary mechanic or plaster shop man who cannot be expected to appreciate various mere suggestions on the designer's preliminary sketches . . . What is needed is one who is fully familiar with the designer's habits of mind, and who can work hand in glove with him.[6]

And again, the maker must be a master of materials and techniques, capable of selecting those most appropriate for the message conveyed. For "The purpose of a model is to illustrate the architect's conception. It has a story to tell . . . To the modeler each design presents its own particular problem. Many

means of expression are at the modeler's command; each has its technical possibilities and limitations."[7]

Initiative is another helpful trait. Sometimes the maker is able to contribute to the design, either by pointing out difficulties inherent in the drawings or by making alternative proposals. Ivan Harbour, an architect at Richard Rogers Partnership, affirms his dependence on the maker's contribution. In discussion with Mike Fairbrass, RRP's model shop manager, he first sympathizes—"You have to understand a garbled set of instructions and a rather grotty set of sketches"—and then he underlines one of the maker's particular values: "Also, you have to input on those. You have to come back and say, 'Well this isn't very good, is it?' That's the real skill."[8] Certainly, one of the gravest misconceptions about modelmaking, as one observer noted in 1975, "is that it consists of patient little men making little things, using tools and following someone else's instructions"; in fact, "show a good modelmaker a drawing and he will show you the design problems. He questions everything because he is forced to answer everything"— in most cases, more than the architect has to, or is able to, at the same stage.[9] This is why, as another observes, "it's often a highly charged moment when architects see their design for the first time."[10]

Trust, and a certain humility in the architect, is necessary for modelmakers to work in this way; they can often contribute most in an in-house situation or when a relationship with the architect has been built up. When this trust has been established, the architect will sometimes give the maker a free hand.

Choice of scale is often left to the professional, and color also offers the opportunity for a significant contribution. To achieve realistic color is surprisingly difficult, requiring both aptitude and experience. Yet even when realism is not the aim, many architects rely on the maker's judgment. Modelmakers generally agree that "architects are amazingly scared of color, which accounts for the number of white and silver models you see." London modelmaker Richard Armiger opines, "I think it's a cop-out . . .

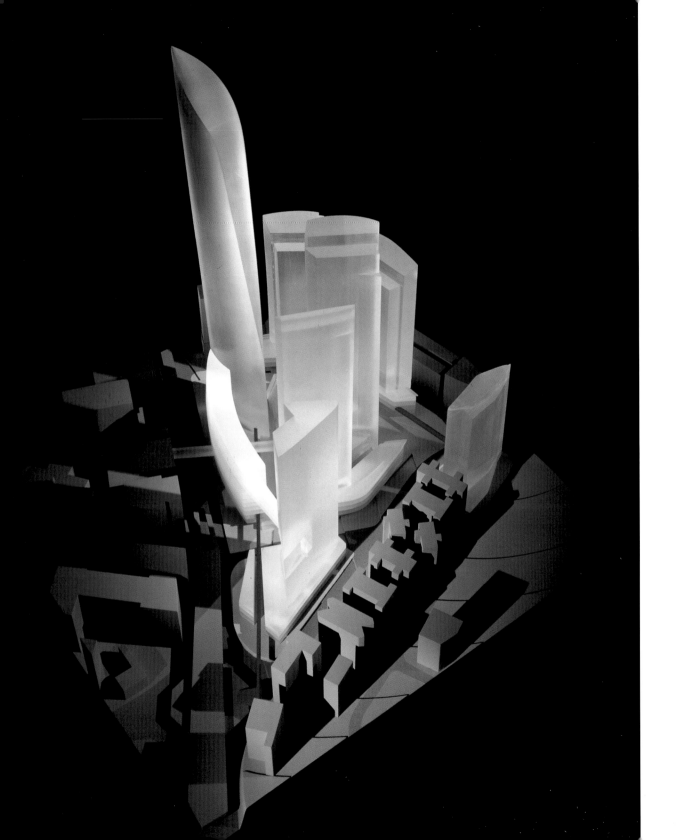

color is critical, but it's seen as a last-minute thing if it's considered at all."[11]

Such participation reinforces the need for that vital piece of the modelmaker's equipment: artistic sensitivity. As LeRoy Grumbine, the early-twentieth-century commentator, insisted, "A good model . . . should be made by an *artist* not a *craftsman*."[12] Others in this period noted specific examples of artistic modelmaking. Alwyn T. Covell drew attention to the work of H. E. Woodsend, an English "artist-architect" who operated a studio in New York around 1914: "The sort of model developed by Mr. Woodsend . . . unquestionably places scale modeling among the fine arts," he claimed. Covell went on to describe Woodsend's philosophy: "the most important thing is to interpret the design in the true spirit of the style and country from which it is adapted and to express as much as possible by means of softness of line, irregularity of surface, and depth and variety of color." Woodsend, according to Covell, believed in "bringing out the *character* of his subject in terms at once subtle and artistic."[13]

Today, Peter Pran of NBBJ reiterates this need for an artistic sense. "Models have to have a kind of poetic touch by the people who have made the model," he says. "You can immediately see it if a model is made by people who are not artistic. A lot of model shops do just the conventional ordinary models. That's not enough; you have to lift it up to the level of artwork."[14] Since architectural models can now rank with works by David Hockney at the prestigious Royal Academy Summer Exhibition, their significance in this respect is not in doubt, but the nature of the maker becomes an object of even greater curiosity.

Among all the abilities of the modern model-maker, interpretation is key. Richard Threadgill of Tetra Models, writing in 1987, explains the model-maker's role:

A model is architecture at its purest, untouched by Building Regulations and door handles.

It's the ultimate expression of the architect's intentions. Our skill lies in understanding the architect's statement and producing something which clearly and sharply reveals the strength of that statement.[15]

Where do such talented and able people come from? Few countries offer opportunities for formal training in modelmaking. In the U.K., for instance, only a handful of universities and colleges offer degree courses; these include architectural projects alongside industrial prototype modelmaking.[16] In the U.S., only one full degree program—at Bemidji State University—is dedicated to modelmaking (the program includes an architectural component).[17] In these and other countries, makers may be introduced to modelmaking as part of a vocational course at a technical college or through studying other disciplines that include the teaching of modelmaking skills, such as interior or industrial design, or architecture itself. But opportunities of this kind are limited, and the majority of practicing modelmakers have arrived at their occupation by other routes.

In fact, the diversity of training of today's model-makers helps differentiate the present-day practitioner from those of the past. Historically, modelmakers came from a small group of specialized backgrounds, trained in either wood- or plasterworking techniques. There were always some models made in other materials—papier-mâché and cardboard, for example, were used in the nineteenth century—but from the earliest years of the Renaissance to the beginning of the twentieth century, the majority of models, certainly of surviving models, were fabricated in either wood (made by joiners, carpenters, and cabinetmakers) or clay or plaster (made by sculptors or ornamental plasterers).

Also in contrast to today's modelmaker, few of these earlier craftsmen dedicated their lives solely to making small-scale models of buildings. Before the nineteenth century in Europe, the makers were usually artisans employed in construction work. Often, as in France, they came from the trade guilds linked

NBBJ (U.S.). Kwun Tong Town Centre, Hong Kong, China, 1998. Concept/ presentation model, acrylic, paint, and electric lighting: Alec Vassiliadis.

The model was made in the in-house workshop of NBBJ's Seattle office for the architectural team headed by Peter Pran.

Sir Christopher Wren (U.K.). St. Paul's Cathedral, London, 1675–1710. Model, 1:24, oak and plaster painted to simulate stone and lead with some gilding of details and relief work, 3.97 by 3.99 by 6.41 meters, 1673–74: William Cleere.

The Great Model of St. Paul's was made by Cleere with a team of craftsmen, including twelve joiners, a wood-carver, a plasterer, and a "sergeant-painter" who carried out the gilding work. It cost six hundred pounds in 1674, has survived for three centuries, and is still considered one of the greatest masterpieces of modelmaking. It is known, of course, as Wren's model, not Cleere's.

to the building sites of cathedrals or other large public works.[18] Even the most celebrated models were sometimes made by craftsmen for whom the activity appears to have been a digression. Antonio Labacco, who supervised the making of Antonio da Sangallo's Great Model of St. Peter's in Rome, worked as the architect's assistant on a variety of tasks. William Cleere, who led the team that constructed the Great Model of St. Paul's in London for Sir Christopher Wren, was a practicing joiner and carver; before taking on this ten-month task, he was engaged in executing the principal woodwork of the Sheldonian Theatre.[19] Similarly, for other modelmakers associated with Wren, the activity was only part of their career. Two John Smallwells (probably father and son) were master joiners in a broad sense: skilled wood craftsmen, each serving as master of the Joiners' Company at different periods. The elder Smallwell, who first worked for Wren some years after the Great Model of St. Paul's was completed, produced models of interior fittings for the cathe-

dral, including the *baldacchino*. Other models by the Smallwells include the Radcliffe Camera model to Hawksmoor's design (the one that later served as a dollhouse), further models for Hawksmoor (and also Vanbrugh) of Castle Howard and Blenheim, and others for Thomas Archer.[20]

The more distinct profession of architectural modelmaking as it exists today had some precedents. Jean-Pierre Fouquet and his son François Fouquet, who worked in France in the late eighteenth and early nineteenth centuries, made a business of producing small-scale building models in plaster and are among the best-known pre-twentieth-century architectural modelmakers. One of Jean-Pierre Fouquet's first recorded commissions was for Thomas Jefferson in 1786, when the latter was ambassador to Paris: Fouquet senior made a model of the capitol of Virginia at Richmond. On the whole, however, the Fouquets' work for architects was subsidiary to the production of historical replicas of classical buildings made for collectors and for students and

Architectural modelers in the workshop of the Philippson Decorative Company in 1891 on the grounds of the forthcoming World's Columbian Exposition in Chicago.

Ornamental plasterworkers dominated architectural modelmaking in America in the nineteenth and beginning of the twentieth century. The modelers in the picture are working on ornamental panels for buildings being constructed for the 1893 World's Fair.

BELOW

Henry Ives Cobb (U.S.). U.S. Post Office/ Courthouse, Chicago, Illinois. Model: Emile Garet.

This photograph may have been used for publicity by the modelmaker.

connoisseurs on the Grand Tour.[21] The eighteenth-century Italian modelmakers Giovanni Altieri and Antonio Chichi, who worked in cork, are also remembered as architectural modelmakers, but they had a similar, nonprofessional clientele.[22]

While modelmakers from the fifteenth to the eighteenth centuries boasted mainly woodworking skills, many in the nineteenth and early twentieth centuries, like the Fouquets, worked in plaster.[23] This was particularly true in the U.S., though the major-

ity of the makers, unlike the Fouquets, were ornamental plasterers and worked to a much larger scale. The American craftsmen were often immigrants who had acquired their training abroad, and among them were many Italians: Ricci, Ardolino, and Di Lorenzo made models for New York architects Dennison & Hirons; the Menconi brothers were employed by Egerton Swartwout on his Denver Post Office project; C. G. Girolami & Sons worked—and continues to work—in Chicago.[24] The chief focus of these companies was the sculptural and decorative elements of a building, the only aspect regularly studied in three dimensions at the time; Girolami & Sons has records of only one scale model of a complete building made throughout the company's existence.[25] In the same way, Alexander L. Sampietro in New York, who took on a large model of the choir of the Cathedral of St. John the Divine for the office of Heins & La Farge around 1899, explains in his letterhead the many aspects of his work: "Artistic decorations in Plaster, Stucco, Papier Mâché and Carton Pierre; Models for Bronze, Wood and Stone Carving; Scale Models of Buildings and Monuments."[26] A French émigré, Emile Garet, who worked in Washington, D.C., on the large plaster model of the U.S. Capitol during the same period (see page 151), appears to have been more specialized,

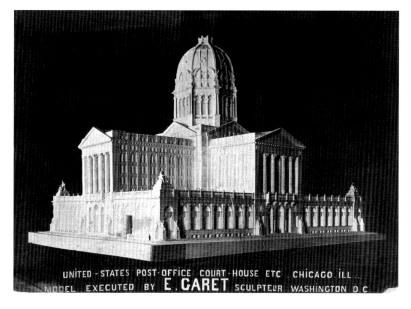

UNITED-STATES POST-OFFICE COURT-HOUSE ETC CHICAGO ILL. MODEL EXECUTED BY E. GARET SCULPTEUR WASHINGTON D C

John B. Thorp with the cupola of Sir Edwin Lutyens's model for Metropolitan Cathedral of Christ the King, Liverpool, England, c. 1933.

Thorp's timber model (see page 94) stood over twelve feet high and took ten men more than a year to build, at the staggering cost, for its time, of five thousand pounds.

describing himself as "Sculpteur, Architectural Modeler and Carver. Specialty: Scale Models of Buildings and Monuments."[27]

Before the twentieth century, a few individuals operated solely as architectural modelmakers in the present-day sense, not only in the range of work but in the type of practice, that is, they devoted the most substantial part of their business to making models for architects of the building and its parts (and not just the decorative elements). Nineteenth-century references imply that some earlier makers subsisted on just such a pattern of work. "Mr. Dighton" and "Mr. Day" were mentioned summarily in *The Builder* in the 1840s; several other British practitioners, including C. N. Thwaite and the firm of Jackson's, were noted by John Physick and Michael Darby in *Marble Halls*.[28]

One of the most distinctive precursors of today's professional modelmaker is found in late-nineteenth-century London. The career of John B. Thorp (1862–1939) illuminates early modern modelmaking practice; it is perhaps not entirely by coincidence that Thorp's company also appears to be the only architectural modelmaking business from the era that still operates today.[29] Thorp trained as an architect, at a time when modelmaking was unlikely to have been prominent in his studies, if included at all. Instead of going into practice, he set up his reprographic Drawing and Tracing Company in 1883. An advertisement in *The Building News* of 1885 shows the services offered: "All Kinds of Architectural and Engineering Drawings and Tracings Made. Bird's Eye Views of Estates, &c. Perspectives in Ink and Color. Designs Prepared, and Working Drawings Made from Rough Sketches, &c., &c."[30]

Thorp had an interest in and an aptitude for three-dimensional work, for at some point between 1885 and 1897 models came to be included in the list (as did blueprints, invented in the intervening years).[31] At this time his models were designed primarily to clarify points in legal cases, but toward the end of the cen-

Label on an album of photographs of the work of John B. Thorp's model-making business.

The label is decorated with foliage entwined with the modelmaker's tools.

Craftsman turning the dome for Lutyens's Liverpool Cathedral model in the workshop of John B. Thorp, early 1930s.

tury this was changing. "Mr. Thorp is very successful as a modelmaker," one commentator remarked on his "very ingenious" architects' models of 1901, further noting, "Architectural models might be much more frequently employed than they are."[32] Thorp was of the same mind. Tapping into the growing interest among his architecture clients (who soon included Sir Edwin Lutyens and Sir Giles Gilbert Scott), he made models a major portion of the firm's work.

Unlike American models of the period, Thorp's were most frequently a combination of cardboard and wood, with various other materials introduced where necessary. His techniques appear to have been picked up by trial and error, and his skills honed through experience on the job. Soon he was employing additional craftsmen. For Lutyens's design for Liverpool Cathedral (the model Thorp saw as his supreme creation), the maker called on traditional wood craftsmen, but for many of his models, wood was only a framework or not used at all, and a wider range of skills was necessary. A hundred years later, the firm—now Thorp Models—still constructs its products in a variety of materials.

Apart from the embryonic modern professional represented by Thorp, most modelmakers at the beginning of the twentieth century worked in the medium in which they were skilled. Commentary in articles up to World War II reflects this material-based division in the industry. In the U.S. in 1939, "models [fell] into three general classifications

according to the basic materials from which they are made and the corresponding techniques; those made of clay or plastelline [*sic*] (which may later be cast in plaster), those made of cardboard, and those made of wood."[33] (Cardboard workers were, by the second quarter of the twentieth century, among the professionals.) However, by this time the professional sphere was changing. Some makers were beginning to experiment with new materials, others with new combinations. It had become clear that with the growing use of models by architects, increased pace of construction, and concurrently rising wages, the painstaking work of the traditional plaster craftsman was no longer viable. The turmoil in modelmaking during this period of changeover was expressed by a bemused writer in 1939: "Modelmaking, it appears, is essentially the adaptation of numerous tools and materials to the purposes for which they were not originally intended."[34]

Regimented machinists in the workshop of Lester Associates, c. 1963, making parts for the massive Panorama of New York City for the 1964–65 New York World's Fair.

After World War II, a new breed of modelmaker emerged, one who worked in different materials, often on different building types (commercial rather than public), to tighter deadlines, and with increasing reliance on machines rather than hand tools. And thus, by 1950, the modelmaking industry was transformed. No longer was it an extension of traditional craft practices. Versatility and ingenuity became more essential than conventional craft skills. Some of the new modelmakers had a background in machine tooling. Mechanization helped with the precision, speed, and repetition required in models for multistory commercial buildings, skyscrapers, office blocks, and large housing projects. It also suited the processing of some of the new materials adopted in this period.

Mechanization had been encouraged by the war effort: in particular, workshops were set up in the U.S. for the fabrication of strategic models during World War II. The success of these facilities—seen at the time as powerhouses for the development of modeling ideas—contributed to a desire for factory-style production in modelmaking.[35] As the model boom continued over the next three decades, the influence of mechanization could be seen in the organization of some of the larger in-house workshops, like the one at I. M. Pei & Partners, set up by George Gabriel around 1956. (There were other notable workshops at Skidmore, Owings & Merrill, Perkins & Will, and the offices of Norman Foster and Philip Johnson.) Gabriel remembers, "Mine was 4,500 square feet. [It was] like a laboratory. The people were lined up on each side, the support tables in the middle, and you could wheel the models like patients to the doctor."[36]

Specialization and division of labor were part of the system, and efficiency was the goal. Some workers would concentrate on landscape elements, others on paint spraying and mixing. In Gabriel's workshop, which employed thirty-five at its peak, some were kept full-time on research, scouring for new ideas to improve the products and aid their making:

I had groups of people, like top modelmakers and support modelmakers, I had tree makers and cabinet makers and crate makers and research guys that were on the phone constantly trying to find different adhesives and different methods and so forth from other industries.[37]

However, the men (almost always) who staffed these workshops were not restricted to machinists; they came from a wide mix of backgrounds. "Employees of the highly mechanized shops," Sanford Hohauser explained in his American modelmaking book of 1970, "usually start their careers as pattern makers, cabinetmakers, sculptors, toolmakers, architectural draftsmen or graduates of trade schools."[38] The situation in London was much the same. The trainees in Piper Models' smaller workshop in 1975 were "pattern makers, woodworkers, and engineer's toolmakers," and the company looked for others with experience in technical drawing, hobby modeling, or "a flair for art in its widest sense, including pottery, sculpture and painting."[39] Modelmakers continue to emerge from such varied backgrounds (combining art, handicraft, and technology) today, though few of the ambitious in-house workshops that had helped to establish this approach survived the recession of the 1980s and early 1990s.

The influx of women makers in recent years has added to the industry's diversity. If modelmakers through the ages have generally been unsung heroes, female makers have been almost invisible. Before the twentieth century, sources suggest, makers were exclusively male.[40] While both Eero Saarinen's and Peter Pran's mothers were modelmakers, and while there is rare evidence of female makers in the 1920s on both sides of the Atlantic, it is probable that women in the field throughout most of the twentieth century worked mainly on an informal basis in a home studio, rather than in a professional workshop.[41] It was not until the 1920s that modelmaking began to be recognized as a task "admirably suited to women," and not until the last

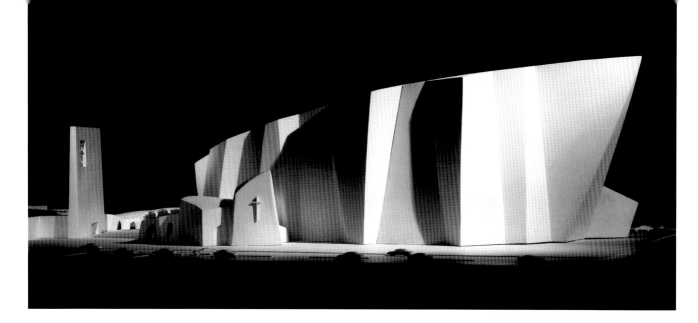

Philip Johnson/Alan
Ritchie Architects (U.S.).
Cathedral of Hope,
Dallas, Texas, 1995.
Model, vinyl: Richard
Tenguerian.

Many contemporary
models require artistic
understanding on the part
of the modelmaker as
well as an aptitude for
advanced technological
and computer-based work.
This model combines
traditional sculptor's skills
and modern materials:
vinyl sheets that were
shaped and formed with
different types of tools.

few decades that many women were to be found in the professional arena.[42] Today's modelmakers are, of course, both men and women, and often evenly divided between the two.

Changes in architectural style can demand a different mix of practitioners. Frank Gehry's and Will Alsop's complex curves, like those of the Art Nouveau and Expressionist periods, and the vogue for computer-modeled forms require makers with a sculptural understanding. The multistory office blocks and housing of the modernist period, on the other hand, may have seemed a more attractive challenge to engineers.

With the lack of any centralized training for modelmakers for most of the twentieth century, traditional skills have also remained a useful starting point for an activity that itself is no longer so. Countries in which traditional crafts survive have continued to provide skilled workers to more industrialized nations. Several of I. M. Pei's modelmakers have been Lebanese, their skills originating from the filigree work common in the country.[43] Others from that region have set up independent modelmaking companies in New York and elsewhere. Changes in manufacturing processes and communication systems, including the introduction of computerized

programming of machines (known as computer numerical control, or CNC), computer-aided design (CAD), and drawings sent electronically, have also had a direct, but contrasting, impact on the makeup of the industry's workforce. Now, few modelmaking companies run without at least some computer-trained staff and many have been using CNC machines for decades.

Modelmakers today offer an even greater range of skills to architects, and models, as a result, have increased potential for expression. These significant changes in the character of the model have inevitably influenced the architect's relationship with the maker. Today's modelmakers are best employed when given the opportunity to work *with*, rather than *for*, the architect.

The contemporary professional can choose between two principal modes of operation: in-house or independent practice. When an architect's office depends a great deal on models for design development, the swift movement of ideas and the rapid redundancy of models can make the use of an outside maker impractical. In smaller offices as well, like those of Steven Holl and Asymptote in New York, Zaha Hadid in London, Odile Decq in Paris, and Daniel Libeskind in Berlin and now New York,

Office of Metropolitan
Architecture
(Netherlands). Los
Angeles County Museum
of Art, California,
c. 2001–2. Model (above)
and model interior (left).

New materials enable the
representation of current
forms and effects.

Michael Gruber, director of the Richard Meier & Partners model shop (right), working with a colleague on a 1/8"-scale auditorium model for the Getty Center, Los Angeles, California, 1990.

The wall of the design-development model has been left off so that the interior is clearly visible.

a large proportion of models are made in-house. For these firms, a model made outside is more likely to be a finished presentation model, needed when the design is mostly resolved.

In-house makers are often drawn from the ranks of junior architects in the practice, though in some cases senior architects may be more involved. Of Gehry Partners' 115 architect employees, about 55 are involved in modelmaking from the outset of the project to the final levels of detail. This is a collaborative process, as one of them explains: "Frank does make some of the models himself, but generally other staff members will make the first models with Frank. He'll direct them and they'll rip the paper, for example, and he'll critique and adjust and shape."[44] Other practices establish fully equipped in-house model workshops staffed by specialists. Because of the costs involved, this arrangement is restricted to larger architectural firms.[45] More com-

monly, presentation work is contracted to an independent modelmaking company. Still other offices rely almost exclusively on independent makers, liaising with them throughout a project or, when depending largely on other means of representation, commissioning models for their clients only at a later stage.

Different strengths in the modelmaker are sometimes appropriate for different relationships. In an in-house workshop, the majority of models may be made before working drawings are prepared. Mike Fairbrass explains the staff makeup and needs of the job at Richard Rogers Partnership's workshop: "They're from different backgrounds. Some have studied modelmaking, interior design, spatial design, sculpture, but I tend to go for people who may not have as many hand skills, or technical skills, but have the right attitude." He describes this attitude as "being able to communicate effectively with the architects they are working with and translate that into models, rather than just being told, 'Cut that to that shape and spray it this color.'" Physical skills are still vital, he emphasizes, "but these can be learned, whereas attitudes take longer to form or change." The critical factor for in-house modelmakers is that they are all part of a team. Fairbrass refers to the "'us and them' outlook that used to prevail in independent model-making companies—that's the essential one to get rid of, especially in-house, as it is joining a team that gets best results and is most rewarding."[46]

Independent professionals, on the other hand, tend to work more on presentation models, and for these they must recruit makers with the highest levels of skill, patience, and experience in detail and finishing. Attitude is still crucial: drawings alone rarely convey the architect's intentions for a particular model, and it is critical that the modelmaker draws from the architect, when he or she visits, a dialogue and response that will inform the model.

Other skills, like the ability to estimate accurately, are vital for independent makers, and total, selfless commitment to the job is essential, since all architects—modelmakers are united on this—want the work done "yesterday." Burning the midnight oil is an industry standard. For Emile Garet, the U.S. Capitol model was a labor of love. "Next to my family, my deepest interest is centered in my great model of the Capitol," he wrote in 1904.[47] Such sentiments are not unusual in modelmaking. The pressures of the work demand dedication, and the industry attracts only the most motivated individuals. This is not by any means a conventional career.

Tensions in the relationship between architect and maker are inevitable, and not just because of time constraints and the dedication required. Last-minute changes that seem minor to an architect can require fundamental changes in a model's construction. Architects can as easily misunderstand the maker's concerns as the maker can misunderstand

Emile Garet with his ⅕"-scale model of the U.S. Capitol, Washington, D.C.

Garet made the model under the direction of Carrère & Hastings in 1904; it was shipped to Seville, Spain, in 1928 for the International Exposition of 1929.

Cartoon by Louis Hellman, mid-1980s.

Mistaken conceptions of the time consumed by making models lead to tensions over cost between the architect and the modelmaker. The escalating price of professional models in the 1980s prompted this cartoon.

the architect's. Cost is a perennial cause of friction. Architects may or may not be paid by the client for the model; sometimes it is included in the overall cost of design.[48] For unpaid competition entries, the outlay on a model is always a risk, especially since models can cost thousands, if not hundreds of thousands, of dollars. Their small scale or apparent simplicity often belies the labor-intensive, and thereby costly, effort to make them. Charges of payment oversights have filtered through the obscurity of time. Language alone identifies this complaint by the modelmaker Giovanni Battista Montano as one from the past: the intermediary Emilio dei Cavalieri wrote on his behalf to the client, Grand Duke Ferdinando I de' Medici, "M. Giovanni Battista tells me that, since he has waited five months for payment of the model, he is beginning to receive bills and must therefore claim his own. And he begs for payment, for the love of God."[49] Battista at the outset of the seventeenth century was nevertheless better off than William Ross in 1931, although this time it was the architect who took the modelmaker's part. "We are again advised by William F. Ross Company," wrote C. N. Godfrey of Cram and Ferguson to the client, "that they have received no payment in connection with their work of constructing the model [for the Cathedral of St. John the Divine] which has been going on for several years."[50] It is probably best not to extend such examples to recent times.

An issue hardly less aggravating to modelmakers is lack of proper credit. Concerns over this subject have risen with the modern-day reliance on models and in relation to the broader acknowledgment of those on the architectural team and in supporting services like graphic design and photography. Modelmakers are expected to get the model out on time and to produce the extra magical touch that wins over the client or clinches the competition. They are trusted to find a way to express the architect's vision with skill and taste and to interpret his or her intentions when little or inadequate detail is given. Yet when it comes to credit, the modelmaker is frequently overlooked. It is difficult to say why, for most architects deny the allegation when charged. In some cases, the modelmaker's contribution, lauded at the time, is simply forgotten when the project moves on to construction and the architect's attention is directed elsewhere. Some in the profession, however, have suggested that architects deliberately keep their makers' identities secret because they are too valuable to lose. And some architects, certainly, are suspicious of anyone stealing their glory. (Alberti's comment—that the model should "demonstrate the ingenuity of him who conceived the idea, and not the skill of the one who fabricated the model"—comes again to mind.)[51] There is an understandable concern to keep attention focused on the design, and for honesty in presentation, but this does not exclude giving credit where it is due. Some architects are known for their arrogance and should beware the modelmaker's wrath. Makers can become so alienated that they turn down architects' work or retaliate clandestinely with miniaturized revenge. One modelmaker recalls with undisguised pleasure,

> I adapted a figure by grafting extra bits of leg to make it super tall and drilling out the eyes to give it a piercing stare in order to resemble a universally disliked architect. [I] placed it on the model. Photos of it were later blown up, and there he was, staring over the crowds. All agreed it was hilarious. We once made a tiny gravestone engraved with the name of the awful architect we were working with and placed it in the trees.[52]

One factor in this equation is the absence of formal organization in the modelmaking industry. Most modelmaking concerns, if not one-person endeavors, are tiny companies that operate in isolation. Much of their work is gained by word of mouth, and they depend on the relationships they build. Modelmaking has not provided the craft-based continuity, educational tradition, or subsequent unionization found in other architectural adjuncts such as photography, which, significantly, has a wider existence in other fields. Recently established professional societies, like the Association of Professional Model Makers in the U.S., and the lengthening history of formal training in the U.K. suggest that improvements may come in time.

The lack of security in the field, especially when demand for models weakens, has led some makers to diversify. Models made for legal use still form a part of present-day architectural modelmakers' work. Some produce models for the film industry or expand into the area of prototype models for industrial design—the route by which Thorp Models successfully avoided bankruptcy in the recession of the 1980s. Fluctuations in workload, even today, can prompt the question of viability. Just how much worse was the situation in the mid-nineteenth century, when demand for models was "so small as to

offer little inducement in a pecuniary point of view to the men fitted to produce them"? A writer in *The Builder* recorded with pathos the plight of "Mr. Day":

> There are few architects who are not acquainted with the admirable models of Mr. Day. We are sorry to hear, that after struggling for some years to make a living by the practice of his art, he finds his efforts fruitless, and that he must either seek some other occupation or starve. It seems sad as well as surprising, that with the ability he has acquired in this particular path he should not be enabled to maintain himself by the exercise of it. Some of our readers may, perhaps, be disposed to aid him.[53]

When it comes to the question of acknowledgment, the lack of industry muscle, the personal insecurity, and the close relationship of modelmakers with their clients incline them to avoid confrontation.

Modelmaking has also been regarded traditionally as merely a service industry, practical rather than creative. Some modelmakers may merit this description, but an element of class consciousness lingers here. Even architects themselves have suffered such snobbery from others. In a recent description of seventeenth-century architectural training, there is evidence of the all too familiar prejudice against the practical crafts:

> As for studying the technical or practical aspects [of building] . . . In the scale of values of pure art, these were considered much too close to common craftsmanship. While a preliminary training in painting and sculpture were highly esteemed, it is significant that any previous activity as a bricklayer, carpenter or cabinet-maker, which involved a far more solid technical preparation, was looked upon as a rather negative qualification.[54]

However far we may have come since then, these sentiments can sometimes persist, and with them the patronizing opinion that it is neither necessary nor appropriate to acknowledge a tradesman's contribution.

Misunderstandings may sometimes cloud relationships, but modelmaking has many rewards. Each job provides new challenges, and the production of fine craftsmanship is always satisfying. When architect and maker are successfully matched, their creative interaction can generate the most vibrant and innovative models.

Although it is an independent company, the London modelmaking practice A Models demonstrates that independence from the architect's office does not exclude the modelmaker from creative involvement in project development. The rapport these modelmakers have developed with Alsop Architects has generated models that are essentially artistic collaborations. Many architects go to professionals for competition models, and this is a field in which A Models excels. For such projects, the design is usually in a fluid stage, with few details resolved. While some makers may prefer a more formed brief,

A Models thrives on the experimental nature of this work and the opportunities it gives for involvement with both the design process and the designer. The art-school background and industrial-design experience of Christian Spencer-Davies, who leads the A Models team, were good preparation for Will Alsop's S.Z. House project, which Spencer-Davies calls one of his most satisfying modelmaking experiences. Working directly with Alsop from a "mostly verbal" brief, A Models enjoyed far more creative input than usual, on a model that required a great deal of interpretation.[55] Spencer-Davies commented on architect-modelmaker interaction for an article in *Building*, "working relationships with architects are happy if the modelmakers are given creative freedom. 'I get on very well with clients because I enjoy making fun models. We encourage them to be more daring, colourful, use a variety of materials.'"[56] As a result, A Models' productions are lively and

Future Systems (U.K.). Project Zed, London, England, 1995. Competition/presentation model, 1:250, acrylic with scribed and painted vacuum-formed acrylic outer skins, etched nickel silver, and foam: A Models.

Both modelmaker and photographer have contributed to creating a striking image for the architect. The novel form of this building was developed through research into sustainability conducted in collaboration with scientists at Cambridge University. The design harnesses the free energy sources of wind and sun, making the building almost entirely self-sufficient in terms of energy.

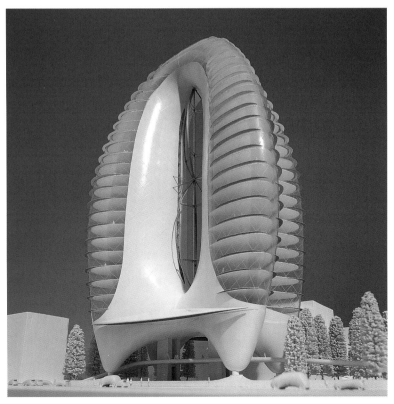

exciting, contributing significantly to both the development and the presentation of their clients' projects.

Like A Models, New York–based modelmaker Richard Tenguerian focuses on personal understanding and interpretation of ideas. Craftsmanship is key to this native of the Caucasus region, where filigree work is an ancient tradition, as it is in Lebanon. Tenguerian sees every model as an original piece, rather than as an assemblage of familiar parts, and compares his job to that of a chef imaginatively combining ingredients or a tailor working with a fashion designer. As soon as the job is seen in terms of mass production or assembly, he believes, the model loses something. He is wary of the application of new technologies. People think he's old-fashioned, he says, but lots of clients go to him

because he "knows the feel of what they want."[57] His clients also value his ability to resolve complex design problems. Kohn Pedersen Fox wrote to him regarding his model for T'aichung Tower II in Taiwan: "It is very reassuring to work with someone who can address the challenges of an unusual design and solve them with imagination and technique. I hope that the contractors who build this tower are as perceptive and capable as you have been with the miniature version."[58] Independent professionals also have the satisfaction of making finely crafted presentation models primarily for display at a late stage in the project and the challenge of inventing working mechanisms or devising intricate and spectacular lighting.

Many of the best modelmakers pride themselves on an ability to respond to a variety of clients with

Alsop Architects (U.K.). S.Z. House. Competition model, 1:50, laser-cut acrylic, vacuum-formed acrylic shells, folded stainless-steel and copper mesh: A Models, 2001.

different requirements and taste in models. Deft handling, needed for model construction, is a useful talent with clients as well, since occasionally makers find themselves working for different entrants to the same competition. London modelmaker Richard Armiger of Network Modelmakers, whose clients have included Richard Rogers, David Chipperfield, Nicholas Grimshaw, and Zaha Hadid, has found it essential to develop diplomatic skills and ingenious ways with office management to prevent one architect from seeing another's work, but his central aim in modeling also helps to overcome such problems: "We try very hard in each case to draw out the essence of the architect's intention."[59] Like A Models, Armiger's company is known for both its artistic sense and its understanding of clients' aesthetic concerns. Network is preferred by architects who "don't want a 'developer's model' or a 'model-railway model,'" Armiger explains. While architects are

discriminating in their choices, modelmakers can be equally picky. "It's difficult when people try to co-opt our expertise in order to pull the wool over people's eyes," he says. "We turn away that work."[60]

Alternative challenges greet the in-house maker. After a varied career as an independent maker in Europe, Alec Vassiliadis now works at NBBJ in Seattle. Although he originally trained as an architect, the seminal influence on his career was his working association with the sculptor Sir Anthony Caro. This experience, he contends, was "more important to my development as a modelmaker than any of the architects with whom I have worked." It taught him to deal with models in a freer, more sculptural, and less representative way. As with all successful modelmakers, a close relationship with architects is central to his approach. For Vassiliadis, whose clients have included Ron Herron, Peter Cook, Richard Rogers, and Daniel Libeskind, the excitement of his present

Alsop Architects (U.K.).
Hôtel du Département,
Marseilles, France,
1990–94. Model, 1:200:
Network Modelmakers,
1992.

OPPOSITE
Architect Peter Pran (left)
and modelmaker Richard
Tenguerian with model of
the Graha Kuningan,
Jakarta, Indonesia, 1996.

NBBJ (U.S.). Telenor
Headquarters, Fornebu,
Norway, 1997–2002.
Model, 1:1000, acrylic
with compact fluorescent
lighting: Alec Vassiliadis,
1997.

in-house job is that he is part of a design team in a
practice where modelmaking is highly valued. His
brief is to help the architects think in three dimensions, conceiving the idea in solid form from the
outset: "We encourage them to join us in the workshop and make models, or partner up with a modelmaker, in order to bypass drawings, and design
directly in three dimensions."[61] (It is interesting, he
notes, that the recognized "best designers" are the
ones most likely to do this.) This approach can result
in purely conceptual sketches, like his U.S. Federal
Courthouse cube (see page 93), or in more detailed
resolutions of the design idea. Michael Gruber in

Richard Meier's model shop, Mike Fairbrass at
Richard Rogers Partnership's, and Chris Windsor
at Foster and Partners' work in a similar way,
supporting the lead designers and contributing to
proposals as they take shape.

The requirements of the job are diverse, and
successful makers a rare breed—as hard to find, in
fact, as the perfect member of a professional dancing team. Architects, for their part, must choose with
discretion, selecting the partner who best suits the
performance required. The increasing importance of
models in recent design practice has opened the way
for such partnerships to flourish. Egerton Swartwout

caught the emerging rhythms of present-day modelmaking in comments of 1911:

> It is needless to say that much of the success
> or failure in this class of work lies with the
> modeler, and in the care and accuracy with
> which he conducts his work. In the present
> instance we were extremely fortunate in
> securing the services of Menconi Brothers,
> with whom I have worked for many years,
> and who were as much in sympathy with the
> work as they were skillful in executing it.[62]

Modelmaker working on
the lobby area of the
huge ¼"-scale model of
the Getty Center in Los
Angeles (see page 50), in
the office workshop of
Richard Meier & Partners,
Los Angeles, 1993.

CHAPTER 7

Material Matters

The change in the skills profile of modelmakers in the twentieth century was initially driven by the desire to broaden the use of models in architectural practice. New materials and manufacturing processes were needed that would make modelmaking more accessible within the office and provide less costly options for project presentation. As the century opened, this search began and led to an enlargement of choice that has had enormous impact on the model's expressive potential.

In the early years of the twentieth century, cardboard, available in a far wider range of qualities than it had been in the past, generally won out as the medium of choice: clean, easy to cut with the ubiquitous scalpel or X-Acto knife, quickly fabricated, and capable of being colored in a variety of ways. But as the century progressed, alternative materials were constantly tested, and more options continually became available. Before, the selection of materials might have meant settling on pear wood rather than mahogany; now the possibilities seem endless. Wood is still used for models, as are plaster, clay (or similar substances), metal, and glass (the latter two enterprisingly incorporated for specific purposes by some early modelmakers); countless other choices have been added: laminated papers, flexible and rigid foam plastics of varied densities, sheet plastics, metal and plastic combinations, epoxy resins, fiberglass, metal foils, perforated sheet metals and meshes, and paints of every level of sophistication. These changes in materials have been not so much a matter of the new supplanting the old as a process of continual and ever more rapid accumulation of alterna-

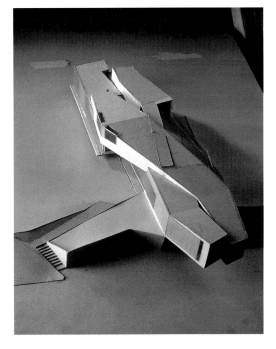

UN Studio (Netherlands). Möbius House, Het Gooi, Netherlands, 1993–98. Model, card.

OPPOSITE
Vladimir Tatlin's assistants building the model of his Monument to the Third International from wood held together with metal plates, 1920.

Models are often the best way to resolve and display novel architectural forms, like this avant-garde Russian Constructivist design.

tives. As the materials pile grew in the modelmaker's store, the nature of models changed. As a medium of expression, they blossomed.

As soon as card was established as the most popular material between 1910 and 1930, its disadvantages became apparent. It was neither strong nor easy to join cleanly; its surface was susceptible to damage and humidity, as was the finished model. It was as difficult (if not more so) to work to fine tolerances as plaster, and certainly wood. While other materials in succession claimed pride of place, however, its services were retained, chiefly due to its low cost and accessibility.

After World War II, new materials—aluminum and acrylic plastic—became the focus of attention. Theodore Conrad and Raymond Lester were among the modelmakers working with these in America in the 1950s, though Conrad had been using plastic since before the war, in 1939.[1] An article covering their work at the end of the 1950s reported that by then "plastics [had] all but pre-empted the materials formerly used in the model-building field"—at least as far as professionals were concerned.[2] Significantly, the similar methods of working required for both new materials were in direct contrast to those of the formerly popular clay and plaster. Professional modelmaking had ceased to be the plastic activity of a sculptor and had instead become the processing of rigid materials that lent themselves naturally to machining. This transformation from soft to hard, from hand manipulation to machining, neatly matched the transition from the organic curves of the Beaux-Arts, Art Nouveau, and Art Deco to the crisp geometry of the Modern Movement, proving that modelmaking was evolving as much in response to changes in architecture as to needs for new methods of making.

Though subsidiary to the rigid materials of the postwar era, sculptural materials were still necessary. The search for an alternative to clay and plaster ("disagreeable stuff to have around in an architect's office") continued.[3] Plasteline, or plasticine, a mix of clay and oil, was already in use by modelmakers before 1900; the oil prevented the clay from drying and cracking. As early as 1897 New York architect Henry Rutgers Marshall had described how to apply the material as a surface on a wooden base, providing a medium for the detailing, then finish it with shellac and paint.[4] These, and their synthetic counterparts, remain in use.

Carving rather than plastic modeling became a popular alternative for sculptural form as new materials offered themselves to the inquisitive maker's hand. Just as turnips had been briefly claimed for modeling purposes in Renaissance times, so a number of enthusiastic architects in the late 1920s felt they had found the answer in soap.[5] Balsa wood, too, was favored for a while, but the rigid foam plastics that entered the modelmaking scene in the 1960s provided a long-term solution.

New plastics were constantly being developed. The granular nature of the first low-density polystyrene foams restricted their usefulness. Detailed work was impossible unless the surface was coated with plaster or other filler. Paolo Soleri was nevertheless an early champion of the material, which he used for sketching and developing the forms of his experimental cities, later to be constructed in acrylic. Polystyrene was soon adopted more widely as an excellent base for landscape work. In the 1970s, denser foams, both rigid and flexible, became available to modelmakers. Found to be as useful for quickly rendered sketches as for more permanent parts, these rapidly became a staple of the industry. One architect recalls, "I remember the excitement with which this high-density foam was greeted, . . . and I remember getting incredibly excited about how you could carve this material. It was relatively inexpensive, and easy to use, and very quick."[6]

Electric lighting, incorporated in the early years, has also transformed the model's potential. Light, though not a material as such, has come a long way since Franz Alois Mayr set a mirror inside his eighteenth-century church model to reflect light and reveal paintings in the dome.[7] From the early twentieth century, when lightbulbs were first included in models, electrification began to revolutionize their ability to convey atmosphere and ideas about the design and is without question an essential ingredient of the current model scene.[8]

By 1980, the basic materials of the contemporary model were established, but there would be improvements and refinements, and the materials would come in an ever-growing number of available finishes and forms. As each new introduction was claimed by modelmakers, the pool of options expanded. The widening acceptance of abstraction in this period allowed makers to explore these materials to their full expressive potential, producing more visually diverse and exciting models and enabling them to communicate more clearly. Even quick sketch models with little detail or finish convey more of the architect's idea when appropriate materials are selected. Zaha Hadid's concept model for the Zollhof 3 Media Center in Düsseldorf, for instance, effectively reveals her vision, above all because of her materials choice: shards of sandblasted acrylic reflecting against a mirrorlike metal sheet (see page 97). Her model is simple; its materials express her intention and inspiration as clearly as the words she chooses to describe her project: "a fragmented series of slabs set perpendicular to the street like glass splinters that have broken free from the wall."[9]

None of the basic materials in contemporary modelmaking has been quite so widely and effectively used as acrylic, known commonly as Perspex in the U.K. and Plexiglas in the U.S. Its success is a result of its many useful properties: it is easy to work, easy to join, easy to finish finely, stable and durable, available in a multitude of colors, and able to transmit one of the other basic components of present-day models, namely light.[10] In fact, transparent materials in general have proved important in modelmaking since the early twentieth century, chiefly because of the importance during this period of glass and transparency in architecture: from Mies van der Rohe's Glass Skyscraper projects of the early 1920s to buildings of every type today. Mies used actual pieces of glass to construct his models, as had been done in earlier times with smaller frag-

Zvi Hecker Architect (Germany). Mountains Housing Project, 1994–2001. Study model, polyurethane foam.

ments for the authentic representation of windowpanes.

Because of the difficulty of working with glass, other materials have regularly been employed as substitutes, including horn, mica, tracing linen, and isinglass (a gelatin produced from fish).[11] Celluloid was the earliest synthetic plastic used for the representation of glass, appearing in models before World War I.[12] Cellophane and acetate sheet were other alternatives applied before acrylic was introduced in the 1940s.[13] The miracle material has dominated the field ever since. Glass, by contrast, has dropped almost entirely from the modelmaker's repertoire, though occasionally it can achieve effects not viable through other media. Thom Mayne of Morphosis had the firm's evocative model of the Kate Mantilini Restaurant made entirely of glass.

For more realistic models, however, the use of glass has been abandoned.

One disadvantage of acrylic has been largely overlooked. Spencer de Grey of Foster and Partners maintains that it does not truly represent the visual appearance of glass. "The building can look more transparent than it should, and you also see inside the model more clearly," he says. "It gives a very misleading feel about the building, and you need to find a way of compensating—to be accurate, it should be something closer to black or dark gray."[14] Mies van der Rohe's trials with real glass no doubt fortified him against any subsequent problems with acrylic: "My efforts with an actual glass model helped me to recognize that the most important thing about using glass is not the effects of light and shadow, but of the rich play of reflection."[15] Be this as it may, acrylic has transformed modelmaking, and it continues to be the primary material for the representation of glass in the twenty-first century.

Transparency as an idea has in itself profoundly influenced recent architecture, and acrylic has had a distinct role to play here as well. Peter Pran's models are often specifically designed to convey the sense of transparency that inspires his work. Many of his simpler models, like one for the Portofino Diamond C Apartment Tower in Florida, demonstrate how acrylic can be used as a material in the abstract yet still retain a considerable degree of realism and accessibility for the client.[16]

Paolo Soleri was among the first to use acrylic in this way—as a material on its own rather than as a model component. He achieved a dramatic effect at his Corcoran Arcology show by combining transparent acrylic with light, setting an electric bulb beneath the models so they appeared as if illuminated from within.[17] This ingenious conjunction of media has become a standard feature of today's models. Sometimes parts of the model are lit to emphasize portions of the design. Thus Thom Mayne lights the river—that vital nerve of a city— in his master plan for the Spreebogen in Berlin.

Morphosis (U.S.). Kate Mantilini Restaurant, Beverly Hills, California. Model, glass, 1985.

NBBJ (U.S.). TNB
Headquarters Tower,
Kuala Lumpur, Malaysia,
1995. Model, acrylic:
Richard Tenguerian.

Paolo Soleri in the photo studio with an Arcology model, c. 1970.

Experiments in photography went hand in hand with architectural investigation at Arcosanti.

Richard Rogers Partnership (U.K.). Southbank, London, England, 1994. Competition model, wood and acrylic.

A vacuum-formed acrylic roof and acrylic floors allow the viewer to see the interior spaces of the building.

Blocks (colored, transparent, or opaque), rather than sheets, of acrylic may be used for the impressionistic representation of buildings in a site model, transforming each into a glowing bar of light. This can convey a general idea of the intended impact of a design and add considerable sophistication to what is basically a simple block model. By this means, Steven Holl highlighted the project buildings on his model for the Nelson-Atkins Museum in Kansas City. Yet this combination of acrylic and light is also indispensable for realistic representation of the architect's idea—to show, for example, the effect of an occupied building at night. Countless varied and spectacular results have been achieved through this marriage of materials and technology. Nonetheless, it is difficult to tire of the progeny.

Transparency has also been central to Rem Koolhaas's work (see page 149). The architect Bill Price remembers, from the time he was working with Koolhaas, that "Rem was very much into researching transparency, . . . transparency in

building—but also in modeling. At one point in almost every OMA project the models were constructed to be transparent. It was like X-raying the program arrangement." While ideas of architecture inspire such models, the relationship is symbiotic: models can also inspire architecture. Here Price's ardent evocation suggests the imagery of models as a motivating idea: "When we were working on the Porto concert hall, I started thinking about how the complex might be seen from above. I saw it as a glowing ember in the landscape—a sort of light bulb on the skin of the Earth." An even more tangible example of the model's suggestive influence is manifest in Price's development of an unusual project. The idea was sparked by a model of the concert hall, the one made with translucent materials to show the model's structure more easily. Koolhaas had questioned, "Could we make the concrete translucent?" The two architects then "started to wonder whether the actual concert hall could be built so that it resembled the translucent model. That meant finding a way to make concrete transparent." Price is now involved in the development of "transparent" concrete.[18]

Acrylic is valuable for its ability to transmit light, but also to portray what would otherwise not be visible, as in Hadid's diagrammatic model for the Zollhof 3 Media Center, which shows the internal floor arrangement of the building, information that would be difficult to reveal as simply and explicitly

Morphosis (U.S.).
Spreebogen Urban
Design Competition,
Berlin, Germany, 1993.
Model, acrylic, foam core,
wood, and paste, approximately 38 1/2 by 54 by 12
inches, 1992–93 (detail).

Alsop Architects (U.K.).
Palestra, Southwark,
London, England, 1999– .
Presentation model,
acrylic laminated with self-
adhesive films printed
with computer-generated
graphics, resin board,
timber, and acrylic components: A Models, 2000.

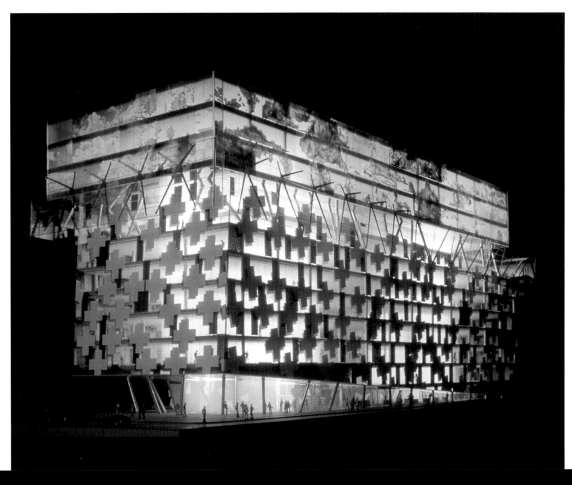

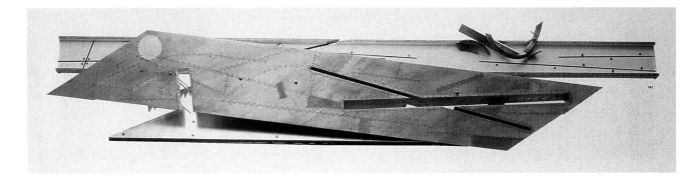

Studio Daniel Libeskind (Germany/U.S.). Aleph Wing, Berlin, Germany. Model, metal, wood, paper, and paint, 335 by 85 by 30 centimeters, 1988.

in any other material (see page 14). And acrylic is also valuable as the basic material of construction for most presentation models. Window areas remain transparent, and other areas are painted opaquely. Rods, blocks, and sheets of acrylic are all used for model building.

As acrylic is one of the core modeling materials of today, so metal is another, but one that has a considerably longer history in modelmaking. Jacob van Campen's seventeenth-century wooden model of Amsterdam Town Hall, for instance, had capitals of brass. Details of Vasily Ivanovich Bazhenov's Kremlin model (1769–73) were cast in lead.[19] In 1792, Sir John Soane commissioned coppersmith Samuel Rehe to make a model for the roof of the Bank of England Stock Office mainly in brass, with rafters, pillars, and fretwork in iron.[20] This last was unusual. As the other examples imply, metal has mostly been used for details on models made from other materials. Like glass, metal is difficult to work and cannot be easily processed in the average office or workshop. Despite the ambitious all-metal model proudly displayed in Edward W. Hobbs's 1926 *Pictorial House Modelling* (produced in the workshops of Twining Models, Northampton, England), which might have signaled a twentieth-century change, all-metal models are still relatively rare, although less so now because of the wide availability of accessible sizes and wafer-thin sheets.[21]

Like acrylic, metal allows the architect to play with light, reflection, and color. Its high-tech image

also has clear architectural implications suggestive of the materials of construction. Often, it is used to convey the materials effect that inspired the idea of the building. As with all materials, this can be done in an evocative way, not necessarily with realistic precision. Ross Wimer of Skidmore, Owings & Merrill describes one of the firm's project models for the Pennsylvania Station redevelopment in New York City:

You can see in those models, they weren't exactly factual, they were somewhat abstract. The building, for instance, was made of wood to convey the sort of weightiness of the existing Post Office building. We built the shell structure out of brass that was plated with nickel, which is not in fact what it's going to be made out of, but it was meant to reinforce the design idea, more so than present the fact.[22]

Attempts are occasionally made to reproduce the effect of the building by using the exact materials of construction in the model. Mies van der Rohe's real glass model of his Glass Skyscraper was followed by one of the Seagram Building fabricated in composition stone, tinted glass, and polished bronze. The idea seems logical, but in fact is usually compromised by the impact of scale. Such "real" materials are not only difficult to work, but they often appear rather clumsy in use, especially if the model is meant to be a realistic representation. Yet while authentic materials can look "wrong" on a realistic model, the same materials used in the abstract can

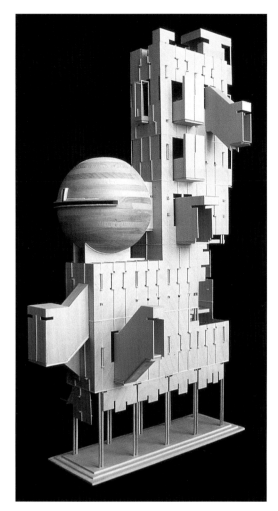

George Ranalli, Architect (U.S.). Tower of Silence, K Project for the Dentsu and Toyota Motor Corporations, Tokyo, Japan, 1990–91. Model, wood, 1990.

genuinely convey the architect's idea. Peter Pran's JFK model (see page 96) did just that. Daniel Libeskind's model of the Aleph Wing also successfully communicates the reflective qualities and dynamic strength of metal, the outsize nuts and bolts reinforcing the effect. In recent years, architects have made much use of perforated sheets and metal meshes, which, available in miniature, allow for manipulation in model form. Experimentation with these materials in models has almost certainly contributed to the development of architects' ideas.

Sheet metal is the most common form in which the material is used. However, blocks can be machined, and rods used as columnar supports; wire also provides exciting possibilities for expression, as in Zaha Hadid's many experiments or in Peter Eisenman's model for the Hotel am Spree (see page 66). Foils and metallized papers are available and widely exploited.

Another of today's primary modelmaking materials is wood. Because wood, unlike plastics and metal, has a grained surface and is susceptible to atmospheric variation, it is no longer used when accuracy is paramount. Even so, it has maintained its position in the modelmaker's pool. Architects' preference for wood as a material for building only partly explains its continued appeal for models. Wood is valued for its appearance; its surface, when

Gehry Partners (U.S.). Ray and Maria Stata Center, Massachusetts Institute of Technology, Cambridge, 1998–2004. Model, wood and paper, 1998.

Michael Sorkin Studio
(U.S.). Animal Houses:
Dog, 1991. Model, wood
and metal.

Wood has a more struc-
tural presence than card.
For architects with in-
house workshops, the
material continues to be
useful for exploring or presenting a developing idea.

finely finished, improves with age, imparting to
models a feeling of quality and timelessness. When
wood is used in a minimal, abstract way, the viewer
can dwell on its warmth of color and lustrous depth,
which subtly associate the architectural concept with
ideas of comfort, natural beauty, and craftsmanship.
Many models by architects such as Tadao Ando,
Renzo Piano, and Arata Isozaki are exquisite objects
in themselves. Another interesting quality, modelmaker Mike Fairbrass explains, "is that they are well
received by 'the public,' who are able to appreciate
abstraction in wood without taking it literally,"
which can happen with acrylics and other materials.[23]

On the other hand, wood's practicality for quick
site block models and for sturdier or larger studies

goes virtually unchallenged. Only a few simple
machines are needed to produce a variety of model
types. The material has convenience value. Michael
Sorkin explains, "I like working in wood. It's ready-
made, available in terms of dimensions; it's very
malleable with certain kinds of tools." It is a utilitarian
material but also has a particular resonance. "Why
do I work in wood?" he muses. "I like the smell of it
and the way it takes the paint, and it has the right
level of abstraction for what we're doing."[24]

Last among the basic materials of modelmaking
are paper and its products. Paper, too, has been used
for a long time. Among surviving early models is
the fifteenth- to sixteenth-century representation of
St. Maclou, Rouen, made from papier-mâché, and

Zaha Hadid Architects (U.K.). Illinois Institute of Technology Campus Center, Chicago, 1998. Study model, card.

Architectural forms are suggested by a series of simple shapes cut from card sheets and assembled vertically.

another of "pasteboard" (similar to cardboard) of a design for University College at Oxford, made shortly before 1634. In the latter, the elevational details are drawn on a sheet of paper that is glued to a pasteboard base sewn together at the corners with thread.[25] (The practice of pasting drawings to a base is still used today for quick sketch models.) Several models have survived from the Victorian period in England, constructed from card fixed to a stabilizing wooden core.[26] Around 1859, the Gothic Revival architect George Edmund Street had a beautiful model of his design for St. James-the-Less in Westminster made in this way and then delicately painted by professional modelmaker C. N. Thwaite.[27]

Papermaking was not fully mechanized until the beginning of the nineteenth century, and the grades and types of paper products available to model-makers have multiplied ever since. While professionals rarely construct models from paper today, it is unlikely to lose its popularity within the office. The material is familiar to the architect and conveniently at hand, and its construction methods are clean and therefore compatible with desktop activities like drawing and computer work. Modern developments have increased the amazing utility of paper and paper products for models. Foam core—lightweight, low-density foam surfaced with layers of card—has given "paper" constructions greater structural stability. Paper is by definition a sheet material, which to some extent limits its flexibility, and its use is so ubiquitous that it is in danger of being treated as mundane. Zaha Hadid, in her study model for the Illinois Institute of Technology Campus Center, has shown there is life in the old dog yet.

Beyond these basic materials of modelmaking, which, to use building terminology, form its structural foundation, are many supplementary materials. These include sculptural materials like clay and plaster and their modern equivalents, used almost exclusively in-house. It seems somewhat surprising to find that clay and claylike materials are still quite widely employed. Fairbrass explains that clay was used for the model of the Richard Rogers Partnership's Rest

Zone in the Millennium Dome "because it was a complex organic shape. We made a huge clay model of it, and took a fiberglass cast from that to form the exterior. We also used it for the floor inside because it was amorphous and undulating."[28]

The material is pleasingly versatile. Antoine Predock favors it for his initial studies, which can be "very tiny—three-by-five inches like Cal Poly, or very large, like the one for Agadir which is five feet long and three feet wide."[29] Michael Sorkin, like Predock, uses clay (or plasticine) for large site models, built up on a wooden base. Skyscraper architects, like those at Kohn Pedersen Fox, often prefer malleable materials of this type for much smaller preliminary studies of form.

Clay is also the material most perfectly suited for plastic expression. Sorkin explains its advantages succinctly: "It's infinitely flexible. You can easily mush it down and start again."[30] These are charms to which earlier architects succumbed. For Michelangelo, trained as a sculptor, the attachment

was understandable. Yet Borromini, originally a stonemason, was won over to clay, in the end finding it superior to drawing as an aid to planning.[31] A number of architects today continue to appreciate its properties, and it is a useful addition to other modelmaking media.

Mike Fairbrass's comments on the Rest Zone provide a clue to the lesser popularity of plaster. Traditionally, clay models were molded for the production of plaster casts, but nowadays there are handier alternatives like fiberglass. And where blocks of material are required, for filing, sanding, or carving—earlier the province of plaster—now such products as Bondo (a two-part polyester resin designed to fill dents in cars) are in ascendance. Unfortunately this product's color is as unsophisticated as its name (it has a "weird mottled appearance," according to one user), but this can be overcome quite successfully with paint.

Architects like Frank Gehry and Philip Johnson, whose buildings have complex curves that lend

Antoine Predock Architect (U.S.). Spencer Theater for the Performing Arts, Alto, New Mexico, 1994. Model, plasticine.

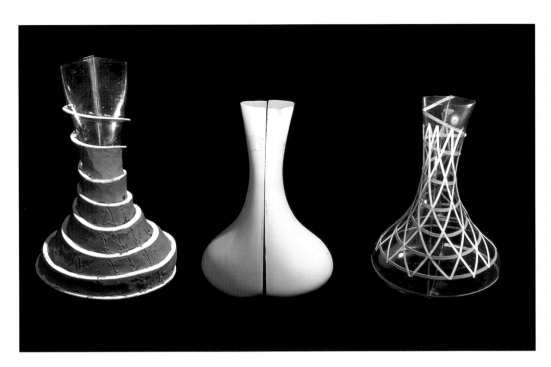

Foster and Partners (U.K.). City Hall (Greater London Authority Headquarters), Southwark, London, England, 1998–2002. Sketch models, 1:200, 1999.

Three study models of the flask-shaped debating chamber and ramp of City Hall demonstrate three facets of the design thinking for the new GLA Headquarters. In one, plasticine and red clay form the ramp; vacuum-formed styrene emerges at the top (left). Prolab 65, an inert epoxy-based board used in the toolmaking industry, was rough-cut in two halves on a CNC router, hand finished, and then used as a forming tool for the vacuum-formed portions of the other models (center). Thin strips of white adhesive tape applied to the base form allow study of structural ideas (right).

themselves to hand modeling in malleable materials, continue to find plaster appropriate, whether for casting forms based on clay or Bondo studies or (more rarely) for carving while still soft. Yet professional modelmakers almost never use plaster in contemporary practice, and since the introduction of foam and products like Bondo, its use in modelmaking has plummeted. Its messiness has certainly contributed, and modern quick-setting materials dry more rapidly. Ironically, plaster was used for the highest levels of detail in nineteenth- and early-twentieth-century models; today it is more likely to be used for the simplest formal sketches. Its nonreflective surface absorbs light, thereby highlighting form, and it conveys a sense of solidity.

Sculptural materials in general are limited in their color range and potential for surfacing and have a more distant relation to the materials of construction (though plaster can successfully be used to represent stone). These were among the reasons for the downfall of such materials. As one writer commented in 1936, "Plaster models are losing favor as they do not lend themselves to delicacy or refinement in the representation of materials."[32] Still, they have not fallen entirely from favor. These traditional materials continue to be useful in the office, giving creative freedom in the development of form. Early-twentieth-century writer LeRoy Grumbine makes a helpful distinction: "Clay is useful where the draftsman draws freehand: cardboard where he uses T-square and triangle. To make a scale model of a building in clay is like drawing an elevation freehand."[33]

While most of the basic materials of modelmaking are shared, some are divided unequally between in-house makers and professionals. Michael Sorkin elucidates, "The models obviously shake out in two kinds. One is the kind of working model, and wood and plasticine are very useful for that, and then there are the after-the-fact models in which you are essentially representing something which has already been designed."[34] Alec Vassiliadis, working in-house at NBBJ, lists his main materials as acrylic and styrene sheet, all kinds of wood and plywood, rigid foam, and paper.[35] In Japan, Toyo Ito's list is

Member of the design team at Toyo Ito & Associates, Tokyo, working on an in-house, paper and plastic study model of the Sendai Mediatheque, Miyagi, Japan, 2000.

Gehry Partners (U.S.). Lewis Residence, Lyndhurst, Ohio, 1989–95. Model, wax-impregnated fabric, 1994.

OPPOSITE
Richard Rogers Partnership (U.K.). Tomigaya Exhibition Space, Shibuya-Ku, Tokyo, Japan, 1990–92. Model, Meccano parts, wood, acrylic, and string: Tim Price Associates.

The model is a schematic early study for an exhibition building in which the floor area can be increased by adding temporary mezzanines.

similar: "For in-house constructions we use balsa wood, sponges, styrene panels, acrylate, PVC, and other easily handled materials."[36] There is considerable unanimity that paper, plastics, and wood are the most useful materials for the in-house task. Even at Gehry Partners, where a wide range of materials is used, "by far the most common are wood, foam core, paper, and Plexiglas," comments Keith Mendenhall. "Nearly all of our models are made of these materials . . . If I walked around our office right now, 95 percent or more of the models would be made of these materials only."[37]

Metal, on the other hand, is more typically used by professionals, though several architects, like SOM, use metal-sheet surfacing on wood-block models built in-house (see pages 54 and 192). But paper, and often wood, are almost absent from the arsenal of professional makers. The London-based company A Models uses acrylic as its principal material (either in block or sheet form), as well as foam block in different grades and densities and wood; these are supplemented by numerous metal components including etched brass and stainless steel, metal rods, metal meshes, and perforated metal sheets.

An infinite variety of other materials can play a part in specific circumstances; used alongside ready-made "finds," they provide limitless opportunities for expression. Richard Rogers Partnership built a model from Meccano—a child's construction toy—to emphasize the moving nature of parts of a design. One of Odile Decq's models has part of a building sunk into the thickness of an open book. Frank Gehry's Lewis Residence project prompted a model made from fabric coated in wax. This idiosyncratic choice is included on Mendenhall's shortlist of occasional additions to the basic repertoire: "In rare circumstances, we play with other materials including felt, waxed velvet, clay, heat-formed plastic, lead, plastic mesh, wire mesh, aluminum, copper, and molded plaster."[38] Gehry also uses different types of foil and metallized papers to represent metal finishes. Adding to this variety for all modelmakers are the

Eric Owen Moss Architects (U.S.). The Umbrella, Culver City, California, 1996–2000. Model, 1:50, foam core, Gator board, basswood, and plastic, 1997.

OPPOSITE
West 8 Urban Design & Landscape Architecture (Netherlands). Living in the City, Bishopsgate, London, England, 1999. Model, wood and wood veneer, cast acrylic, aluminum sheet: Made By Mistake.

Site models allow for considerable flexibility. Here, the designers use color and contrasting materials to distinguish the project buildings from other constructions on the site. The huge "Arcadian" rocks that dominate the scheme "will be icons of urban nature" and are an essential part of the design. West 8's models balance realistic demonstrations with conceptual interpretations.

many specialized materials for vegetation and landscape, including sponges, dried plants, and wire wool.

This wealth of materials prepares the maker for a contemporary challenge: finding methods to represent new building materials and new architectural ideas and forms in a way that communicates the intended effect. Eric Owen Moss's Umbrella project in Culver City included an irregular roof section made from gunite sprayed to the ceiling (gunite is a type of sprayable concrete more typically used for surfacing pools or preventing erosion). So experimental was Moss's design that large-scale and full-scale mock-ups were made to test the idea. Sprayed plastic foam represented the gunite.

The physical realities of contemporary architecture may challenge today's maker, but so may virtual realities. Hani Rashid of Asymptote remembers,

One day I had a major breakthrough. I knew what I could do on the computer, but I couldn't do it with my materials. I went out and bought water jugs, you know, for bottled water, because it was preformed in the shape I was looking for. And I brought it back here. What I realized I was looking for was a preformed materiality with shapes and quality of light that I could get on the computer.[39]

The tasks facing the present-day modelmaker are challenging indeed.

While the range of materials in itself is broad, so are the effects of different finishes or other surface treatments. The concept of "finish" can include the removal of surface material by cutting, sandblasting, or etching—Zaha Hadid's and Will Alsop's models of sandblasted acrylic come to mind. The designers of the Dutch practice West 8 enthuse over the possibilities of working the surface of acrylics:

The casted acryl is chosen because of the complete freedom in choosing colours and modelling the shape, creating transparent sculptural blocks with interesting light

reflections and coloured shadows. The casted
acryl is sawn into blocks and sandpapered
with a very fine grind to achieve different
transparencies and reflections. For more
sculptural blocks, the blocks are treated as a
sculpture and with use of electrical tools for
professional modelmaking and restoration-
purposes, such as an electric micro-chiseller,
saws, polishers, grinders and of course
hand-powered-tools . . . Although this is a
pretty intensive and long process, these
[become] the eye-catching elements of the
models, and therefore the attention and care
taken for the modelling pays off.[40]

Then more obviously, there is the direct application
of paint, ink, and the like, or the attachment of a
laminate or other material with adhesive. The last
methods, in particular, offer extensive opportunities
for expression.

Painting the surface directly or applying pencil
or watercolor drawings onto a base has been common for centuries. Early-twentieth-century variations on this theme included bizarre-looking models
constructed from blueprints, which were recommended by a writer in *Architecture* in 1926.[41] But the
seventeenth-century pasteboard and paper model of
University College at Oxford is an example of precisely the same type of layered application: the
drawings were made on paper and then attached to
the rough model surface. With this method, the
quality of the drawing or painting has a dramatic
impact on the model. Cesar Pelli is known for the
colorful hand-drawn renderings with which he has
faced his models. Experiments by Daniel Libeskind
go a conceptual step further. His surfaces are col-
lages of significant (or intentionally insignificant)
printed fragments. His model for City Edge in
Berlin, as much a sculpture as a model, emphasizes
the random patterning of urban existence, and is
poetically described by the architect:

A voyage into the substance of the city and its
architecture entails a realignment of arbitrary

Studio Daniel Libeskind (Germany/U.S.). Extension of the Berlin Museum with the Jewish Museum Department, Germany, 1989–1999. Model, printed paper and wood, 1989.

The names printed on the paper covering the base of the model record the identities of German Jewish Holocaust victims, whose history is interpreted in the museum.

Studio Daniel Libeskind
(Germany/U.S.). City Edge
Urban Competition,
Berlin, Germany, 1987.
Site model, paper, wood,
metal, and paint, 270 by
155 by 40 centimeters.

points, disconnected lines and names out of
place along the axis of Universal Hope. Very
thin paper—like that of architectural drawings, Bibles, maps, telephone books, money—
can easily be cut, crumpled or folded around
this indestructible kernel. Then the entire
unwieldy construction can be floated on water
like the tattered paper making its Odyssey on
the Liffey.[42]

Libeskind's model for the Jewish Museum in
Berlin is pasted with more poignant matter—the
lists of names of Holocaust victims—layering
meaning onto the model well beyond its representational reality.

Steven Holl's models are also treated with an
artist's sensibility. He is known for his delicate
watercolors, which have surely inspired the painterly
surfaces of his three-dimensional objects. Thom

Mayne, too, has approached his models as an artist
might a canvas, working up a heavy impasto of
modeling paste. One description of his models
notes: "[They] appear with a patina and coloring
that evokes the impression of the monolithic, as if
they were objects cast in bronze or some other dense
metal with polished surfaces . . . [an] aesthetic of
proudly hand-worked surfaces . . ."[43]

The need for accurate representation of reality
has encouraged an altogether different line of
inquiry, with photographed images of real materials
being reduced to the correct miniature scale and
then applied. In the past, trompe l'oeil skills could
create a similarly convincing effect. Carefully reproduced moldings and marbling were painstakingly
painted by hand on many Baroque pieces large and
small. Today these skills have largely been replaced
by sophisticated paint-spraying techniques, which,

Steven Holl Architects (U.S.). Sarphatistraat Offices, Amsterdam, Netherlands, 1996–99. Model.

with their fineness of texture, produce finishes that appear perfectly in scale.

In models like NBBJ's Kwun Tong Town Center or Hadid's Zollhof 3 Media Center, we see that the simple use of materials emphasizes the architect's idea and is usually highly effective. Elaborate finishing or sophisticated layering of materials, on the other hand, intimates a series of complex ideas that build up a picture of the fuller architectural concept, but such complexity requires a great deal of subtlety if it is to avoid confusion and carry the project idea successfully. Alec Vassiliadis of NBBJ maintains that "the most basic *basic* models are very often the most evocative."[44] Simple combinations can also successfully suggest the convergence of real materials, as

indicated in a description of freely assembled developmental models by Gehry Partners:

At this point the model's components will somewhat represent materials, meaning you'll see perhaps clear acrylic, clear plastic sheets used to represent glazing; you'll see sheets of silver paper used to represent metal; sometimes you'll see sheets of colored paper used to represent painted metal; and sometimes we'll leave areas just as raw wood block, which is intended to indicate either a stone of some kind, whether it be marble or just a plaster stucco.[45]

There is plainly a need for an accurate depiction of materials in order to understand the built effect,

Morphosis (U.S.). Berlin
Wall Competition,
Germany, 1988. Model,
wood, card, and paste,
approximately 78½ by 39
by 15 inches, 1986 (detail).

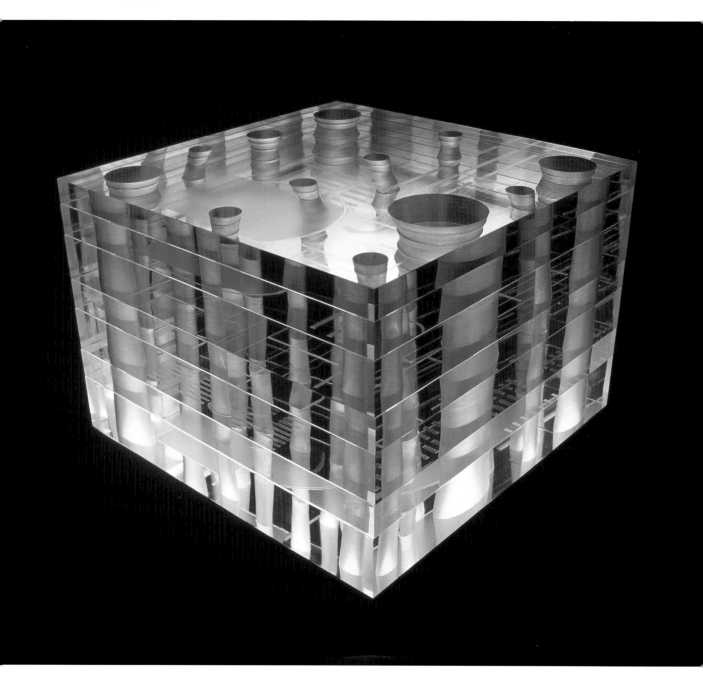

Toyo Ito & Associates
(Japan). Sendai Media-
theque, Miyagi, Japan,
1995–2001. Exhibition
model, acrylic, 1999.

but in many other models, suggestion can be more effective than replication for the expression of ideas. Experimentation with the model as a medium aids communication. This is where the wealth of materials in present-day modelmaking plays its part. And architects do not doubt the importance of their choices—these are deliberately made. Michael Schumacher, of the German firm schneider + schumacher, stresses, "The choice of material is very important, because the atmosphere of the model is usually very closely related to the material. The material tells you if we want to talk about precision, or emotion or logic."[46] Jun Yanagisawa writes, of Toyo Ito's work:

> The material too constitutes an important factor for defining the character of a model. Our choice of material for the model depends on where we wish to focus attention . . . I get the impression that the choice of material [in the models accompanying the essay] was made according to which materials permit the clearest and most successful depiction of the concept of the envisaged building . . . Not made according to formal criteria, but instead according to the suitability within the scope of the particular project.[47]

An open approach to materials can stimulate architectural ideas, and it is possible that the reverse could have a stultifying effect. Hani Rashid is not the only one to have suggested that limiting the choice of materials for models may have a negative impact on the architecture produced; modelmakers have made this point before. As a student, Rashid considered the work of a group of architects of the 1960s and 1970s. "As I looked at their work," he remembers, "I couldn't help but notice that their window cutouts were all a result of the fact that they were working with a material called foam core which gave you certain limits in the way they were made."[48]

Is it going too far to suggest that limiting the materials of models can limit the flow of architec-

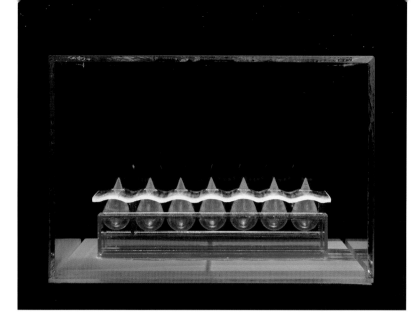

tural ideas? Certainly the materials of the model can influence and inspire architecture. Frank Gehry has pondered the ambiguities involved in the choice of model materials:

> The models are ephemeral, and it's like ripping a piece of paper. The ripped edge can be beautiful. But you can't make architecture do that. I think I'm starting to explore that in [Jay Chiat's Telluride house]. That indeterminacy that you get when you're not certain what it is. The Ron Davis house is a clear trapezoidal shape. You can read it, and you can remember it. Jay's house you remember as crinkled-up paper. Now, how do you get that into final form?[49]

Undoubtedly, experimenting with materials can enrich the message of models and influence the generation of ideas as the materials are worked. The twentieth-century revolution in materials opened modelmaking to vital new possibilities, and with each addition of the twenty-first there will be more: more ways for architects to express and understand an architectural concept, and more ways for modelmakers to resolve the model's design.

Richard Rogers Partnership (U.K.). Tribunal de Grande Instance, Bordeaux, France, 1992–98. Minimodel, Plexiglas ELiT, 1999.

"Live edge," "light gathering," and "lit edge" are all terms used to describe the relatively new acrylic sheet material used in this model, which gathers light into the face of the sheet, traps it inside with a high refractive index, and transmits it again only at the edge. This model, like that of the Millennium Dome (see page 61), was one of a series of minimodels used as a table centerpiece at the office's 1999 holiday party and afterward auctioned to raise money for charity.

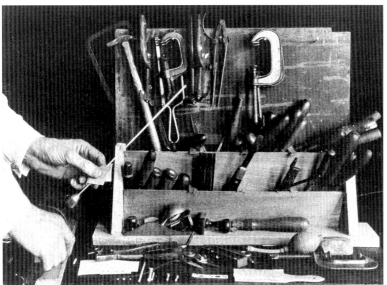

LEFT
Harvey Wiley Corbett's toolbox, from *Pencil Points*, August 1922.

The illustration accompanied an article by Corbett; in addition to showing the collection of tools used for the models he discussed, it demonstrates his method of turning columns.

Workshop of John B. Thorp, modelmaker, London, from *American Homes and Gardens*, August 1915.

Although the model workshop in the photograph is unidentified, the article notes that Thorp "has at present in his workshop a model of the mansion built by the late Whitaker Wright," and the model shown under construction can indeed be identified as Witley Park (previously Lea Park), near Godalming, Surrey, England, which was purchased by Wright in 1890.

CHAPTER 8

A Process of Change

The model's story is one of continuity and change. While many models are still made in small, low-tech workshops, the technologies of making have advanced so far and so fast that it sometimes seems that the modelmaker, or indeed the physical model itself, is becoming obsolete. Computers have accelerated the model's evolution, providing alternative means for three-dimensional study and presentation and prompting the model enthusiast to pause a moment and take stock. Yet rather than throwing doubt on the role of the physical model, the computer instead seems to clarify its purpose and put its contribution into better focus.

In 1922, New York architect and modelmaking advocate Harvey Wiley Corbett wrote an article on cardboard models in which he illustrated his box of tools. This contained an assortment of conventional hand implements like pliers, a drill, saws, a vise and steel clamps for holding small objects, manicure scissors, and "I must not omit mention of the humble spring clothes pin of wood."[1] His cardboard models were carefully made, delicately detailed, and highly presentable; the surroundings were peopled with pedestrians and sported streetcars and trees. Corbett's models were made in-house. It is not impossible that such a modest collection of tools might be found in an architect's office today; in fact, the only equipment necessary for a model made from foam core (cardboard's present-day substitute) is an X-Acto knife or scalpel and a metal rule.[2] An independent modelmaker, too, could plausibly start out with not much more and provide a basic service for a local architect, turning out models to

the architect's specifications with just that much more detail than the architect has time to make personally—and with little or no overhead, in the basement or garage, at a very competitive price.

Nevertheless, the most significant developments in modelmaking during the twentieth century have come from the hands of the professional modelmaker, and the other side of the coin shows a very different picture—that of high-tech processing and space-age machines. A professional's workshop featured in *American Homes and Gardens* in 1915 presents some compelling contrasts to Corbett's in-house toolbox. Here, the showpiece is a belt-driven table saw, with a complement of various hand tools and clamps.[3] But while the basic cutting tasks are now powered, and the table saw indicates the use of wood, rather than cardboard, the differences from Corbett's equipment are mostly of quantity and size rather than character. Barring the table saw, a Renaissance workshop may have looked similar. The workshop, however, was no doubt advanced for its time and was presumably that of the forward-thinking British modelmaker John B. Thorp, whose models are illustrated and whose name is mentioned in the text.

Only ninety or so years later, a visitor to a similarly state-of-the-art workshop might be confronted with a large CNC (computer numerical control) milling machine, a laser cutter, and a three-dimensional printer, with no modelmaker in sight. The operator is likely to be in an adjacent room in front of a keyboard and screen.

The revolution came in stages. The career of Theodore Conrad, who, while he was an architectural student, made cardboard models for Corbett, illustrates the early mechanization of modelmaking by professionals. In addition to his paperworking skills, Conrad had experience in machine tooling and, around 1939, was one of the first individuals to set up a workshop with industrial equipment. Perhaps he was inspired by the model workshops of the New York World's Fair of that year (these had been in operation since 1936 or so) or their employees, to whom he was known.[4] The fair's workshops, like Thorp's in 1915, included a table saw as well as a jigsaw, lathe, and sander assembly, ingeniously belt-driven from a single motor. Conrad was experimenting with new construction methods himself, and he shared their outlook: his intention was to machine rather than hand-work as many parts as possible for greater efficiency.

Conrad's collection of tools swiftly multiplied. The success of his business contributed to the proliferation of highly mechanized workshops set up in the post–World War II period. Nearly twenty years later, in 1958, Jane Jacobs reported, "The range of milling machines, drill presses, lathes, saws, grinders, polishers, and paint-sprayers which Conrad uses (he has seventy basic machines and 120 electric motors in the shop) is no longer unusual for professional model makers."[5] At one point in the 1950s, Conrad employed twenty-six workers to operate these machines.[6] George Gabriel, who worked with Conrad before moving to an in-house position at I. M. Pei & Partners in the mid-1950s, remembers, "Conrad was a machinist. All his models were made on machines: stamped, metal parts that he would use as overlays . . . He would just sit making parts and putting them together."[7] Though apparently Conrad had taken over a former diamond shop for his workspace (and presumably some of its fine cutting tools), "his models were huge. He couldn't go very small because he couldn't produce those parts."[8]

Conrad's models, according to Gabriel, lacked finesse and were unwieldy as a result of the technology used. To make the parts smaller, using machines, required making (or having made) special fittings for standard machines or building new machines from scratch. Gabriel continues:

> For miniaturization you have to kind of shrink the tools, and shrink everything because you've got to put your nose into the machine, and you can't have a ten-foot machine to cut these little pieces. The hole where the blade comes through was bigger than the pieces you're trying to cut. So I use blades that are used in the jewelry industry. I invented precision-type machines that were doing extreme precision for this trade: circular saws made from scratch with adapters and rigs that gave the precision of milling machines, machines for topo work . . .

Much high-precision equipment of this type was brought into modelmaking workshops during the 1970s, along with various complex processes. Gabriel adds: "We did casting in lead, metal casting, plaster casting, plastic casting, all kinds of techniques and methods from different trades."[9]

Not all parts could be manufactured in the workshops, however. Even in the seventeenth century, William Cleere had been obliged to subcontract components for his Great Model of St. Paul's: despite the range of craftsmen under Cleere's command, he had still found it necessary to have statuettes for the model made through a separate commission.[10] Such subcontracting has been a regular practice in modelmaking through the years. In the 1970s, the outsourced tasks included "sand blasting, plating and the vacuum molding of large objects."[11]

Gabriel's was an in-house workshop. A model construction book written in the U.S. by Sanford Hohauser in 1970 describes the broader scene: "Many professional modelmaking workshops can be found throughout the country. These range from one-man operations to large shops equipped with a hundred or more machine tools, and provisions for precision large-scale casting, and sufficient space for big models and even full-size mock-ups of parts of

schneider + schumacher (Germany). KMPG Building, Leipzig, Germany, 1994–97. Model, 1994.

The precision and realism that are standard today were unthinkable in models a century ago.

CNC milling machine in the workshop of Kenneth M. Champlin & Associates cutting acrylic components for a presentation model of the Miglin-Beitler Tower, Chicago, for Cesar Pelli & Associates, 1990.

OPPOSITE
Preparatory sheet of drawings by Harvey Wiley Corbett for cut-and-fold cars for use as accessories on architectural models, c. 1925.

In the early twentieth century, almost everything included in the model had to be made by hand.

buildings."[12] The large workshops of this period were certainly impressive, and it is possible that independent modelmaking companies were bigger between 1950 and 1980 than at any other time in the history of architectural modelmaking.

The significance of the move to machine tools was that they allowed for greater accuracy at faster speeds. Models would advance to ever higher levels of finish and verisimilitude in the 1980s and 1990s as the processes of making became more sophisticated. By the late 1970s, the linkup between computers and machines was already developed, and CNC operation was becoming a potential method of production for the model workshop. The CNC process permits the direct transfer of drawings (made on a computer) to a machine; parts can then be "ordered" and cut with minimal supervision. However, the cost of equipment is extremely high, and was an even greater investment in the early days of the technology. Computers themselves were expensive; the large three-axis milling machines most useful for creating three-dimensional forms more so. Thorp Models in London, for example, acquired its first CNC machine, computer, and operating software around 1984 for about £12,000 ($17,400). This

secured only a fairly basic piece of equipment with a relatively small cutting bed (approximately fifty by forty centimeters, or twenty by sixteen inches) that was built for the engraving industry and adapted to suit modelmakers.[13] Kenneth M. Champlin & Associates (KMCA), a model workshop in New Haven, Connecticut, purchased a CNC milling setup in 1988; the computer (constructed from parts to reduce cost) was $7,000 and the milling machine $65,000, a considerable outlay for a small company. The high value put on models during this period made such technological advances possible for the industry, both in Europe and the United States.

An article in *Architects' Journal* in 1990 summarized some of the merits of the CNC process: "Accuracy is the most obvious advantage of CNC machines. They can do difficult three-dimensional work such as glazing bars on domes. They can also work to a smaller scale than was ever possible before. And they can cut harder materials than have been used in the past such as metals."[14] Once set up, these machines could then repeat a task endlessly, liberating the maker from the type of work that, done by hand, "would bore you senseless" (as one modelmaker puts it) and thus allowing time for more creative tasks.[15] A cursory look at the pattern of an early-twentieth-century modelmaker's job demonstrates the radical impact of mechanization on the modelmaking process. Expatriate Emile Garet (struggling a little with the language) reported on his progress on the U.S. Capitol model around 1903. After some months of work, a number of pieces had been individually prepared:

About 60 models: doors, capitals, brackets, modillions, etc. All the details models for the DOME are done. All the details models for the wings are quite done except balustrade, roofs and steps. All the columns are turn and fluted by hand (200 was made again. But I use the first one and turn them again). On the casting about 2000 separate pieces are cast if it is not more (I have no time to count them).

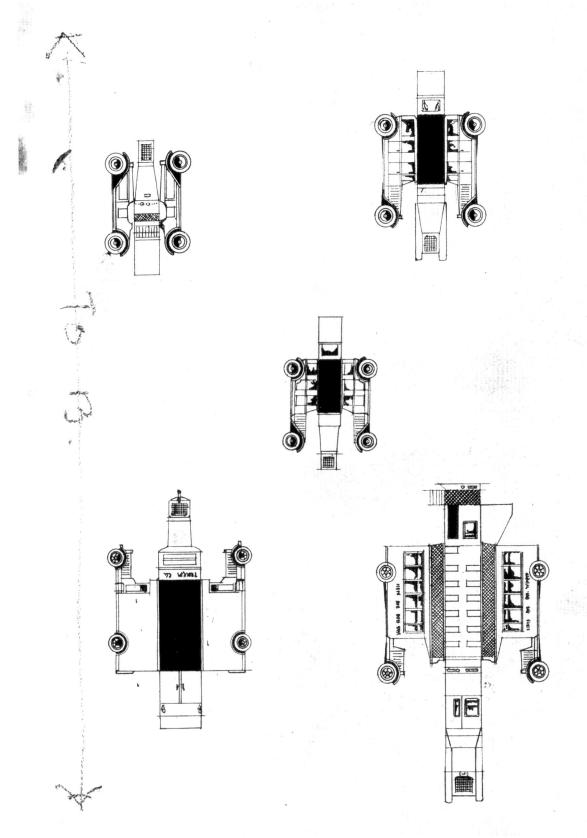

More of 200 gelatine moulds were made for cast . . . All skeleton's are quite made and 2 new fronts which we can move alternatively . . . Columns with all the bases, 250 about, altogether are done with caps fluted columns and they are beautiful and all the work is so far first class. About 60 running moldings was done.[16]

The final decades of the twentieth century saw increasing computerization of modelmaking tasks. Cutting and engraving by laser with a CNC-operated machine was developed specifically for model part production at the large in-house model workshop of Skidmore, Owings & Merrill in the mid-1980s.[17] For most in-house shops and professionals, laser cutting was first available through service bureaus, but by the end of the 1980s a machine was available "small enough to fit into a designer's office and as easy to use as a pen plotter."[18] This meant that, besides the benefits to modelmaking businesses, the quality, quantity, and speed of production for in-house mod-

els could be transformed. The laser cutter would eventually become a design tool for the architect's office, producing parts quickly for the rapid visualization of complex ideas. By 1990, presentation models, to which these CNC technologies were usually applied, had reached a new peak in their ability to replicate the details of a design. It was not only the maker who benefited from these changes. Architects were able to convey more information in the model. Clients had more confidence in its veracity.

In parallel with the advances in parts production, other inventions and improvements have been added from the early twentieth century on, contributing to the high-tech model of today. The painting of models has become ever more sophisticated; spray techniques are now essential to professional modelmaking, and even small in-house model workshops often include a spray booth. Professional modelmakers with an engineering bent have regularly fertilized the medium with fresh ideas and new methods, including the electrically powered innovations that are always attractive to clients. The spectacular City of Light model displayed by Consolidated Edison at the 1939 World's Fair (see page 72), which simulated natural and interior illumination—both day and night—in a scale replica of the New York skyline, set the stage for future lighting extravaganzas.[19] Theodore Conrad was experimenting with fluorescent and neon lighting in his models in 1959, and the soon-to-be-added attractions of automated illumination of individual apartments, complete with fading and timers, were popular with clients. In 1990, one British article reported on the current state of play:

> The marketing departments of the big developers are asking for bigger and more detailed marketing models. These often have to be built on split baseboards so they can be opened up for viewing of internal areas such as atria. Recently Piper's, and others have started using power operation to open them. This can make the front of a model sink down

Kohn Pedersen Fox Associates (U.S.). Rockefeller Plaza West, New York, New York, 1987–93. Client presentation model, acrylic with fiber-optic lighting components: Kenneth M. Champlin & Associates, 1989 (opposite); KMCA modelmakers working on the structure (right).

The electronic signage on the building is represented on the model by hand-painted acrylic panels back-lit by fiber-optic rods. The internal structure of the model is all acrylic.

into its plinth at the touch of a button for the ultimately slick presentation.[20] Lighting technology continues to grow more complex with fiber optics and increasingly elaborate electrical systems.

Kohn Pedersen Fox Associates' model for Rockefeller Plaza West in New York, made in 1989 by KMCA, epitomizes the integration of technology current at the time. Laser-cut elevations masked an all-acrylic interior structure ingeniously threaded with multiple fiber-optic rods. These illuminated acrylic panels at the base of the building (simulating lively backlit billboards and other colorful images intended for display) as well as portions of the articulated fenestration at the top of the model. The complexity of such models was reflected in their price, and this was the period in which modelmakers were to earn the label "special effects consultants to the architecture profession."[21]

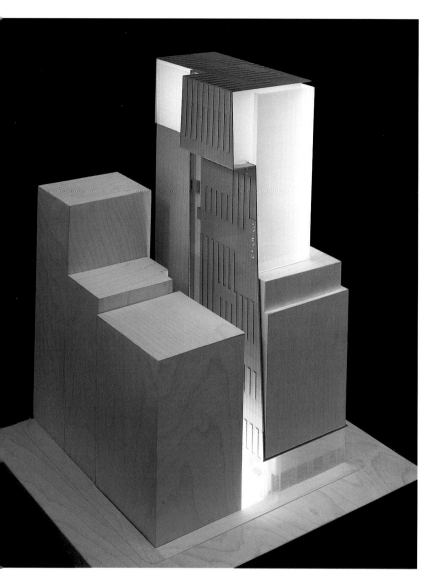

Skidmore, Owings & Merrill (U.S.). 350 Madison Avenue, New York, New York, 1998–2000. Model, 1/16" scale, basswood, birch veneer, painted acrylic, and lighting components, 1998.

The second of two made for the 350 Madison Avenue project, this model was illuminated by light transmitted from a slide projector to a system of mirrors; a built-in light had melted the first model. The materials of the building are represented in the model in a suggestive rather than a realistic way.

The wizardry of these models was not infallible. Modelmakers sometimes overstretch their ingenuity, and overambitious models have—literally—gone up in smoke. Twelve thousand tiny lights in SOM's model for the Pepsi-Cola Building in New York (a project completed in 1960) were too much for the model's plastic structure, and the timer of its inbuilt cooling system failed. "In spite of the efforts of a courageous maintenance man, the plastic block went up in flames and the whole model was destroyed— together with most of the furniture of the conference room it was standing in," reported *Architect and Building News*.[22] This was not an isolated occurrence. In fact, so notorious were such incidents that in 1970 the model even merited the attention of a Monty Python sketch in which "architect" John Cleese witnessed his residential block bursting into flames during a presentation to a client. Neither has the problem gone away. SOM had similar trouble with a 1998 model for a Manhattan office building, 350 Madison Avenue, though this time the story had a happier ending. Ross Wimer recalls,

> We were trying to show a volume of light in the model. The lobby of this building is in a dark slot on Madison Avenue, between two tall buildings. The first model we made, we built a light into it, in the bottom of it, and during the presentation to the client the thing started to melt and to smoke, which wasn't quite the desired effect but it actually helped to sell them on the idea.[23]

In a later model they resolved the technical difficulty presented by the bright light:

> We made a hole in the back of the model and built a system of mirrors in its base, and we put a slide projector against the back of it. There is a three-hundred-watt bulb in the slide projector, the brightest light we could find. It blasts the light up through this slot in the model without overheating it. It was extremely effective.[24]

Richard Rogers Partnership (U.K.). Turbine Tower, Tokyo, Japan, 1993. Model: Tim Price Associates.

The Turbine Tower—named for its power-providing wind turbine—was a key research project for RRP, involving the engineering firm Arup Associates and London's Imperial College of Science and Technology. The model has an LCD sheet wall; the liquid crystals turn from opaque to clear with the application of an electrical charge, conveying one of the other architectural concepts explored—the idea that the skin of the building would react to sunlight, changing its opacity.

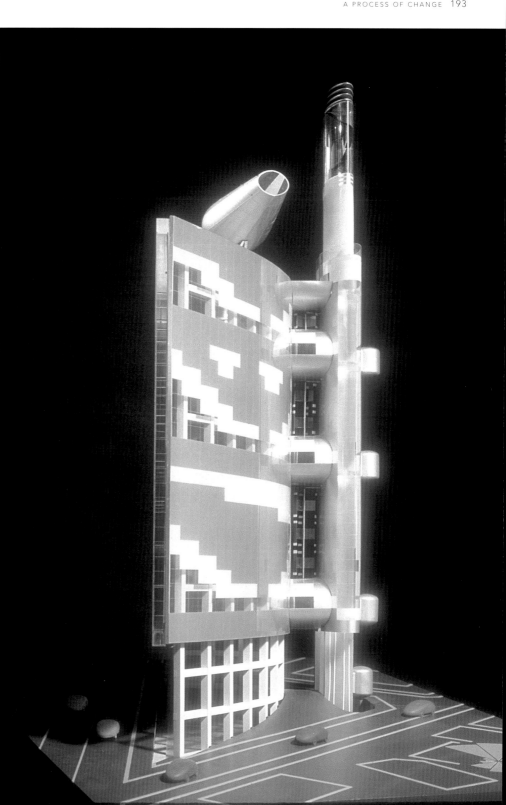

As early as the 1950s, metals and plastics and new machining processes facilitated the production of sharply defined models with an increasingly high level of detail. Even in 1958, before the finer tolerances of the 1970s were achieved, the impression created was of "fantastically precise, gleaming, plastic and metal models."[25] By the end of the 1980s, the ability of the no longer virginal model to replicate reality appeared magical. This "new-age exactitude" (as Akiko Busch described it in her 1991 ode to the presentation model) fascinated clients, who were proud that their projects could show off the latest marvels of modelmaking.[26] In fact, from the 1970s on, to some extent "developments in modelmaking [were] being driven not by architects but by clients," one U.K. observer noted in 1990. "The big developers want huge and super-realistic models for their marketing programmes . . . Olympia and York is the biggest developer and has the largest budget. Every year it spends a seven-figure sum on models . . . There is a constant pressure from O&Y to raise the standard of workmanship as better techniques become available."[27]

High-tech manufacturing processes and electrical components of one sort or another have continued to increase in importance in the more complex and ambitious presentation models of recent years.

Modelmaker Kenneth Champlin's representation of the Petronas Towers in Kuala Lumpur, for example, which became the world's tallest buildings upon their completion in 1998, required 126,000 volts to run its neon lighting system. It would have been impossible, both economically and physically, to construct without CNC production (both milling and laser cutting) thirty thousand tiny computer-generated sunscreens of identical size, among other parts.[28] Modern engineering processes and electrical additions have created a whole new strata of model style. They not only suggest new ideas for model construction, but inspire new ideas for expression in models that may not aim for such an engineered overall effect.

But high-tech models are not necessarily ostentatious. Slide projection, for instance, has found its way into a number of model presentations in recent years, and not necessarily the most elaborate. NBBJ's competition model for the Seoul Dome conveys clear information about the building while remaining elegantly understated. The exclusion of unnecessary detail gives its technological additions particular power. Made in-house by modelmaker John Lodge, it includes images on electronic screens and "exquisite metal roofs," as Peter Pran, one of the lead designers on the project, describes it. The combined effect of the materials, detailing, and articulation gave the model an "incredible richness."[29]

Neither is realism always the goal. Many architects prefer simpler models to identify themselves with less commercial aims. A more abstract rendering of a project or a traditionally made wooden model may better portray an intention. And not all modelmakers have, or desire to have, complicated equipment, perhaps choosing instead to specialize in a more interpretive, impressionistic style or to respond to situations in which CAD files are not available. The cost of equipment also restricts the acquisition of the newest technologies to bigger model firms or architectural practices, frequently those who build large commercial projects. It is not until prices go down that smaller ventures begin to find state-of-the-art technology accessible.

The embrace of new technologies has varied at the international level. At the beginning of the twenty-first century, a significant number of both small and large modelmaking companies in the U.S. have their own laser-cutting equipment; in Europe the laser has been slower to gain ground. There, until recently, CNC milling and photo etching were the standard processes for high-quality models. Photo etching (an industrial process of much longer standing) can produce finely perforated parts such as railings in soft metals like brass and copper and also in stainless steel.[30] The higher cost of the laser cutter in Europe may be one reason for the discrepancy, but other factors are relevant: in Europe, more small-scale, less detailed models are made, partly because of the greater number of competitions. The time pressure of competition work also reduces the reliance on computer-aided design, and thus more

NBBJ (U.S.). Seoul Dome, LG Twins Baseball Stadium/2002 World Championship Football Stadium and Entertainment Center, South Korea, 1997. Competition model, laser-cut acrylic, acid-etched stainless steel, acrylic components, lacquer paint, and incandescent lighting: John Lodge, 1997.

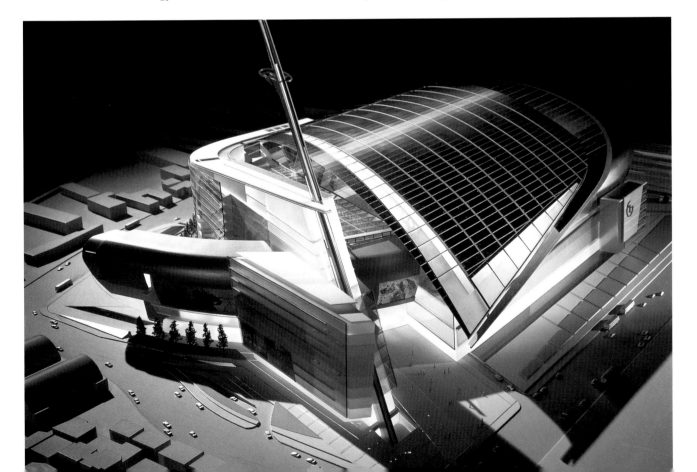

presentation models are based on preliminary sketches. In 1995, Richard Armiger of London's Network Modelmakers described his situation: "We use CAD where appropriate; it's good for repeated forms, like punching out 200 window frames. But the key developments for us are photo acid etching and materials like chemical wood, which is light-weight and sandable."[31] Modelmakers who have experience on both sides of the Atlantic are generally agreed, too, that Europe is more sympathetic to the qualities associated with traditional handcraftsman-ship, while, Alec Vassiliadis remarked after his move to the U.S., "here they're a little more attracted to the toys you use to create what you're creating."[32] Nevertheless, the laser is becoming increasingly popular with European modelmaking firms.

At each stage in the development of model-making technologies, the process of production has been removed further from the modelmaker's hand. With conventional and CNC machining, production mostly entails the creation of model parts, which then have to be assembled (and the assembling of thirty thousand sunscreens is no mean task). With the introduction of rapid prototyping (RP) in the early 1990s, however, a whole new order in computer control arrived: the final step in the "dehuman-ization" of the process has made it possible for the machine to take over the role of the modelmaker entirely.[33] Rapid prototyping technologies, which involve using software files to build the model in layers, can be used to complete the job in one blow. No longer is the machine hand-fed, nor is it set up by hand. No longer is assembly required once the parts are made. With RP technologies, an entire model can be made at the proverbial push of a button.

RP comes in several forms, distinguished by the materials and method of building in layers. In stereo-lithography (SLA), the oldest and most popular RP process, ultraviolet laser radiation is directed onto a vat of liquid polymer resin following the specifica-tions of a CAD drawing. Where the laser beam passes, the material solidifies, and when cured, the

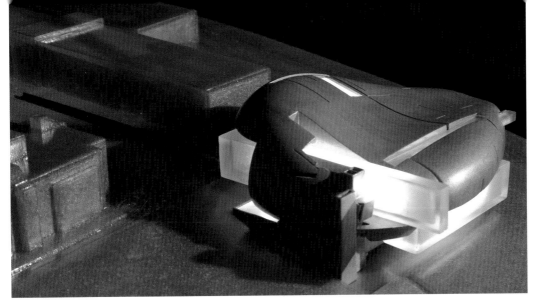

Morphosis (U.S.).
Experimental Media and
Performing Arts Center,
Rensselaer Polytechnic
Institute, Troy, New York,
2001–3. Competition
model, three-dimensional
printed resin, 2002–3.

object can be polished, painted, or treated with metallic finish. Other RP processes construct models by using lasers to cut, cure, or sinter material into a layer or by ejecting material from a nozzle to create a layer. Depending on the process, many different materials may be used, including plastics, paper, wax, and metallic powder. Recently a three-dimensional printer has been developed that offers RP production in a small, less costly machine. Using ink-jet technology, it builds up layers by spraying tiny droplets of thermoplastic material onto a platform surface. Its description as a "printer" was cannily chosen. Comparable in size and convenience to a photocopier, it can be marketed to both architects and model-makers as an office-friendly modeling solution. The limitations of RP products, in size and finish as well as cost, have until recently reduced the usefulness of this ultimate CNC process for the architect and modelmaker, but these difficulties will surely pass.

In the early days of CNC, the technologies were most useful for commercial modelmaking, where high-quality models are produced for maximum profit. As the machines came down in price and as architectural practices rebounded from the economic slump of the late 1980s, CNC production began to move in-house for use as a design tool. But the bulky CNC mills found their way into the work-shops of only the larger architectural offices with dedicated model-building staffs, whereas the laser cutter is more easily installed and used. In-house, a laser cutter can quickly facilitate such tasks as the rapid production of alternative designs for fenestration or repetitive facade detailing. Ross Wimer describes the impact that the acquisition of a laser cutter has had on the design process at Skidmore, Owings & Merrill:

> I'd say the most significant effect of the laser cutting is the fact that the designers on the team can more easily make more detailed models. You could argue that with the model shop in the past, with conventional wood-working-type equipment, you could do a very detailed model. These guys were extremely skilled, but it took longer and it required skilled craftsmen to build them. The way it works now with the laser, because it's so precise and so fast, is that you don't have to be a skilled craftsman. The architects on the team do the drawing on the computer, and the laser cuts it out very precisely, so it sort of eliminates the need for a professional model builder to actually execute them.[34]

With the advent of the three-dimensional printer, and as the more established RP equipment comes

OPPOSITE
Cesar Pelli & Associates
(U.S.). Petronas Towers,
Kuala Lumpur, Malaysia,
1996–98. Presentation
model, 1:150, acrylic:
Kenneth M. Champlin &
Associates, 1993 (top);
model under construction
(bottom).

Kenneth Champlin and his
team took a year and used
the most advanced
processes to produce this
model, which is close to
fifteen feet tall (including
the base).

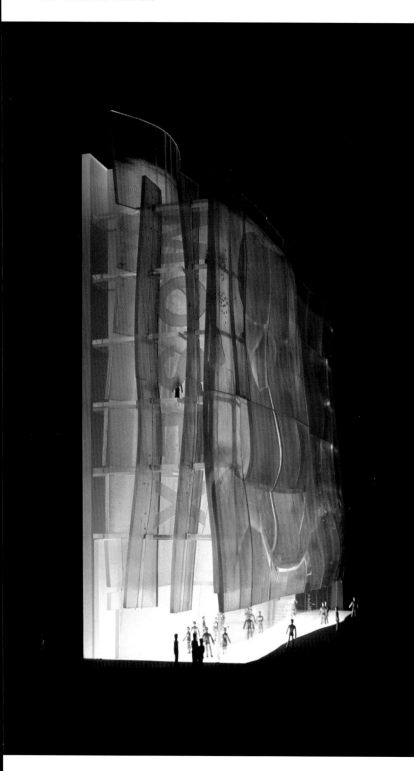

down in price, these solid imaging systems are likely to become increasingly common in architectural offices. Many practices are already appropriating RP technologies through the agency of service bureaus. Some have a three-dimensional printer in-house. Models produced entirely by machine are potentially an efficient way of resolving questions about a design proposal. A detailed RP model of a section of a design, or an accurate model of a complex shape, can readily contribute to discussion and aid decision-making in design development.

There is a danger, however, in considering such "push-button models" as the ultimate architect's aid. Precise reproduction of a design drawing or three-dimensional modeling file can be informative both for design study and for presentation, but the process tends to eliminate the opportunity for interpretation. The potential for textural effect and materials choice is, in any case, restricted. And once the hardware is purchased, the temptation to accept the all-in-one solution, rather than to fabricate with a variety of processes and materials, is strong. With the possibilities for expression curtailed, the emphasis and refinement of the model's message can easily be lost.

There are further limitations. All these processes require data that have first been developed on the computer screen. As Ivan Harbour of Richard Rogers Partnership remarks of the CNC process, "The problem with CNC milling is you need to have a drawing. For conceptual models, forget it."[35] CNC models can only be what Michael Sorkin describes as "after-the-fact models," useful as a "reality check" and having no experiential benefit unless the resulting parts are combined or manipulated in some way after production.

The idea of the instant, totally machine-made model is in reality something of a dead end for the model as a medium. Yet when seen as an addition to the repertoire, it becomes a new opportunity with a potential for expression equal to any. The new technologies can be used with imagination not just by professionals for the showy developer's model but down the line (most likely as an outsourced service) by the smaller in-house practice. SHoP/Sharples Holden Pasquarelli of New York has taken up the opportunities offered by stereolithography alongside the use of more traditional techniques. The firm creates design files with the three-dimensional modeling program MAYA and sends them out for production as SLA parts. On their return, the pieces are assembled in the office.[36] The choice of technology reflects the partnership's outlook. SHoP's practice "is based on the vertical integration of theory, design, and technology," one of the firm's designers, Gregg Pasquarelli, explains, and "SLA combined all of these aspects." The firm's seemingly simple model for the Museum of Sex in New York has a subtlety and depth of information made possible only through the use of this rapid-prototyping process. Pasquarelli expands on the choice of stereolithography: "Its precision is far superior to heat forming or vacuum forming, and it offers the ability to insert structure and architectural details 'inside' the volumes, such as the staircases that are built inside the thickness of the MoSex facade."[37] This model—futuristically lit like Soleri's early essays in

acrylic—conveys an elemental, sensual effect of rippling transparency, as of a body seen through water. It vividly captures the ideas behind the design, as detailed in the project description:

> The extremely narrow floor plan suggested the use of a layered organizational device, and the generative concepts of organic form, tactile expression, exposure and concealment led to thinking of this device as "skin." The exterior envelope is a play of several translucent layers of steel and glass, sometimes fusing in a readable thickness, sometimes peeling apart to allow vertical movement, light filtration, or to house displays. With variations of transparency, the facade becomes part of a flirtatious game played between the building and the city.[38]

While the overall appearance of the model is decidedly abstract, the SLA-formed panels simultaneously communicate such intricate details as the built-in staircase structures.

SHoP's inventive approach has enabled the firm to find equally effective and appropriate applications for laser technology, says Pasquarelli:

> As for the Columbia School of the Arts, the laser-cutting technique allowed us to use the model as an interactive tool to study the sections, since we could "pull" any slice of the building out of the main volume, refine it, and feed it back into the computer. In fact, we produced two identical models. One for the client and one for our office, so that we could use it as a design tool—not simply for representation.[39]

Incorporated creatively, these new techniques and technologies enable models to convey ever more complex ideas about a project. SHoP's models are successful not just because they are the result of a particular process but because that process was chosen for its qualities and their suitability for a predetermined effect.

While three-dimensional computer modeling has naturally led to the increased use of computer-

SHoP/Sharples Holden Pasquarelli (U.S.). Museum of Sex, New York, New York, 1999–2002. Model, ⅛" scale, stereolithography resin (below and opposite).

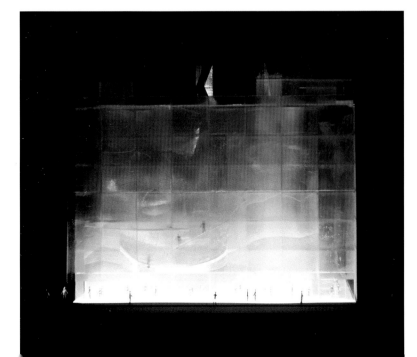

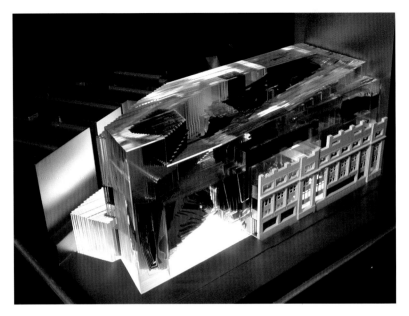

SHoP/Sharples Holden Pasquarelli (U.S.). Columbia School of the Arts, New York, New York, 2000. Model, ¼" scale, acrylic and chipboard.

The model for the School of the Arts was built from over a thousand laser-cut acrylic pieces. Like the model for the Museum of Sex, it was built "to coalesce the operative diagrams into a tangible set of spatial relationships so the client could begin to understand the proposed solutions three-dimensionally."

generated models, it has also affected our thinking about the model's theoretical existence: the relationship between two dimensions and three dimensions is becoming confused. The still relevant question of the 1970s—the nature of the model and its relationship to other forms of representation—has resurfaced.

Since the mid-nineteenth century, technology has generated new forms of representation that have compromised the physical nature of the three-dimensional model on several occasions. Model photography was the first, capturing the model's substance on a two-dimensional plane. Experiments with film and video in the 1970s also removed the model's third dimension, but added a new "dimension" of time by simulating movement through a building in its future state of completion. Holography, with which architects briefly flirted in the same period, appeared to offer another alternative, one suggesting full three-dimensionality, yet without the object's material properties.[40] With computer three-dimensional modeling, a new representational system emerged that no longer needed the construction of a physical model as the first stage. Computer

modeling provides a means of exploring three dimensions without the presence of a physical object; it also combines many of the benefits of other forms. It can set the building in its context, like a photomontage. It can simulate movement, like a video or film. And it can create the effect of three-dimensionality in the round, like a hologram (though instead of circumambulating the model, the object is rotated on a screen).

The three-dimensional computer model, or virtual model, is still young, yet it has burst upon the scene with force. Its advantages are apparent at many points in the design process, and its relationship to the physical model is still being explored. Gehry Partners was among the earliest architectural offices to embrace the new technology. Originally, the office found CATIA (a computer modeling program used primarily in the aerospace and automotive design industries) a useful aid as the conventional model-based design process was drawing to an end. "Once we had achieved a design that we were pleased with and that met all of the client's requirements for the program of the building," explains Keith Mendenhall, "we would develop the design entirely in physical models, get to the final physical model, and then digitize that model into CATIA. Then we would begin to create the computer model, which, for us, is the primary source of data for construction."[41] Having built up a database of costs over a number of years, Gehry Partners can utilize the software earlier, to the same purpose:

> We now come in fairly early in the design process, at the point where we have some of these more expressive models, and we begin to digitize portions of those models. For example, where there are very, very complex curves, we digitize that area of the model or the whole model and use our database of costs to give us an idea of where we stand at that point in terms of budget and constructability.[42]

Gehry finds that this use of the computer allows him greater freedom in his approach to physical

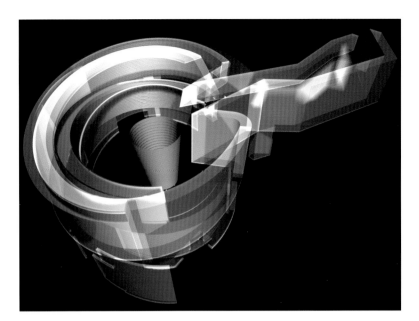

Morphosis (U.S.). Lutèce
Restaurant, Las Vegas,
Nevada, 1998–99. Three-
dimensional computer
rendering, 1998 (right);
model, acrylic, card, and
foam core, 1998 (below).

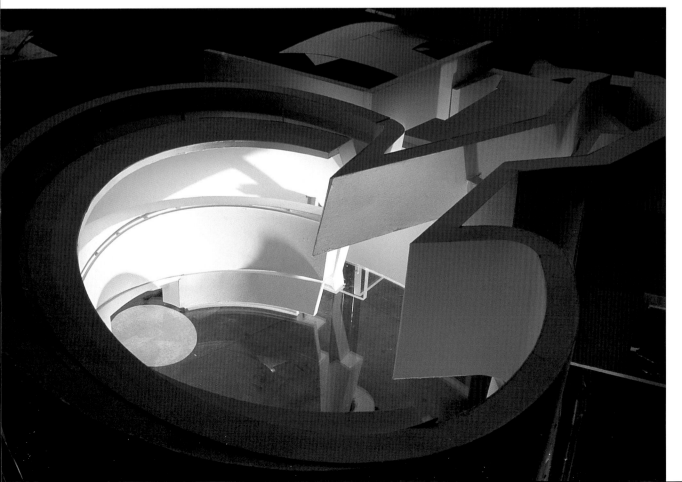

Final design model for Marques de Riscal Winery, Elciego, Álava, Spain, being digitized by a Gehry Partners employee, 2000.

models, particularly in his experimentation with form. He has described how this works:

> I start manipulating the shapes. Because of the computer, we know the quantities we can afford. Some of the models look very voluptuous and way-out. They're overblown, they are not economically feasible, but they do relate to the programs. You pare away the stuff and get down to the essence of it. And because we have the computer monitoring it, we know what the economic essence is, and all we have to do is correlate that with the visual essence. And when you finish, it all fits. It's like a Swiss watch. But it looks like you just threw it up in the air and it lands. That's what I like the most, to maintain spontaneity while responding to specific needs.[43]

For Gehry, the computer validates the design he has produced with physical models and thereby his traditional reliance on the medium. Others use computer modeling as an alternative to physical models for some aspects of design development. One of the advantageous points of application, says Peter Pran, is that "you can more quickly develop highly refined curtain-wall details visually, and it's better on a computer in that it looks like it's almost built. It takes longer to do those refined details in models."[44] Cesar Pelli elaborates,

> Many details we now study in computer renderings instead of building models because the computer rendering shows the details more accurately and it can simulate materials, textures, reflections, so the computer rendering gives me a clearer representation—for instance, of a piece of curtain wall, or the way a railing may come around.[45]

Many of today's younger architects (but not exclusively so) have engaged with virtual modeling more comprehensively, abandoning traditional drawing and modeling techniques for a direct exploration of form, and movement through space, within the computer. Even an office like Morphosis, with an early output that was in part defined by the use of physical models, now uses virtual modeling in conjunction with physical, three-dimensional studies. One recent critic has described the outcome: "[The architects] employ the computer to work continuously on a single object—manipulating, rescaling, stretching, amending, subtracting and prying it apart until a design solution is reached."[46] This last approach to computer modeling draws the most attention to the ambiguity of the medium's claim to "three dimensions." Morphosis's use of virtual modeling appears to supplant the physical manipulation of material objects. According to the firm's principal designer, Thom Mayne, it's like "building, unbuilding, building again . . . very direct, very 'physical' . . . We just build, construct in one-to-one scale within the virtual space of the computer . . . no plan, no section, no elevation . . . It's more like shaping clay."[47] Yet however strong the inclination may be to forget the distinction between virtual and physical, it is both real and significant. In computer modeling, forms can be explored in "space," but they have no substance. The pixels create the illusion of an object, but the object does not exist. The screen is flat; our

Jürgen Mayer H. with
Sebastian Finckh
(Germany). Scharnhauser
Park Townhall, Ostfildern,
Germany, 1999–2001.
"E.gram" model, glass,
1999.

Asymptote (U.S.).
M. Scapes, 2001. Model
(below); model with pro-
jected digital drawings
(bottom).

Part of the exhibition
"Stratascape: A
Collaboration by Hani
Rashid and Lise Anne
Couture of Asymptote
and Karim Rashid" at
the Philadelphia Institute
of Contemporary Art,
M. Scapes ("motion-
scapes"), as described

by Asymptote, involved
"computer generated
studies of the tectonics of
movement manifest[ed]
through automotive
styling and modeling . . .
assemblies that addressed
the formal aesthetics of
movement and speed as
static artifacts."

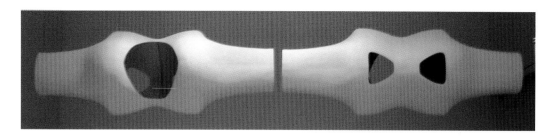

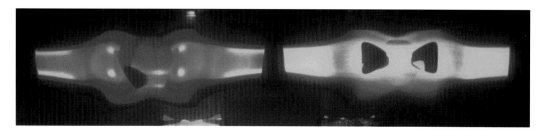

understanding of three dimensions has lost its meaning.

The model for the Scharnhauser Park Townhall in Ostfildern by Jürgen Mayer H. with Sebastian Finckh acts as a kind of parable of this enigmatic relationship between the virtual model and the real.[48] Fittingly, it is a creation only possible through the computer-controlled operation of a laser beam. This magical model-object has embedded within it the negative equivalent of a wire-frame model of the building. The laser beam has splintered the glass into microscopic fragments, leaving a series of CAD-guided, minuscule voids

that record, in diagram form, the skeleton lines of the building. Here, like the virtual model, is an apparently existing object. And like the virtual, it is a model inside a box, removed from the sense of touch.

The rise of the virtual model also prompts us to look again at the physical model's relationship to the building. Gehry's method in particular offers food for thought. His final design models in paper, wood, and acrylic, rather than merely providing a visual guide to the final scheme, are digitally captured to create the computer model, which then forms the construction data for the building. Here the building, in one sense, *is* the model, by virtue of a mathematical correspondence in which the computer acts as intermediary. Marvelous though the technological wizardry of the process and the consequent intimacy of the model with the finished structure may be, it is worth bearing in mind that such a relationship does not in fact depend on the computer. A 1920s critic pondered exactly the same idea of correspondence while examining Dennison & Hirons' development of the Liberty Tile and Trust Company building in Philadelphia. At the end of a lengthy model-based design process (not entirely foreign to Gehry's), the final models return from the architectural sculptor's studio:

> The casts from [the] final models are brought back to the architect's office where all dimensions of piers, window openings, set-backs, etc., are established for the last time. Working drawings are then made by taking the dimensions directly from the ½″ scale and ⅛″ scale models. It can easily be seen how, through this procedure, the finished building, as far as the exterior is concerned, is made an exact enlargement of the final studied models.[49]

With nonrealistic models, the relationship is less simple. These have a conceptual correlation with the building that cannot be defined by measurement, though they may relate to the architect's theoretical purpose or vision more precisely than to the final product. Nonrepresentational computer images relate to the building in a similar way. However, the physical character and aesthetic quality of the model are essential to its message. The ideas conveyed through these models are dependent on the choice of the representational form, its materials and textures, attributes that cannot be readily exchanged. The physical and virtual models each speak about the meaning and intentions of the architect in a separate language.

While each form of representation operates in its own sphere, interaction with others is catalytic.

The advent of computer modeling has stirred architects' imagination, spurring them to think afresh about media and representation. The new tendency is toward a synthesis of motivations and input, which blurs the old distinctions between forms of representation and even the building itself. The architectural monograph, when assembled by the architect, provides the ideal outlet for this approach. Many of the images in *Asymptote: Architecture at the Interval* are based on models. Hani Rashid comments, "Our whole book is computer-generated that way. It's all been redrawn, and redrawn again and redrawn again and rephotographed again, until ultimately we have this strange surreal state."[50] Describing his physical models as "analog productions," he expresses the direction of his and Lise Anne Couture's work at Asymptote:

> I think eventually what we're looking at is a fusion. That's what we're trying to do in this office: fuse visual production with analog production, with thinking, with program, and ultimately what comes out at the end is not so clearly one thing or another; that's what we're striving for.[51]

Many architects have concluded that such a coalescent, multimedia approach, where each element is woven into a fabric in which virtual imagination, model, and reality merge, is the only viable way forward in this brave new world. In this mode, the richness and vividness of the exploratory process can become the ultimate architectural reality—as real, or more so, than the building itself. The recent volume *Toyo Ito: Blurring Architecture* belongs to this journey of discovery, revealing such a direction of thought in the context of Ito's practice:

> On the brink of the new millennium it is shown here that investigation or mediating study on the one hand and implemented reality on the other hand are no longer fundamentally contrasting aspects. The boundary between reality and virtuality becomes diffuse: "blurring architecture."[52]

At the outset of the twenty-first century, the model seems unaltered in many ways, yet it is also substantially different. While there have been huge changes in design and technology, the model's purpose remains essentially the same: it is used at various scales for design development and to communicate architects' ideas to others.

Perhaps the most important change in models is in what can be expressed—which is far more now than in the past. The greater diversity in modelmaking processes and the much wider availability of materials are only part of the story. The self-consciousness of the model in the twentieth century has enlarged its agenda, the acceptance of abstraction has enriched its purpose, and the diversity of skills among makers has freed its form. Models have become a platform from which architectural theory as well as matters of design can be usefully explored, and from which messages of intention as well as image can be delivered. Quite apart from other forms of representation, they offer an alternative sphere of activity in which architects can experiment with, and communicate, design ideas.

It is vital to recognize the breadth of the contribution that models can make, a contribution conveniently thrown into relief by the ever more virtual character of architectural design. The model's true three-dimensionality is unique within the design process, and this confers distinctive value on it. The power of the model both as object and as miniature continues to engage, and its importance in communicating ideas is unlikely to pass. Additionally, its superior accessibility for the layperson remains unchallenged.

Architects are voluble on their understanding of the model's crucial role in the design process, even at a time when virtual modeling is in its honeymoon phase. "I think we'll be seeing models in use for some considerable time, and maybe they will never get replaced as a form of communication," muses Spencer de Grey of Foster and Partners.

Because ultimately a physical model— made out of wood, or foam, or Perspex, or whatever—is in fact, in one way or another, a scaled-down version of a building, which in itself is a three-dimensional, finite object. I think that if you can see it in those terms, it is difficult to understand what would replace it. I think there will always be a demand. It is difficult to see that fundamentally changing.[53]

"Computers," insists Cesar Pelli, "can give me very good views of interiors, but the views are flat. A model is three-dimensional. As I move my head, I see relationships that I would not see in any other way. We will be building—we are probably already building—fewer models than we did before, but the key use of the model has not changed, which is to understand the whole building, its spaces, its volume, the relationship of the building to the surroundings."[54]

Nor, despite Asymptote's swing to computer-based design development, will Rashid be abandoning models:

My passion for the computer really started with a realization that I can make equally compelling structures with digital media. Now we're in a process where we're figuring out how to take those structures out into real space again and make models from them, so we've gone full circle.[55]

There are still many areas in which the substitution of computer for physical modeling would provide no contribution. Steven Holl comments, for instance, on the importance of the model's physical qualities:

Properties of light . . . provide the organizing concept for the Museum of the City we designed for Cassino, Italy. We attempted to model the light on computers and quickly realized physical models were necessary. In fact, light should be modeled full-size, as it falls off a wall at the square of its distance to the source.[56]

Peter Pran believes, "It's the tectonic qualities of a building that you can really get through in a model that you can't quite in a three-dimensional computer model."[57]

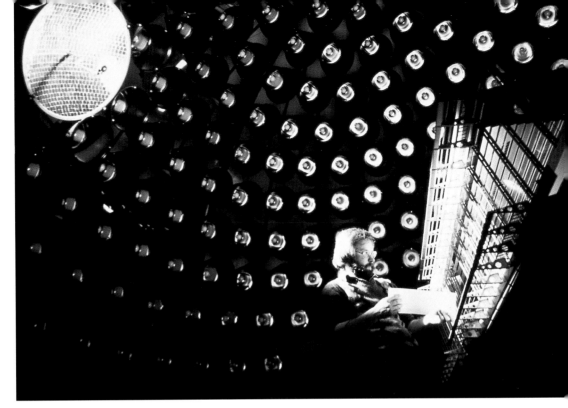

Model of Foster and Partners' Hong Kong and Shanghai Bank Headquarters during daylight testing in Innsbruck, 1982.

The lighting rig at Innsbruck can simulate daylight conditions anywhere in the world. Daylight testing of physical models gives a more direct and visible understanding of the effects of natural light on a three-dimensional object than does a computer simulation.

Models offer another key benefit. Their construction and handling keep architects in contact with the real world, a world where buildings are still fabricated individually from real materials and unique components, where handcraftsmanship and real production have permanent value. Relating to models, as well as to theoretical and computer-based study, enables architects to connect more readily with the practical implications of their work. The physical activity of fabrication, requiring both tactile and visual judgment, aids the appreciation of structural and sensual considerations in a way that would be impossible on a computer: the properties, color, texture, and finishes of real materials; their qualities of weight, mass, and balance. A concern among modelmakers is that the handcrafting and constructional activities traditionally experienced in childhood, and the consequent skills acquired, no longer feature so largely today. For the modelmaker, this affects recruitment. For the architect, concerned with physical construction, it is a critical lack. As

Hani Rashid remarks, "We have a vested interest in making."[58] While Michael Sorkin recognizes that his affinity for handcrafts is partly a matter of aesthetics and personal preference, he sees fundamental merits in the modelmaking process: "Given that one of the crises of architecture is about the way in which the body is installed in it, giving up these tactile contacts, however removed from the final product, entails a certain amount of risk."[59]

The stimulus generated through this physical activity complements other architectural tasks, and can be inspiring in itself. Keith Mendenhall's lively description of Frank Gehry's office transmits the atmosphere of creative excitement that exists in the physical world of making:

Our office is messy. Our floors are buckling and chipped and cracked plywood. Everywhere there are models, pieces of models, ripped paper. Glue guns lie on the floor next to cans of compressed air, next to boxes of wood blocks. People are crawling and

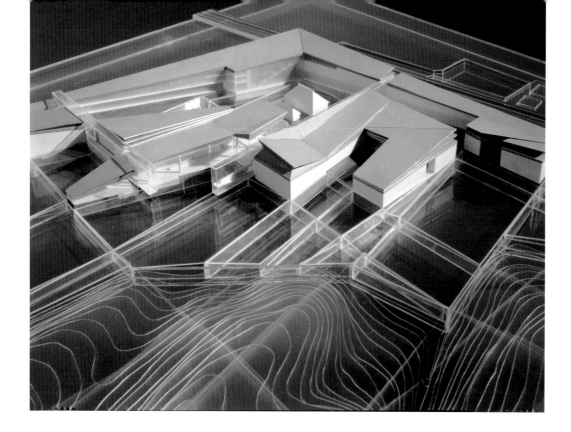

Asymptote (U.S.). Tohoku
Historical Museum,
Sendai, Japan, 1994.
Competition model.

climbing over tables, reaching down into models. Computers are arranged in almost random fashion around the edges of the modelmaking areas. Our walls are covered with more models and pieces of models, and photographs and color Xeroxes and pages ripped from magazines and Star Wars action figures and movie posters and exhibition-catalog covers and anything else that might be somehow inspiring. Papers are everywhere. Most of the models are rough, expressive, abstract.[60]

This could almost be a building site.

The physical nature of models has other, less obvious, advantages. Unlike computer images, models cannot be easily filed away. While the space they demand can be a drawback, their permanence also holds bonuses that have not gone unnoticed. Hani Rashid remarks:

The most important thing about a model is, at the end of the day, the fact that its physical quality persists and is somehow always available, whereas in the digital media you can call something up on a screen but it disappears. The thing about models is that they hang around, even when you don't want them to hang around, and they become something you look at and meditate upon, or comprehend or think about. And that would be happening inadvertently. It's not a conscious effort to look at the model. That's when they're most valuable to me, and that's why I like the fact that somehow or another every project we do generates some kind of what I call "analog" projection. So that it's there, and available for chance mechanisms, for inadvertency.[61]

The architect Stefan Behnisch has made precisely the same point: "models are always physically visible in the studio, inviting contemplation, comment and change—a process of ripening."[62]

Morphosis (U.S.). National Oceanic and Atmospheric Administration Satellite Operation Facility, Suitland, Maryland. Model, polyester resin, fiberglass, and silver powder, 2002.

The building portion of the model is printed by the firm's three-dimensional powder model printer and finished with polyester resin and more silver powder. The fluorescent lights are encased in polyester resin.

Three directions in the development of the contemporary model help demonstrate the extent of its integration in and the value of its contribution to current design practice. As technologies advance, the high-tech presentation model continues to become an ever more impressive and spellbinding object, conveying for the architect a level of precision and information hitherto unthinkable. A second, contrasting propensity of the model is the importance of conceptual and nonrepresentational examples in present practice. These are crucibles of creativity, powerful contributors to architectural dialogue at the nucleus of the architect's visionary world. Even so, Rashid believes that models could yet become "much more pertinent pieces of work around the meditation, theory, and kind of assemblage of ideas, more conceptual, and more compelling, and more real."[63] A third strength of today's model is its utility in the design process. In the twentieth century, architects rediscovered the model's significance for design development, and the regular use of this three-dimensional form has contributed to the enhanced understanding of twenty-first-century spatial and geometrical complexities.

In the last decades of the twentieth century, a delicate balance was struck between differing forms of representation. An overconcentration on computers (like the overemphasis on plan and elevation a hundred years ago) could easily unsettle this balance and have unfortunate effects on design quality. It would be wise to learn from history. Virtual modeling is making a huge contribution to architecture,

but it should not be at the expense of a breadth of vision that has only lately been achieved. Of course, an overemphasis on physical models would be equally limiting. Michele Saee has devised a method that maintains the critical balance:

> If I get too involved with the models, I lose the overall view of the project. So if I think of something, I build it three-dimensionally in cardboard, metal, or whatever material I think is appropriate, and then I photograph it and think about it that way, and digitize it sometimes, and work on it on the computer, and then rebuild it. And then my assistant develops it until it's a little bit more refined, and then I can come back again and tweak things and change things as it's developing.[64]

Many architects (and at least one critic) comprehend the need for divergent forms of representation and temper their enthusiasm, realizing that both are required.[65] With too great a concentration on computer modeling, Ross Wimer fears, the

> risk is that you deceive yourself of what is achievable. Typically at SOM we do both digital and physical models because the computer allows you to get a clearer understanding of interior spaces, which can't easily happen with a model unless you have gotten to enormous scale. The computer will let you add detail that would take you much longer to show in a model, so it's a very convincing tool for a lot of things. But we still find that making architectural models is the best way to understand physically how they come together. The risk with a rendering is that people can delude themselves into thinking that what they see is buildable; when your design is grounded in a physical model, you can't cheat as much.[66]

Spencer de Grey, too, maintains the need for breadth in the representational medium:

> I think that certainly the sort of photomontages, or computer montages, we can do now

are very sophisticated, but they are still two-dimensional views. I know they are "three-dimensional," but they are flat. You can then translate those into fly-bys or walk-throughs—we did some very interesting versions of the British Museum—and they give you, obviously, a much greater feeling of reality because you're actually moving through the spaces. But if you're reliant on just those two things, I still think there would be a gap, and I think you need the three-dimensional model as well.[67]

"Virtuality," concurs Peter Pran, "is another, different dimension with possibilities and opportunities of its own. It is not a replacement. I think having more and more advanced computer work gives an extra dimension to architecture, but it will never, ever take away the importance of physical models."[68]

Variety in forms of representation is unquestionably beneficial. Virtual models remedy the distorting effect of the physical model's reduced size. Physical models counter the immateriality of the virtual model. Perhaps virtual technology will one day prevail. But again, the lessons of history are relevant, and in this case, they suggest otherwise. Through many centuries of existence, models have survived similar challenges. They may succumb for a time, but their disappearance has never been permanent. Even as architecture moves beyond the realm of the material, the physical model—contrary to expectation—may not lose its purpose. A new relationship between virtual and physical models is emerging in a project by Asymptote, the Guggenheim Virtual Museum, a "structure" existing solely in cyberspace (on a Web site). Nevertheless, Rashid and Couture have turned to the physical model as an aid to understanding the navigation of their museum's "architecture." If there were to be a final test of the model's resilience, this might perhaps be it.

Computerization of the design process can get out of control, and the same may be the case with model production. Just as Peter Eisenman is obliged

---

Asymptote (U.S.). FluxSpace 3.0/M. Scapes Installation, Documenta XI, Kassel, Germany, 2002.

The installation projected the abstracted skylines of Hong Kong, Tokyo, and New York—"image maps"—onto a large suspended form that functioned as a receiver or absorber of information. The seemingly infinite environment of animated digital data related to contemporary urbanism influenced the Guggenheim Virtual Museum environments and architecture.

to call back his "dancing partner," it is sometimes necessary to pause and reassess. An effective model speaks to its audience and expresses the architect's vision. The production of models from computer files may offer precision, a particular level of detail and finish, and easier shaping of difficult forms; but if taken as the fallback for model production, it would mean the loss of many characteristics unique to the medium. Consider the burnished impasto of Morphosis, the layering of Libeskind, the clay forms of Predock, the spontaneous crumples of Gehry. Models produced at the push of a button cannot offer the individuality and range of expression requisite for the task, nor can the imagination of architects be satisfied in this manner. The most basic hand-building processes, the finest expressions of craftsmanship, and the diversity of materials and technology will continue to be necessary to get the most from the medium.

Some modelmakers, concerned that the skills of the hand will be lost, are rightly wary of too great a dependence on computer-aided manufacture. In envisaging the consequences, Richard Tenguerian discovers an alarming prospect. The idea of a modelmaker who can "[move] magically to a professional level through the acquisition of CAD/CAM, laser cutters" confounds his reason: "I am hard-pressed to understand how buying high-tech machines and CNC machines . . . can confer on someone the skills necessary to make him/her a professional . . . does this make him a model maker? Do we infer from this that the model maker is no more than an assembler?" Tenguerian relates a typical occasion on which such a person would be flummoxed. Hellmuth, Obata + Kassabaum wanted a "museum-quality" model produced over a weekend. The information presented to the modelmaker took the form of a few basic drawings and some unresolved ideas. "Short deadlines and cursory sketches are but two of the parameters model makers must contend with," continues Tenguerian. In such circumstances

technology is no substitute for skill and experience in the progenitor. "Tools such as CAD/CAM," he concludes, must be "at the service of the model maker, not the other way round."[69]

Architects, similarly, are aware of this risk. Seeking a modelmaker in a new location, Timothy Johnson, now at NBBJ, wrote,

> We visited four modelmaking shops . . . that had all sorts of hi-tech equipment like laser cutters, CAD/CAM and CNC machines. We couldn't find any individual who could understand our vision, whom we could trust to take charge of the model and give it personal attention . . . Since the project was done in design study stages, there was no concrete information and many last-minute changes. We wanted a Savile Row tailor so to speak.[70]

Such sentiments should serve as a warning.

To retain a rich diversity of materials and a high level of craftsmanship within the medium will have its costs, but just as architecture would be impoverished without variety in representation, so would models be impoverished without variety within the medium. Craftsmanship, creativity, imagination, and artistic input are needed to make the model convincing and enable it to communicate. The introduction of a new form of representation—computer modeling—highlights the model's distinctive purpose and value, the prodigality of its parts and its capacity for expression.

The model will continue to evolve, and the possibilities are exciting. Models are currently at the peak of their ability to communicate. The freedom to use computer-aided manufacture alongside the most simple and most complex hand techniques is keeping the medium healthy. Daniel Libeskind has likened the relationship between architect and model to that between puppet and puppeteer.[71] The electricity between them makes the model come alive. When models are removed from the hands of the maker, the strings are cut.

Alsop Architects (U.K.). Met Office Headquarters Relocation, Exeter, England, 2000–2001. Competition/presentation model, 1:1000, vacuum-formed acrylic, silver paint, and acrylic components: A Models, 2000.

This model, developed from early drawings, is described by the maker as "a simple sketch to capture the essence of the building."

NOTES

PREFACE

1. Henry A. Millon and Vittorio Magnago Lampugnani, eds., *The Renaissance from Brunelleschi to Michelangelo: The Representation of Architecture* (New York: Rizzoli, 1994); Henry A. Millon, ed., *The Triumph of the Baroque: Architecture in Europe, 1600–1750* (New York: Rizzoli, 1999). Two publications of the late 1970s and early 1980s were dedicated to the contemporary model as it emerged: Suzanne Buttolph, ed., *Great Models*, vol. 27 of *The Student Publication of the School of Design* (Raleigh: North Carolina State University College of Design, 1978); and Kenneth Frampton and Silvia Kolbowski, eds., *Idea as Model* (New York: Institute for Architecture and Urban Studies/Rizzoli, 1981). There is a surprising coincidence in the content and overall concept of these two volumes that is difficult to resolve. Although *Great Models* was published first, the catalog *Idea as Model* was based on an exhibition of 1976 and presumably represented its format as well as its content. The "Idea as Model" exhibition is discussed in chapter one, "The Model Defined." The year 1991 saw the first publication, in recent years, of a book that studies the model as a medium of representation rather than serving as a manual of model construction. Akiko Busch, *The Art of the Architectural Model* (New York: Design Press, 1991) provides a valuable introduction to the subject, focusing primarily on presentation models and the realistic portrayal of architectural proposals, while largely ignoring conceptual, sketch, and visionary productions or any concern with the model as a platform for dialogue or with a historical perspective. A more recent book by Tom Porter and John Neale, *Architectural Supermodels* (Oxford: Architectural Press, 2000), more directly addresses contemporary process models and their part in design development.

CHAPTER 1:
THE MODEL DEFINED

1. Peter Pran, interview with author, January 25, 2000.
2. Hani Rashid, interview with author, March 3, 2000.
3. Except perhaps in the case of Peter Eisenman's axonometric model of House X, or other experiments at making a model correspond to a drawing. See Kenneth Frampton and Silvia Kolbowski, eds., *Idea as Model* (New York: Institute for Architecture and Urban Studies/Rizzoli, 1981), 82–83.
4. Luca Galofaro, *Digital Eisenman: An Office of the Electronic Era* (Basel: Birkhäuser, 1999), 30.
5. http://www.predock.com/clay.html, February 2001.
6. Rashid, interview.
7. Heinrich Klotz, ed., *Paper Architecture: New Projects from the Soviet Union* (New York: Rizzoli, 1990), 11.
8. Jaquelin Robertson, "Madden House I," in Frampton and Kolbowski, *Idea as Model*, 60.
9. Michael Graves, "The Wagenman House and the Crooks House," in Frampton and Kolbowski, *Idea as Model*, 38.
10. Leon Battista Alberti, *De Re Aedificatoria* (1452); English trans., Joseph Rykwert, Neil Leach, and Robert Tavernor, *On the Art of Building in Ten Books* (Cambridge, Mass.: MIT Press, 1988), 34.
11. Cited in Judith Davidsen, "Light-Hearted Models for Serious Results," *Architectural Record* 180 (July 1992): 31.
12. A. E. Richardson, "Fitzwilliam Museum: Exhibition of Architectural Models and Drawings," *Cambridge Review* 63 (November 29, 1941): 118.
13. John Wilton-Ely, ed., *The Architect's Vision* (exhibition catalog, Nottingham: University of Nottingham Department of Fine Art, 1965). The quotation is from the first paragraph of the introduction. The exhibition ran from March 1 to March 21, 1965, at the Nottingham University Art Gallery.

14. John Frederick Physick and Michael Darby, *Marble Halls: Drawings and Models for Victorian Secular Buildings* (exhibition catalog, London: Victoria and Albert Museum, 1973).

15. Sam Lambert, "Model Architecture," *Architects' Journal* 160 (December 4, 1974): 1317. See also David Lewis, "Models on Show for Sheffield Society," *RIBA Journal* 81 (November 1974): 8. A further U.K. exhibition, entitled "Model Futures" (1973), showcased the work of a group of professional modelmakers.

16. "Italian Renaissance Architecture: Brunelleschi, Sangallo, Michelangelo; The Cathedrals of Florence and Pavia and Saint Peter's, Rome," was organized by the National Gallery of Art, Washington, D.C., in collaboration with the Palazzo Grassi, Venice. It appeared at both institutions, as well as at the Musée National des Monuments Français, Paris, and the Neue Berliner Galerie, Altes Museum, Berlin, between December 1994 and January 1996. "The Triumph of the Baroque: Architecture in Europe, 1600–1750" was organized by the National Gallery of Art, Washington, the Palazzo Grassi, Venice, the Montreal Museum of Fine Arts, and the Musée des Beaux-Arts, Marseille. It appeared at the National Gallery, the Montreal Museum of Fine Arts, the Musée des Beaux-Arts, and the Palazzina di Caccia, Stupinigi, Turin, between July 1999 and March 2001.

17. "The Triumph of the Baroque," for example, was intended to stimulate an awareness of the importance of models in the history of Baroque architecture in Europe.

18. Frampton and Kolbowski, *Idea as Model*, 1.

19. For Eisenman, see Frampton and Kolbowski, *Idea as Model*, 124. Stanley Tigerman was quoted in Stanley Abercrombie, "Creative Playthings," *Horizon* 21 (July 1978): 79.

20. Richard Pommer, "Postscript to a Post-Mortem," in Frampton and Kolbowski, *Idea as Model*, 10. The exhibition "The Architecture of the École des Beaux-Arts" was on view at the Museum of Modern Art, New York, from October 29, 1975, to January 4, 1976.

21. Pommer, "The Idea of 'Idea as Model,'" in Frampton and Kolbowski, *Idea as Model*, 3. SOM refers to Skidmore, Owings & Merrill.

22. Edward Lucie-Smith, *Late Modern: The Visual Arts since 1945* (New York: Praeger, 1976), 261.

23. B. J. Archer, ed., *Houses for Sale* (New York: Rizzoli, 1980), xiv–xv.

24. Frampton and Kolbowski, *Idea as Model*, 10.

25. Mike Fairbrass and Ivan Harbour of Richard Rogers Partnership, interview with author, August 18, 2000.

26. Spencer de Grey of Foster and Partners, interview with author, August 16, 2000.

27. http://www.herts.ac.uk/extrel/horizon/oct99/christian_info.html, February 2002.

28. Pommer refers to models hung on walls at the Max Protech Gallery. Frampton and Kolbowski, *Idea as Model*, 10.

29. "Architectural Imagination" was shown at the Max Protech Gallery, New York, from March 4 to April 3, 1999.

30. John Wilton-Ely had preempted this view of the model in a historical article on models written in 1968: "I propose to consider some of the finest surviving examples as works of outstanding craftsmanship as well as key documents for the architectural historian." Wilton-Ely, "The Architectural Model: 1. English Baroque," *Apollo* 88:80 (October 1968): 250.

31. Keith Mendenhall of Gehry Partners, interview with author, December 3, 1999.

32. At SFMOMA, from 1989 on, following the 1983 founding of the curatorial department of Architecture and Design. Michelle Barger of SFMOMA, e-mail message to author, January 9, 2002.

33. Besides the catalog to "Architecture of the École des Beaux-Arts," published in 1975, books on architectural representation and the architectural process in this period included Spiro Kostof, ed., *The Architect: Chapters in the History of the Profession* (Oxford and New York: Oxford University Press, 1977, 1986); and Eve Blau and Edward Kaufman, eds., *Architecture and Its Image: Four Centuries of Architectural Representation: Works from the Collection of the Canadian Centre for Architecture* (exhibition catalog, Montreal: Canadian Centre for Architecture, 1989).

34. Museum exhibitions included "Het Kleine Bouwen: Vier Eeuwen Maquettes in Nederland" at the Centraal Museum in Utrecht, May 1–June 26, 1983.

35. *Revue de l'Art* 58–59 (1982–83): 123–43; *Architects' Journal* 182 (December 18–25, 1985): 19–46; *Rassegna* 9 (December 1987): 2, 4–5, 74–75; *Der Architekt* 4 (April 1989): 185–206; *Architecture New Jersey* 26 (1990): 9–10, 18–20, 21–22, 24, 27.

36. That is, excluding manuals of the how-to variety. Akiko Busch, *The Art of the Architectural Model* (New York: Design Press, 1991).

37. "Maquettes Invraisemblables: The Model Is the Message" was on view at Showroom Artemide, Paris, in December 1989, and "Hyper-Tension" was at Galerie Aedes, Berlin, in May 1995.

38. For a similar episode in the Gothic period, see François Bucher, "Micro-Architecture as the 'Idea' of Gothic Theory and Style," *Gesta* 15 (International Center of Medieval Art, 1976): 73.

39. Alastair Best, "Thorp Modelmakers," *Crafts* 64 (September–October 1983): 47–48.

40. Piera Scuri makes this point in relation to the image of Philip Johnson in "Skyscraper Business," *Domus* 660 (April 1985): 24.

41. Jun Yanagisawa, "A Utopia Called Model," in *Toyo Ito: Blurring Architecture* (Milan: Edizioni Charta, 1999), 155.

42. In Scandinavia, among other places, during World War I, several family magazines began to publish paper cutout models illustrating real and imaginary buildings. A number of engineers and architects have recounted how their interest in building and construction started when they built these paper models as children. Gunnar Sillén, e-mail message to author, October 24, 2000.

43. Andreas Papadakis, ed., *Dolls' Houses* (London: Academy Editions/Architectural Design, 1983), 4.

44. Bucher, "Micro-Architecture," 72–73.

45. Officina Alessi, *Tea and Coffee Piazza* (New York: Shakespeare and Company, 1983), 17, 34–37. The tableware was exhibited at the Chiesa di San Carpoforo/Centro Internationale di Brera, Milan, and at the Max Protetch Gallery, New York, in October 1983.

46. Rashid, interview.

47. Michele Saee, interview with author, January 19, 2000.

48. David Welch, *Nazi Propaganda: The Power and the Limitations* (London and Canberra: Croom Helm, 1983), 55. While Hitler's skills, demonstrated in the watercolor sketches and pencil drawings of architectural subjects he submitted to the Vienna Academy of Fine Arts in 1907, were not sufficient for admission to the institution, the rector suggested he take up architectural design. However, his qualifications were not considered adequate for that either. See Sherree Owens Zalampas, *Adolf Hitler: A Psychological Interpretation of His Views on Architecture, Art, and Music* (Bowling Green, Ohio: Bowling Green University Popular Press, c. 1990), 16.

49. Louis Grodecki, *Plans en Relief de Villes Belges Construits par des Ingénieurs Militaires Français XVII–XIX Siècle, Bruxelles, Pro Civitate* (1965), cited in Isabelle Warmoes, *Musée des Plans-Reliefs: Historic Models of Fortified Towns* (Paris: Éditions du Patrimoine, 1999), 10.

50. Henry A. Millon and Vittorio Magnago Lampugnani, eds., *The Renaissance from Brunelleschi to Michelangelo: The Representation of Architecture* (New York: Rizzoli, 1994), 21 n. 9.

51. Ben Elton, *Gridlock* (London: Warner Books, 1991), 53.

CHAPTER 2:
A COMMON THREAD

1. Louisa Rodgers Alger, letter to "The Architect, the Capitol," May 9, 1978, U.S. Capitol Archives.

2. Cited in *Competitions* 8 (Summer 1998): 57, 59.

3. Leon Battista Alberti, *De Re Aedificatoria* (1452); English trans., Joseph Rykwert, Neil Leach, and Robert Tavernor, *On the Art of Building in Ten Books* (Cambridge, Mass.: MIT Press, 1988), 34. Also from the Baroque period: "The model enabled the assessment of the building's volume, together with the estimate of costs, calculated with the craftsmen"; see Elisabeth Kieven, "'Mostrar l'Inventione': The Role of Roman Architects in the Baroque Period; Plans and Models," in Henry A. Millon, ed., *The Triumph of the Baroque: Architecture in Europe, 1600–1750* (New York: Rizzoli, 1999), 204.

4. From Philibert de l'Orme, *Le Premier Tome de l'Architecture* (1567), cited in Monique Mosser, "Models of French Architecture in the Age of Enlightenment," *Daidalos*, December 15, 1981, 85.

5. See J. J. Coulton, *Greek Architects at Work: Problems of Structure and Design* (London: Elek, 1977), 55–57.

6. This translation from "Art Serve" at the Australian National University; http://rubens.anu.edu.au/htdocs/texts/vasari/vasari.brunelleschi.html, March 2002.

7. Margaret Richardson, "Model Architecture," *Country Life*, September 21, 1989, 227.

8. From Wren's report to the commissioners of St. Paul's, May 1, 1666, cited in John Cornforth, "Architects, Patrons and Models," *Country Life* 137 (March 4, 1965): 466.

9. *Engineering Record* 24 (November 7, 1891): 362.

10. Chris Windsor of Foster and Partners, e-mail message to author, October 18, 2000.

11. Kieven writes of the Baroque period: "In the case of large-scale projects, a model was almost always made, on the basis of which the commission was granted. Often the model was deemed the final authentic document." See " 'Mostrar l'Inventione,' " 204.

12. From Wren's report to the commissioners, cited in Cornforth, "Architects, Patrons," 467.

13. An early urban model of Florence was constructed in 1529 to study its siege defenses, and Albert V of Bavaria had models made of his principal towns between 1568 and 1574; from John Wilton-Ely, "Architectural Model," *Grove Dictionary of Art Online*, www.groveart.com. For examples of both strategic- and garden-planning models in the Baroque period, see Millon, *Triumph of the Baroque*, and Isabelle Warmoes, *Musée des Plans-Reliefs: Historic Models of Fortified Towns* (Paris: Éditions du Patrimoine, 1999).

14. Alexander Badawy, "Ancient Constructional Diagrams in Egyptian Architecture," *Gazette des Beaux Arts* 107 (February 1986): 56.

15. Gülru Necipoglu-Kafadar, "Plans and Models in 15th and 16th Century Ottoman Architectural Practice," *Journal of the Society of Architectural Historians* 45 (September 1986): 239–40.

16. Jane Jacobs, "The Miniature Boom," *Architectural Forum* 108 (May 1958): 109.

17. Peter Pran, interview with author, January 25, 2000.

18. Just how much this situation contrasted with former practice is difficult to assess, since material relating to the use of models in the Gothic period is considered ambiguous. Spiro Kostof, ed., *The Architect: Chapters in the History of the Profession* (Oxford and New York: Oxford University Press, 1977, 1986), 74.

19. Kostof, *Architect*, 142–49.

20. For France, see Mosser, "Models of French Architecture," 85; for Germany, see Hans Reuther, "Origin and Development of the Architectural Model in Germany," *Daidalos*, December 15, 1981, 99.

21. Arthur T. Bolton, ed., *Lectures on Architecture, by Sir John Soane . . . as Delivered to the Students of the Royal Academy from 1809 to 1836 in Two Courses of Six Lectures Each* (London, 1929), 191. Reuther writes of Germany: "In the classicist period, many architects lost interest in the architectural model; some architects, like Carl Friedrich Schinkel, did not leave us any known models at all. Only in the period of historism [*sic*], the use of models did prosper again"; "Origin and Development," 106.

22. *Builder* 6 (May 6, 1848): 225.

23. *Builder* 6 (October 7, 1848): 490. The citation refers to a failing model business; see chapter six, "Makers," for details.

24. John Frederick Physick and Michael Darby, *Marble Halls: Drawings and Models for Victorian Secular Buildings* (exhibition catalog, London: Victoria and Albert Museum, 1973), 13.

25. For the model of the Pro-Cathedral in Dublin, see Edward McParland, "Who Was P? An Architectural Model Rediscovered," *Architectural Review* 157 (February 1975): 72.

26. Edwin S. Parker, "The Model for Architectural Representation," *Architectural Forum* 30 (April 1919): 120. See also Alwyn T. Covell, "Architecture in Miniature: The Plastic Model Studies of an English Artist," *Architectural Record* 35 (March 1914): 265: "The use of a scale model seems so logical and so desirable that it is remarkable that its use has been restricted almost entirely to large public buildings."

27. U.S. Capitol Archives; Parker, "Model for Architectural Representation," 120.

28. Henry Rutgers Marshall, "The Architect's Tools," *Architectural Review* 4 (November 1897): 55.

29. William Alciphron Boring, "The Use of Models in the Study of Architecture," *Architecture* 45 (June 1922): 200, 202.

30. J. Price Nunn, "Models and Their Making," *Builder* 162 (June 26, 1942): 553.

31. Maurice Gauthier, "Studying in Three Dimensions," *Pencil Points* 7 (July 1926): 416.

32. Frederic C. Hirons, "The Use of Scale Models," pt. 1, *Pencil Points* 1 (November 1920): 5.

33. For example, see Royal Rook, "Model Making in the Drafting Room," *American Architect* 114 (August 28, 1918): 247–52; Parker, "Model for Architectural Representation," 119–21; LeRoy Grumbine, "Cardboard Models," pts. 1–3, *American Architect* 122 (August 2, 1922): 111–14, August 16, 1922, 135–40, August 30, 1922, 177–79; Harvey Wiley Corbett, "Architectural Models of Cardboard," pts. 1–4, *Pencil Points* 3 (April 1922): 10–14, May 1922, 28–32, 37, June 1922, 14–17, August 1922, 15–18.

34. J. Philip McDonnell, "Models and Their Making," *American Architect* 107 (May 5, 1915): 277–83.

35. "Some Architectural Scale Models Executed by Berthold V. Gerow," *Architect and Engineer of California* 56–57 (June 1919): 83.

36. Alwyn T. Covell, "Developing the Country House: Drawings and Models from the Office of Joseph Bodker, Architect," *Arts and Decoration* 15 (July 1921): 193.

37. LeRoy Grumbine, "The Use of Scale Models as an Aid to the Architect," *Western Architect* 34 (June 1925): 59.

38. Steven H. Waring, "Improved Techniques in Architectural Modelling," *Journal, Royal Architectural Institute of Canada* 25 (February 1948): 58.

39. Waring, "Improved Techniques," 58.

40. Kenneth Reid, "Architectural Models," *Pencil Points* 20 (July 1939): 407.

41. Nunn, "Models and Their Making," 553.

42. John Chisholm, "Rehearsal for Reality," *Architect and Building News* 2 (February 27, 1969): 24; Ray Pfaendler, "Architectural Models," *Architectural Review* 140 (July 1966): 70.

43. For the change in style, see Stanley Abercrombie, "Creative Playthings," *Horizon* 21 (July 1978): 74. For the war-borne advances, see Waring, "Improved Techniques," 58; and Jacobs, "Miniature Boom," 107.

44. David Lewis, "Models on Show for Sheffield Society," *RIBA Journal* 81 (November 1974): 8.

45. Abercrombie, "Creative Playthings," 74.

46. Piers Gough, "Modelmakers," *Architects' Journal* 177 (April 27, 1983): 30.

47. For Russia, see Heinrich Klotz, ed., *Paper Architecture: New Projects from the Soviet Union* (New York: Rizzoli, 1990). For Australia, see "Modelmaking: An Architectural Design Tool," *Architecture Australia* 78 (June 5, 1989): 90. For New Zealand, see Carol Bucknell, "Precision Instruments," *Architecture New Zealand*, July–August 1988, 68–70. For Japan, see "The Exhibition: Design New Wave '86," *Japan Architect* 61 (November–December 1986): 5.

48. Wilton-Ely's "Architectural Model," *Grove Dictionary of Art Online*, has been a useful source throughout this section.

49. Richard Armiger, conversation with author.

50. Percy J. Waldrain, letter to the editor of *RIBA Journal*, cited in John Fitchen, *The Construction of Gothic Cathedrals* (Oxford: Clarendon Press, 1961), 302.

51. Alger to "The Architect, the Capitol."

52. On the Radcliffe Camera model, see John Wilton-Ely, "The Architectural Model: 1. English Baroque," *Apollo* 88:80 (October 1968): 255–56. Cornforth described its condition as "battered" in "Architects, Patrons," 467.

53. Helen Seymour, "Model Maestros," *Architects' Journal* 182 (December 18–25, 1985): 31.

54. Cesar Pelli, interview with author, February 2, 2000.

CHAPTER 3:
A QUESTION OF SCALE

1. Scot Walls, videotaped discussion on models, NBBJ, Seattle, May 5, 2000.

2. Josephine von Henneberg, "Emilio dei Cavalieri, Giacomo della Porta, and G. B. Montano," *Journal of the Society of Architectural Historians* 36 (December 1977): 252.

3. The exact dimensions of the model are 24 feet 1¾ inches long, 19 feet 9 inches wide, and 15 feet 4¼ inches high (736 by 602 by 468 centimeters). Pierluigi Silvan, ed., *Saint Peter's from Sangallo to Michelangelo: Models of the Basilica and the Dome, History and Restoration* (Milan: Bompiani, 1996), 63.

4. Emile Garet, letter to Elliott Woods, superintendent of the U.S. Capitol, May 14, 1902, U.S. Capitol Archives.

5. Edwin S. Parker, "The Model for Architectural Representation," *Architectural Forum* 30 (April 1919): 121.

6. Ross Wimer, interview with author, May 19, 2000.

7. Wimer, interview.

8. Ray Pfaendler, "Architectural Models," *Architectural Review* 140 (July 1966): 74.

9. Wimer, interview.

10. William Alciphron Boring, "The Use of Models in the Study of Architecture," *Architecture* 45 (June 1922): 200.

11. J. J. Coulton, *Greek Architects at Work: Problems of Structure and Design* (London: Elek, 1977), 55–57.

12. For the Farnese Palace, see George C. Bauer, "From Architecture to Scenography: The Full-Scale Model in the Baroque Tradition," in Antoine Schnapper, ed., "La Scenografia Barocca," *Comité International d'Histoire de l'Art* 5 (1979): 143. For St. Peter's, see Henry A. Millon and Vittorio Magnago Lampugnani, eds., *The Renaissance from Brunelleschi to Michelangelo: The Representation of Architecture* (New York: Rizzoli, 1994), 50.

13. Bauer, "From Architecture to Scenography," 143–44.

14. Bauer, "From Architecture to Scenography," 144.

15. Bauer, "From Architecture to Scenography," 143–45.

16. From the minutes of a January 27, 1710, meeting of the Academy of Architecture in France, cited in Monique Mosser, "Models of French Architecture in the Age of Enlightenment," *Daidalos*, December 15, 1981, 87.

17. Egerton Swartwout, "The Use of Large Scale Models in Architecture," *Architecture* 24 (September 1911): 129; Mosser, "Models of French Architecture," 94.

18. Mosser, "Models of French Architecture," 94. The painting is in the collection of the Musée Carnavalet in Paris.

19. Arthur T. Bolton, ed., *Lectures on Architecture, by Sir John Soane . . . as Delivered to the Students of the Royal Academy from 1809 to 1836 in Two Courses of Six Lectures Each* (London, 1929), 191.

20. For examples, see *Illustrated World's Fair* 1:4 (October 1891): 20; and Dennison and Hirons's studies for the National State Bank in Elizabeth, New Jersey, in Frederic C. Hirons, "The Use of Scale Models," pt. 1, *Pencil Points* 1 (November 1920): 4–8.

21. "An Innovation in Architecture," *Architectural Record* 12 (November 1902): 637.

22. For the Department of Agriculture model, see Library of Congress, Prints and Photographs Division, Record No. LC-USZ62 58744. For the New York Public Library, see "Innovation in Architecture," 636. For Boston and New York, see also Swartwout, "Use of Large Scale Models," 129.

23. For Lutyens, see Michael Trinick, *Castle Drogo, Devon* (Plymouth: National Trust, 1976), 10; for Mies van der Rohe, see Phyllis Lambert, ed., *Mies in America* (New York: Abrams, 2001), 221 n. 61.

24. Balthazar Korab, telephone conversation with author.

25. Judith Davidsen, "Light-Hearted Models for Serious Results," *Architectural Record* 180 (July 1992): 33.

26. Keith Mendenhall of Gehry Partners, e-mail message to author, February 25, 2002.

27. Steven Holl, interview, cited in *Competitions* 8 (Summer 1998): 57, 59.

28. Davidsen, "Light-Hearted Models," 30.

29. Marc H. Miller, *The Panorama of New York City: A History of the World's Largest Scale Model* (New York: Queens Museum, 1990), 4.

30. Spencer de Grey of Foster and Partners, interview with author, August 16, 2000.

31. Mike Fairbrass of Richard Rogers Partnership, interview with author, August 18, 2000.

32. R. T. Gunther, ed., *The Architecture of Sir Roger Pratt, Charles II's Commissioner for the Re-Building of London after the Great Fire: Now Printed for the First Time from His Note-Books* (Oxford and New York: Oxford University Press, 1928), 23.

33. Henry A. Millon, ed., *The Triumph of the Baroque: Architecture in Europe, 1600–1750* (New York: Rizzoli, 1999), 483.

34. Millon and Lampugnani, *Renaissance from Brunelleschi to Michelangelo*, 519. Guiliano da Sangallo was the uncle of Antonio da Sangallo, who built the Great Model of St. Peter's, Rome.

35. Millon and Lampugnani, *Renaissance from Brunelleschi to Michelangelo*, 474.

36. Millon, *Triumph of the Baroque*, 567.

37. John Wilton-Ely, "The Architectural Model: I. English Baroque," *Apollo* 88:80 (October 1968): 254.

38. Mentioned in the correspondence of the Marquis de Marigny, governor of building concerns under Louis XIV; Mosser, "Models of French Architecture," 94.

39. Edward McParland, "Who Was P? An Architectural Model Rediscovered," *Architectural Review* 157 (February 1975): 72.

40. Millon, *Triumph of the Baroque*, 411, 587.

41. "On the Proper Display of Models," *Builder* 1 (August 5, 1843): 317.

42. Boring, "Use of Models," 201.

43. Jean Hetherington, "The Value of Models in Architecture," *American Architect* 121 (January 18, 1922): 52.

44. John Frederick Physick and Michael Darby, *Marble Halls: Drawings and Models for Victorian Secular Buildings* (exhibition catalog, London: Victoria and Albert Museum, 1973), 14.

45. Harvey Wiley Corbett, "Architectural Models of Cardboard," pt. 4, *Pencil Points* 3 (August 1922): 15.

46. Robert T. Packard and Balthazar Korab, *Encyclopedia of American Architecture* (New York: McGraw-Hill, 1995), 480.

47. Pfaendler, "Architectural Models," 74.

48. Vincent G. Cling Jr., "The Architect as Film Maker," *AIA Journal* 55 (February 1971): 23–25.

49. Beatrix Potter, *The Tale of Two Bad Mice* (1904; Harmondsworth, England, and New York: Frederick Warne, 1985), 21.

50. Jasper Halfmann and Clod Zillich, "Reality and Reduced Model," *Studio International*, 193:986 (March–April 1977): 99; Susan Stewart, *On Longing: Narratives of the Miniature, the Gigantic, the Souvenir, the Collection* (Baltimore and London: John Hopkins University Press, 1984).

51. William L. Hamilton, "A Whistle-Stop World," *New York Times*, April 11, 2002, D9.

52. Cited in Helen Buttery, "A Present from Pompeii," *World of Interiors*, April 1989, 136. See also Margaret Richardson, "Model Architecture," *Country Life*, September 21, 1989, 225–26.

53. For the Louisiana exhibition, see Garet to Woods; for the other venues, see "Model of the United States Capitol," typewritten record, c. 1956, U.S. Capitol Archives.

54. Bernard Gillroy, letter to Edward K. Warren, May 25, 1938. In the end, the model was not included due to lack of space; Gillroy, letter to A. L. Ferguson, assistant to the bursar of St. John the Divine, January 27, 1939, Archives of the Diocese of New York.

55. Arthur E. Herman, "Models of Plastics and Aluminum," *Progressive Architecture* 40 (December 1959): 9.

56. "Some Architectural Scale Models Executed by Berthold V. Gerow," *Architect and Engineer of California* 56–57 (June 1919): 83.

57. Chester N. Godfrey, letter to the Very Rev. Milo H. Gates, July 19, 1934, Archives of the Diocese of New York.

58. Edward M. Gomez, "From Plaything to Hobby," *Metropolis*, July–August 1989, 65.

59. Hamilton, "Whistle-Stop World," D9.

60. Trevor Fawcett, "Two Eighteenth Century Models of Bath" (unpublished article, n.d., photocopy, Soane Museum, London).

61. Buttery, "Present from Pompeii," 136.

62. Mosser, "Models of French Architecture," 85.

63. Cited in Halfmann and Zillich, "Reality and Reduced Model," 99.

64. Kerry Downes, *Sir Christopher Wren and the Making of St. Paul's* (London: Royal Academy of Arts, 1991).

65. Gunther, *Architecture of Sir Roger Pratt*, 22.

66. Cited in Millon, *Triumph of the Baroque*, 483.

67. Hani Rashid, interview with author, March 3, 2000.

CHAPTER 4: VISION

1. Information from Peter Pran, interview with author, January 25, 2000.

2. John Fitchen, *The Construction of Gothic Cathedrals: A Study of Medieval Vault Erection* (Oxford: Clarendon Press, 1961), 302. In the same period, models were also used for studying and testing masonry vaults.

3. Leon Battista Alberti, *De Re Aedificatoria* (1452); English trans., Joseph Rykwert, Neil Leach, and Robert Tavernor, *On the Art of Building in Ten Books* (Cambridge, Mass.: MIT Press, 1988), 33.

4. Sir Henry Wotton, *The Elements of Architecture* (London, 1624).

5. Arthur T. Bolton, ed., *Lectures on Architecture, by Sir John Soane . . . as Delivered to the Students of the Royal Academy from 1809 to 1836 in Two Courses of Six Lectures Each* (London, 1929), 191.

6. From the minutes of a January 27, 1710, meeting of the Academy of Architecture in France, cited in Monique Mosser, "Models of French Architecture in the Age of Enlightenment," *Daidalos*, December 15, 1981, 85.

7. Cited in the brochure for the exhibition "The Triumph of the Baroque: Architecture in Europe, 1600–1750," on view at the National Gallery of Art, Washington, D.C., from May 21 to October 9, 2000.

8. J. Price Nunn, "Models and Their Making," *Builder* 162 (June 26, 1942): 553.

9. LeRoy Grumbine applauds models "for developing the design . . . made so they can be altered as desired" in "The Use of Scale Models as an Aid to the Architect," *Western Architect* 34 (June 1925): 63. Alwyn T. Covell recommends the use of "plastic" models in "Architecture in Miniature: The Plastic Model Studies of an English Artist," *Architectural Record* 35 (March 1914). Models for study are particularly recommended in the following, among many other examples: Edwin S. Parker, "The Model for Architectural Representation," *Architectural Forum* 30 (April 1919): 119–21; Frederic C. Hirons, "The Use of Scale Models," pts. 1–4, *Pencil Points* 1 (November 1920): 4–8, December 1920, 4–8, 25, *Pencil Points* 2 (January 1921): 22–24, February 1921, 21–25; Grumbine, "Use of Scale Models," 59–63.

10. William Alciphron Boring, "The Use of Models in the Study of Architecture," *Architecture* 45 (June 1922): 200.

11. Berthold Audsley, "Miniatures and Their Value in Architectural Practice," *Brickbuilder* (bound with *Architectural Forum*) 23 (September 1914): 214. The "country" referred to is not altogether clear; although the article appeared in an American periodical, the author was probably British and all the illustrated examples were for projects in England.

12. "Model Making by Architects: An Interesting Communication from a Reader Who Strongly Approves the Work Begun at Columbia University," *American Architect* 118 (December 8, 1920): 749–50. Reference is made to the announcement of "a special course in model making" as part of the "architectural course in the Summer School of Columbia University," in Alwyn T. Covell, "Developing the Country House: Drawings and Models from the Office of Joseph Bodker, Architect," *Arts and Decoration* 15 (July 1921): 193. William Alciphron Boring, who was director of the School of Architecture at Columbia University during this time, describes the staff of this new department, employed to help the students develop detail models in clay, as being "of marked ability"; see "Use of Models," 202. Harvey Wiley Corbett and Wallace Harrison, who were studio critics during Boring's time, were notable for their use of models.

13. Kenneth Reid, "Architectural Models," *Pencil Points* 20 (July 1939): 407.

14. Nunn, "Models and Their Making," 553.

15. Phyllis Lambert, ed., *Mies in America* (New York: Abrams, 2001), 568.

16. Henry A. Millon and Vittorio Magnago Lampugnani, eds., *The Renaissance from Brunelleschi to Michelangelo: The Representation of Architecture* (New York: Rizzoli, 1994), 24.

17. Kenneth McCutchon, "Architectural Models," *Architects' Journal* 84 (October 1, 1936): 459.

18. "TWA's Graceful New Terminal," *Architectural Forum* 108 (January 1958): 78–85.

19. "TWA's Graceful New Terminal," 80–81.

20. Stanley Abercrombie, "Creative Playthings," *Horizon* 21 (July 1978): 79.

21. For Gehry, see Judith Davidsen, "Light-Hearted Models for Serious Results," *Architectural Record* 180 (July 1992): 30; for Perkins and Will, see "The In-House Model Shop," *Architectural and Engineering News* 9 (May 1967): 51. The latter notes, "Some jobs require as many as six or seven models . . . Half . . . are for design purposes and the rest are for presentation." Perhaps three or four study models were the most that others had been making at the time of Saarinen's project.

22. Mildred Friedman, ed., *Gehry Talks: Architecture + Process* (New York: Rizzoli, 1999), 208.

23. Scot Walls, videotaped discussion on models, NBBJ, Seattle, May 5, 2000.

24. Alec Vassiliadis, videotaped discussion on models, NBBJ, Seattle, May 5, 2000.

25. "Preservation of Architectural Models," *American Architect* 114 (August 28, 1918): 252.

26. http://www.predock.com/clay.html, February 2001.

27. Hani Rashid, interview with author, March 3, 2000. (Rashid studied at Carleton University School of Architecture, Ottawa.)

28. Robert Descharnes, *Gaudí, the Visionary* (New York: Viking Press, 1982), 131.

29. Davidsen, "Light-Hearted Models," 30.

30. Ivan Harbour of Richard Rogers Partnership, interview with author, August 18, 2000.

31. Wolf Prix, "Where Space Ends Architecture Will Start: The Concept of the Dissolving of the Space," *From the Center: Design Process at SCI-Arc* (New York: The Monacelli Press, 1997), 93.

32. Jonathan Leah, interview with author, August 16, 2000, and Leah, e-mail message to author, April 10, 2002.

33. Alejandro Zaera Polo, "A Conversation with Steven Holl," *El Croquis* 78: *Steven Holl, 1986–1996* (Madrid, 1996), 18.

34. Michael Sorkin, interview with author, May 12, 2000.

35. John Koga, interview with author, May 23, 2000. This reverse method of working with clay has developed because the modern clay substitute is supplied as blocks.

36. Luca Galofaro, *Digital Eisenman: An Office of the Electronic Era* (Basel: Birkhäuser, 1999), 30.

37. Peter Eisenman, interview with author, February 29, 2000.

38. Cesar Pelli, interview with author, February 2, 2000.

39. Rashid, interview.

40. http://www.predock.com/clay.html, February 2001.

41. Davidsen, "Light-Hearted Models," 30; *Frank O. Gehry: The Architect's Studio* (Humlebaek, Denmark: Louisiana Museum of Modern Art, 1998), 25.

42. Michele Saee, interview with author, January 19, 2000.

43. Wolf Prix, "On the Edge," in Peter Noever, ed., *Architecture in Transition: Between Deconstruction and New Modernism* (Munich and New York: Prestel, 1997), 19–21. Intriguingly, in the partnership's discussions the "more rapid language of the body" has replaced spoken language: "body-language was both the first drawing and the first model."

44. Alec Vassiliadis, videotaped discussion.

45. Scot Walls, videotaped discussion.

46. John Wilton-Ely, "The Architectural Model: 1. The English Baroque," *Apollo* 88:80 (October 1968): 254.

47. John Summerson, "Model Restoration," *Architects' Journal* 192 (November 7, 1990): 30.

48. http://www.theweboftime.com/Issue-3/Jeffcapmod.html.

49. A. L. Frothingham, "Discovery of an Original Church Model by a Gothic Architect," *Architectural Record* 22 (August 1907): 116.

50. Donald Wall, *Documenta: The Paolo Soleri Retrospective* (exhibition catalog, Washington, D.C.: Corcoran Gallery of Art, 1970). The exhibition was held from February 20 to April 5, 1970.

51. *Peter Pran: An Architecture of Poetic Movement* (Windsor, U.K.: Andreas Papadakis, 1998), 24.

52. Pran, interview.

53. *Architectural Monographs* 41: *Toyo Ito* (London: Academy Editions, 1995), 7–9, 11, 15–17.

54. *El Croquis* 80: *Daniel Libeskind, 1987–1996* (Madrid, 1996), 76.

55. Michael Graves, "Thought Models," in Suzanne Buttolph, ed., *Great Models*, vol. 27 of *The Student Publication of the School of Design* (Raleigh: North Carolina State University College of Design, 1978), 43; Kurt W. Forster, "Mildew Green Is the House of Forgetting," in Daniel Libeskind, *Daniel Libeskind, Radix-Matrix: Architecture and Writings* (Munich and New York: Prestel, 1997), 11; *Michele Saee: Buildings + Projects*, introduction by Thom Mayne (New York: Rizzoli, 1997); Prix, "On the Edge," 18.

56. Sorkin, interview.

57. Michael Graves, interview with author, April 14, 2000.

58. Jun Yanagisawa, "A Utopia Called Model," in *Toyo Ito: Blurring Architecture* (Milan: Edizioni Charta, 1999), 155–56.

59. Colin Davies, "Coming to Terms with Construction," *Architects' Journal* 208 (December 3–10, 1998): 51.

60. "Provocative Pyrotechnics," *Architectural Review* 193 (June 1993): 48.

61. Doug Cofer, "Eisenman and Graves: Modeling in Architecture," in Laura Todd, ed., *Crit* 15: *The Design Process* (American Institute of Architecture Students Journal), Summer 1985, 45.

62. Saee, interview.

63. Friedman, *Gehry Talks*, 249.

64. Moholy-Nagy also used models of this kind to undertake "experiments in space" while teaching at the Bauhaus in Weimar and Dessau in the 1920s. See the *Grove Dictionary of Art Online*, www.groveart.com.

65. Prix, "On the Edge," 20.

66. "Odile Decq & Benoît Cornette: Hyper-Tension" (exhibition catalog, Berlin: Galerie Aedes, c. 1995), 9.

67. Yanagisawa, "Utopia Called Model," 154.

68. Hans Reuther, "Origin and Development of the Architectural Model in Germany," *Daidalos*, December 15, 1981, 103.

69. Pierre-Alain Croset, "Architecture on Show: The German Architectural Museum," *Casabella* 47 (September 1983): 63; Heinrich Klotz, ed., *Paper Architecture: New Projects from the Soviet Union* (New York: Rizzoli, 1990), 7–8.

70. Rashid, interview.

71. Joseph Giovannini, "Zaha Hadid: Architecture's New Diva Makes an International Scene," *Architectural Digest* 53 (January 1996): 29; see also Giles Worsley, "Inside the Mind of an Architect," *Daily Telegraph*, December 11, 1999, A5.

72. Rashid, interview.

CHAPTER 5:
COMMUNICATION: IDEA AND IDENTITY

1. Cited in John Swarbrick, "Architectural Models in Relation to the Preservation of Ancient Buildings," *RIBA Journal* 32 (June 27, 1925): 522.

2. Edwin S. Parker, "The Model for Architectural Representation," *Architectural Forum* 30 (April 1919): 119.

3. Jacques-François Blondel, *L'Homme du Monde Éclairé par les Arts* (Amsterdam [Paris], 1774), cited in Monique Mosser, "Models of French Architecture in the Age of Enlightenment," *Daidalos*, December 15, 1981, 95.

4. Alwyn T. Covell, "Architecture in Miniature: The Plastic Model Studies of an English Artist," *Architectural Record* 35 (March 1914): 266.

5. B. J. Novitski, "Computer-Assisted Model Building," *Architecture* 81 (October 1992): 117.

6. Peter Pran, interview with author, January 25, 2000.

7. Spencer de Grey of Foster and Partners, interview with author, August 16, 2000.

8. Stephen Wren and Joseph Ames, eds., *Parentalia, or Memoirs of the Family of the Wrens* (London, 1750), 280, 283.

9. R. T. Gunther, ed., *The Architecture of Sir Roger Pratt, Charles II's Commissioner for the Re-Building of London after the Great Fire: Now Printed for the First Time from His Note-Books* (Oxford and New York: Oxford University Press, 1928), 22–23.

10. Kenneth Frampton and Silvia Kolbowski, eds., *Idea as Model* (New York: Institute for Architecture and Urban Studies/Rizzoli, 1981), 78.

11. Richard Armiger, "My Modelmaking," *Architects' Journal* 201 (February 2, 1995): 50.

12. Ross King, *Brunelleschi's Dome: How a Renaissance Genius Reinvented Architecture* (New York: Walker & Co., 2000), 40.

13. Hans Reuther, "Origin and Development of the Architectural Model in Germany," *Daidalos*, December 15, 1981, 99.

14. From *Civil Engineer and Architects' Journal* (1851), 120, cited in John Frederick Physick and Michael Darby, *Marble Halls: Drawings and Models for Victorian Secular Buildings* (exhibition catalog, London: Victoria and Albert Museum, 1973), 13.

15. LeRoy Grumbine, "The Use of Scale Models as an Aid to the Architect," *Western Architect* 34 (June 1925): 59.

16. Grumbine, "Use of Scale Models," 63.

17. Steven H. Waring, "Improved Techniques in Architectural Modelling," *Journal, Royal Architectural Institute of Canada* 25 (February 1948): 58.

18. Ray Pfaendler, "Architectural Models," *Architectural Review* 140 (July 1966): 70.

19. Jeff Bishop, "Models of Participation," *Architects' Journal* 182 (December 18–25, 1985): 36.

20. Hani Rashid, interview with author, March 3, 2000.

21. Trevor Fawcett, "Two Eighteenth Century Models of Bath" (unpublished article, n.d., photocopy, Soane Museum, London), 3.

22. Physick and Darby, *Marble Halls*, 13.

23. "Report of Committee on Model Exhibition," February 25, 1902, Archives of the Diocese of New York.

24. "Soleri's Cities on Display," *Progressive Architecture* 51 (April 1970): 29.

25. Cited in John Cornforth, "Architects, Patrons and Models," *Country Life* 137 (March 4, 1965): 467.

26. Marcel Aubert, "La Construction au Moyen-Age" (1961), cited in Mosser, "Models of French Architecture," 85.

27. The Rt. Rev. William T. Manning, letter to Ralph Adams Cram, October 23, 1924, Archives of the Diocese of New York.

28. Kenneth McCutchon, "Architectural Models," *Architects' Journal* 84 (October 1, 1936): 459.

29. Helen Seymour, "Model Maestros," *Architects' Journal* 182 (December 18–25, 1985): 30.

30. Berthold Audsley, "Miniatures and Their Value in Architectural Practice," *Brickbuilder* (bound with *Architectural Forum*) 23 (September 1914): 213. Awareness of manipulation in drawings was evident much earlier. In 1838, one critic noted that the attractions of a composition could obscure the lack of architectural interest; such drawings "might be still further improved by painting out the architecture altogether." From *Civil Engineer and Architects' Journal* (1838), 224, cited in Physick and Darby, *Marble Halls*, 15.

31. Parker, "Model for Architectural Representation," 119.

32. John Chisholm, "Rehearsal for Reality," *Architect and Building News* 2 (February 27, 1969): 21.

33. Chisholm, "Rehearsal for Reality," 24.

34. Stanley Abercrombie, "Creative Playthings," *Horizon* 21 (July 1978): 79.

35. Bishop, "Models of Participation," 36.

36. Piers Gough, "Modelmakers," *Architects' Journal* 177 (April 27, 1983): 30.

37. The modelmaker was Theodore Conrad, cited in Jeremy Lebensohn, "Mighty Miniatures," *American Craft* 48 (June–July 1988): 35.

38. From Vincent Scamozzi, *L'Idea dell'Architettura Universale* (1615, Eng. trans. 1669), cited by John Wilton-Ely, "Architectural Model," *Grove Dictionary of Art Online*, www.groveart.com.

39. Cited in Arthur T. Bolton, ed., *Lectures on Architecture, by Sir John Soane . . . as Delivered to the Students of the Royal Academy from 1809 to 1836 in Two Courses of Six Lectures Each* (London, 1929), 191.

40. Philibert de l'Orme, *Le Premier Tome de l'Architecture* (1567), cited in Mosser, "Models of French Architecture," 86. See also Spiro Kostof, ed., *The Architect: Chapters in the History of the Profession* (Oxford and New York: Oxford University Press, 1977, 1986), 142.

41. Janet Abrams, "Models of Their Kind," *Independent*, August 26, 1988, 18.

42. Gunther, *Architecture of Sir Roger Pratt*, 23.

43. Abrams, "Models of Their Kind," 18.

44. Abrams, "Models of Their Kind," 18.

45. Unidentified newspaper cutting, October 1985, Piper Models, London.

46. Fawcett, "Two Eighteenth Century Models," 3.

47. Henry Rutgers Marshall, "The Architect's Tools," *Architectural Review* 4 (November 1897): 56.

48. Alwyn T. Covell, "Developing the Country House: Drawings and Models from the Office of Joseph Bodker, Architect," *Arts and Decoration* 15 (July 1921): 162–63, 193.

49. Harvey Wiley Corbett, "Architectural Models of Cardboard," pt. 1, *Pencil Points* 3 (April 1922): 12–13.

50. Joe Oliver, "Architectural Photocomposition," *Photomethods* 32 (March 1989): 34–35.

51. Oliver, "Architectural Photocomposition," 34. Computer technology has since enabled model and site photographs to be combined and manipulated on-screen, both speeding up the process and making it more broadly available.

52. Piera Scuri, "Skyscraper Business," *Domus* 660 (April 1985): 26.

53. Thomas Fisher, "Model Making: A Model of Practice," *Progressive Architecture* 76 (May 1995): 80.

54. The model was shown in *Architects' Journal* 181 (June 26, 1985): 20–21, and *Architectural Design* 54:3–4 (1984): 32.

55. Ross Wimer, interview with author, May 19, 2000.

56. Nora Odendahl, "The Art of Architectural Representation," *Architecture New Jersey* 26 (April 1990): 22.

57. King, *Brunelleschi's Dome*, 39–40.

58. This translation from "Art Serve," Australian National University; see http://rubens.anu.edu.au/htdocs/texts/vasari/vasari.brunelleschi.html, March 2002.

59. Margaret Richardson, "Model Architecture," *Country Life*, September 21, 1989, 227.

60. Message from Hugh Ferris, "Proceedings at the Dinner in Honor of the Late Harvey Wiley Corbett,

at the Architectural League of New York, Thursday Evening, 17 February 1955, under the Chairmanship of Julian Clarence Levi," transcribed by Jeffrey Ellis Aronin. I am grateful to Scott Springer for this information.

61. Balthazar Korab, telephone conversation with author.

62. Keith Mendenhall of Gehry Partners, interview with author, January 24, 2000.

63. Mildred Friedman, ed., *Gehry Talks: Architecture + Process* (New York: Rizzoli, 1999), 127.

64. Alec Vassiliadis, telephone conversation with author.

65. Friedman, *Gehry Talks*, 262.

66. Michael Schumacher, e-mail message to author, May 8, 2000.

67. Information from Mendenhall, interview with author, December 3, 1999.

68. Odile Decq, interview with author, July 26, 1999.

69. Mike Fairbrass and Ivan Harbour of Richard Rogers Partnership, interview with author, August 18, 2000.

70. Leon Battista Alberti, *De Re Aedificatoria* (1452); English trans., Joseph Rykwert, Neil Leach, and Robert Tavernor, *On the Art of Building in Ten Books* (Cambridge, Mass.: MIT Press, 1988), 34.

71. Alastair Best, "Thorp Modelmakers," *Crafts* 64 (September–October 1983): 47.

72. Cited in the brochure for the exhibition "The Architect's Studio," on view at the Dundee Contemporary Arts Centre, Dundee, Scotland, from July 3 to August 29, 1999.

73. Rashid, interview.

74. Michael Sorkin, interview with author, May 12, 2000.

75. Keith Mendenhall, e-mail message to author, December 7, 2001.

76. From Thomas Fisher, "Communicating Ideas Artfully," cited in "The Representation of Architecture," *Architecture New Jersey* 26 (1990): 10.

77. Alec Vassiliadis, videotaped discussion on models, NBBJ, Seattle, May 5, 2000.

78. De Grey, interview.

79. Covell, "Architecture in Miniature," 266.

80. LeRoy Grumbine, "Cardboard Models," pt. 1, *American Architect* 122 (August 2, 1922): 113.

81. Wimer, interview.

82. Rashid, interview.

83. James C. Rose, "Landscape Models," *Pencil Points* 20 (July 1939): 439.

CHAPTER 6: MAKERS

1. Giorgio Vasari, *The Lives of the Artists*, trans. George Bull (Harmondsworth, Middlesex: Penguin, 1974), 160. For comments on the relationship between Brunelleschi's training and architecture, see François Bucher, "Micro-Architecture as the 'Idea' of Gothic Theory and Style," *Gesta* 15 (International Center of Medieval Art, 1976): 74.

2. Richard Armiger, conversation with author.

3. Peter Eisenman, interview with author, February 29, 2000.

4. LeRoy Grumbine, "The Use of Scale Models as an Aid to the Architect," *Western Architect* 34 (June 1925): 61.

5. Grumbine, "Use of Scale Models," 61.

6. Robert Dennis Murray, "Models and Scotch," *Pencil Points* 20 (July 1939): 429.

7. Grumbine, "Use of Scale Models," 61.

8. Mike Fairbrass and Ivan Harbour of Richard Rogers Partnership, interview with author, August 18, 2000.

9. Joan Llewelyn Owens, "Making Models for Industry," *Daily Telegraph*, September 1, 1975 (cutting, Piper Models, London).

10. Richard Armiger, "My Modelmaking," *Architects' Journal* 201 (February 2, 1995): 50.

11. Armiger, "My Modelmaking," 50.

12. Grumbine, "Use of Scale Models," 61.

13. Alwyn T. Covell, "Architecture in Miniature: The Plastic Model Studies of an English Artist," *Architectural Record* 35 (March 1914): 266.

14. Peter Pran, interview with author, January 25, 2000.

15. "Career Variations: Modelmaking," *Architects' Journal* 186 (July 1, 1987): 79.

16. A number of universities and colleges in the U.K. offer modelmaking courses: the Arts Institute at Bournemouth, B.A. (Hons.); Kent Institute of Art & Design, B.A. (Hons.); Hertfordshire University, B.A.; Rycotewood College, H.N.D.; and Sunderland University, B.A.

17. Bemidji State University is in Bemidji, Minnesota.

18. Monique Mosser, "Models of French Architecture in the Age of Enlightenment," *Daidalos*, December 15, 1981, 83.

19. John Wilton-Ely, "The Architectural Model: 1. English Baroque," *Apollo* 88:80 (October 1968): 253.

20. The elder John Smallwell was master of the Joiners' Company in 1705, and it was probably his son who served for a term in 1735. Wilton-Ely, "Architectural Model: 1," 181.

21. For a detailed history of Jean-Pierre Fouquet (1752–1829) and François Fouquet (1787–1870), see Geneviève Cuisset, "Jean-Pierre et François Fouquet, Artistes Modeleurs," *Gazettes des Beaux Arts* 115 (May–June 1990): 227–40. (An English translation by Margaret Schuelein is available in the Soane Museum, London.)

22. Giovanni Altieri (active 1767–90); Antonio Chichi (1743–1816). Peter Thornton and Helen Dorey, *Sir John Soane: The Architect as Collector, 1753–1837* (New York: Abrams, 1992). For Chichi, see Helen Buttery, "A Present from Pompeii," *World of Interiors*, April 1989, 132–37.

23. Regarding French models of the sixteenth and seventeenth centuries, Monique Mosser comments: "To all appearances the models in France were mostly made of wood, like in Italy, a practice which continued in the seventeenth century." See Mosser, "Models of French Architecture," 86.

24. For Ricci, Ardolino, and Di Lorenzo, see Frederic C. Hirons, "The Use of Scale Models," pt. 3, *Pencil Points* 2 (January 1921): 23. This isolated example is of a portion of a facade; none of the firm's other work is known. For the Menconi brothers, see Egerton Swartwout, "The Use of Large Scale Models in Architecture," *Architecture* 24 (September 1911): 132.

25. This model survives in the company's collection. Pat Brugh, telephone conversation with author.

26. Alexander L. Sampietro, letter to the Rev. Dean Hoffman, secretary, Hon. Building Committee of the Cathedral of St. John the Divine, February 1, 1902, Archives of the Diocese of New York. A number of advertisements placed by other architectural modelers in *Architectural League of New York* in 1890–91 include J. & J. Morrison, New York: "Artistic Models and Decorations, in Plaster, papier mâché, and composition. Models made for Bronze, Wood, Brass, Stone, etc. in an Artistic Manner"; Samuel H. French & Co., Philadelphia: "Peerless colors for Mortar, Ornamental Glass, Slate and Wooden Mantels, Painters' and Builders' supplies, Architectural Modelers"; Ellin, Kitson & Co., New York: "Architec-tural Sculptors, Modelers, Decorative plaster and Papier Mâché work, Carvings on Wood or Stone, all kinds of Wood or Stone Work executed to order from Architects' Drawings, Church Work a Specialty"; and James M. Kerr, New York. "Architectural Sculptor, Decorations in Stone, Wood, Plaster or Papier-Mâché, Scale models of Buildings and Monuments."

27. Emile Garet, letter to Elliott Woods, superintendent of the U.S. Capitol, May 14, 1902, U.S. Capitol Archives. An article published in 1926 gives a summary of the steps followed by an architectural modeler to make a complete building model in plaster: "The plastelline [*sic*] elevations were sent to the architectural modeler's studio in the afternoon and several casts from it were delivered next day. The modeler makes glue moulds from the elevation studies furnished him by the architect, casts the work in plaster of Paris, miters the corners, and fits them together, so that what the architect gets is a cast, or several casts, of the complete building to scale"; Maurice Gauthier, "Studying in Three Dimensions," *Pencil Points* 7 (July 1926): 410–11.

28. For Mr. Dighton, see "Architectural Models," *Builder* 6 (May 6, 1848): 225; for Mr. Day, see "Day, the Architectural Modeller," *Builder* 6 (October 7, 1848): 490; John Frederick Physick and Michael Darby, *Marble Halls: Drawings and Models for Victorian Secular Buildings* (exhibition catalog, London: Victoria and Albert Museum, 1973). In general, the transition to modern modelmaking practice was smoother in Europe, and the limitation of materials less extreme, especially in countries like Britain, where the Beaux-Arts influence was less dominant.

29. Some ornamental plasterers have also survived this long, including C. G. Girolami & Sons in Chicago, though the firm's work concentrates on details and has rarely included complete building models.

30. *Building News*, July 3, 1885 (cutting, Thorp Modelmakers).

31. *Builder*, November 27, 1897 (cutting, Thorp Modelmakers).

32. *Builders' Journal*, January 9, 1901 (cutting, Thorp Modelmakers).

33. Kenneth Reid, "Architectural Models," *Pencil Points* 20 (July 1939): 407. A similar comment appeared in an article the following year, giving one practical reason for this separation of materials in model work: "Professional modelmakers ordinarily specialize in one basic material—cardboard, plaster, wood, clay or plastelline [*sic*]," since they find that mixing materials causes warping and cracking of the model through differences of expansion and contraction. G. A. Jester, *"Architectural Models,"* *Industrial Arts and Vocational Education* 29 (October 1940): 341.

34. Robert I. Hoyt, "World's Fair Models," *Pencil Points* 20 (July 1939): 420.

35. Steven H. Waring, "Improved Techniques in Architectural Modelling," *Journal, Royal Architectural Institute of Canada* 25 (February 1948): 58–60. War has had a hand in the development of modelmaking techniques at other times. In late-seventeenth-century France, as in World War II America, the decision to use models for strategic and offensive planning led to the creation of large modelmaking workshops, the development of new techniques, and the standardization of practices that have had lasting effects on the industry as a whole. See Isabelle Warmoes, *Musée des Plans-Reliefs: Historic Models of Fortified Towns* (Paris: Éditions du Patrimoine, 1999), 18–21. For another type of war model—made for articles in *Life* during the World War II years by Norman Bel Geddes—see "Prefabricated History: Designer Geddes Makes Battles to Order for *Life* Magazine before They Happen," *Architectural Forum* 80 (March 1944): 4.

36. George Gabriel, interview with author, February 2, 1999.

37. Gabriel, interview.

38. Sanford Hohauser, *Architectural and Interior Models: Design and Construction* (New York: Van Nostrand Reinhold, 1970), 10.

39. Owens, "Making Models for Industry."

40. Women were, however, employed as sculptors. Several women were recorded working on models of some of the large figure sculptures for the buildings of the World's Columbian Exposition of 1893 and are illustrated with their models in *The Illustrated World's Fair* (Chicago: Illustrated World's Fair Publishing, 1890–93).

41. Catharina Pran started making models for her father, who was an architect, in Norway from around 1950. She mostly made them herself but sometimes subcontracted work to others. "They were so good all the best architects in Norway came to her," says her son Peter Pran. "She was the first in Scandinavia to use Plexiglas for models." For Loja Saarinen, see Michael A. Capps, "Eero Saarinen: Architect with a Vision," http://www.nps.gov/jeff/ar-eero.html, February 2002. An article by Jean Hetherington included illustrations of some of her own models: "The Value of Models in Architecture," *American Architect* 121 (January 18, 1922): 51–52. "Miss Swift" was the maker of several models in William Harvey, *Models of Buildings: How to Make and Use Them* (London: Architectural Press, 1927). Miss Joyce Inall's work is featured in Edward W. Hobbs, *Pictorial House Modelling* (London: Crosby Lockwood and Son, 1926). A detailed article on models by Ethel Bartholomew, "Architectural Model Making as Part of the Technique of the Drafting-Room," *Architecture* 54 (September 1926): 200–202, suggests that the author was a maker.

42. Hobbs, *Pictorial House Modelling*, x.

43. Ilona Rider (now at Kohn Pedersen Fox), telephone conversation with author, May 10, 2001.

44. Keith Mendenhall of Gehry Partners, e-mail message to author, December 7, 2001.

45. Armiger suggests that only offices with a staff of one hundred to two hundred could afford this.

46. Fairbrass and Harbour, interview, and Fairbrass, e-mail message to author, May 22, 2002.

47. Garet to Woods, January 23, 1904, U.S. Capitol Archives.

48. Architects may not get paid at all; in fact, payment problems have always been a source of vexation for architects. Michelangelo wrote in 1555 that he had been forced to work on St. Peter's for eight years without pay; letter to Vasari, May 11, 1555, in *Lettere*, ed. Milanesi (Archivio Buonarroti), 537, cited in James S. Ackerman, "Architectural Practice in the Italian Renaissance," *Journal of the Society of Architectural Historians* 13 (October 1954): 5.

49. Emilio dei Cavalieri, letter to Grand Duke Ferdinando I de' Medici, November 17, 1600, cited in

"Documentation: Emilio dei Cavalieri, Giacomo della Porta, and G. B. Montano," trans. Josephine von Henneberg, *Journal of the Society of Architectural Historians* 36 (December 1977): 253.

50. Chester N. Godfrey, letter to the Very Rev. Milo H. Gates, April 24, 1931, Archives of the Diocese of New York.

51. Leon Battista Alberti, *De Re Aedificatoria* (1452); English trans., Joseph Rykwert, Neil Leach, and Robert Tavernor, *On the Art of Building in Ten Books* (Cambridge, Mass.: MIT Press, 1988), 34.

52. Fairbrass, e-mail message to author, May 10, 2001.

53. The comment on demand is from an article on modelmaker T. D. Dighton: "Architectural Models," *Builder* 6 (May 6, 1848): 225. For Mr. Day, see "Day, the Architectural Modeller," 490.

54. Elisabeth Kieven, " 'Mostrar l'Inventione': The Role of Roman Architects in the Baroque Period; Plans and Models," in Henry A. Millon, ed., *The Triumph of the Baroque: Architecture in Europe, 1600–1750* (New York: Rizzoli, 1999), 174.

55. Christian Spencer-Davies, e-mail message to author, November 8, 2001; Hannah Baldock, "It's a Small World," *Building* 265 (June 30, 2000): 28–29.

56. Baldock, "It's a Small World," 29.

57. Richard Tenguerian, interview with author, February 28, 2000.

58. William Louie of Kohn Pedersen Fox, letter to Richard Tenguerian, September 24, 1997, courtesy of Richard Tenguerian.

59. Armiger, "My Modelmaking," 50.

60. Armiger, "My Modelmaking," 50; other quotes from Armiger, interview with author, November 21, 1999.

61. Alec Vassiliadis, conversation with author.

62. Swartwout, "Use of Large Scale Models," 132. The "present instance" refers to models for the Denver Post Office.

CHAPTER 7:
MATERIAL MATTERS

1. See Robert I. Hoyt, "World's Fair Models," *Pencil Points* 20 (July 1939): 422, which refers to Conrad's use of aluminum plates for the model's roof. Aluminum was not really new; it started to move out of the luxury market around 1900. See http://www.carnegie museums.org/cmag/bk_issue/1997/sepoct/dept7.html, February 2001.

2. Arthur E. Herman, "Models of Plastics and Aluminum," *Progressive Architecture* 40 (December 1959): 11. On the influence of military models in World War II, see Steven H. Waring, "Improved Techniques in Architectural Modelling," *Journal, Royal Architectural Institute of Canada* 25 (February 1948): 58–60; and chapter six, "Makers."

3. Henry Rutgers Marshall, "The Architect's Tools," *Architectural Review* 4 (November 1897): 55.

4. Marshall, "Architect's Tools," 56.

5. For the use of turnips, see Vasari on Brunelleschi: "He carefully examined the stones of the stonecutters to see that they were hard or if they contained any flaws, and showed them the way to make the joints by models made of wood and wax, or even of turnips, and doing the like with the ironwork for the smiths." This translation from "Art Serve" at the Australian National University; http://rubens.anu.edu.au/htdocs/texts/vasari/vasari.brunelleschi.html, March 2002. For soap, see Margaret J. Postgate, "Architectural Models from Ivory Soap," *Pencil Points* 10 (June 1929): 392–96; and Francis Keally, "The House of a Thousand Bubbles," *House and Garden* 58 (November 1930): 67–69.

6. Spencer de Grey of Foster and Partners, interview with author, August 16, 2000.

7. Henry A. Millon, ed., *The Triumph of the Baroque: Architecture in Europe, 1600–1750* (New York: Rizzoli, 1999), 411, 587, 600. For previous reference to Mayr, see chapter three, "A Question of Scale."

8. Some pre–World War I British models were electrically lit (see Percy Collins, "Architectural Modeling," *American Homes and Gardens* 12 [August 1915]: 263), as were those of British maker L. H. Partridge, M.C., of London, in 1920 (see "Architectural Models," *The Architect* 104 [September 17, 1920]: 1790). The American Harvey Wiley Corbett included miniature electric bulbs in the arched recesses of a model church interior in 1922; see Corbett, "Architectural Models of Cardboard," pt. 2, *Pencil Points* 3 (May 1922): 29.

9. *Zaha Hadid: The Complete Buildings and Projects*, essay by Aaron Betsky (London: Thames and Hudson, 1998), 68.

10. Styrene sheet has similar properties and is also used by modelmakers, but the quality is not as good.

11. Horn was used in the model of St. Maclou in Rouen. Corbett used mica; see "Architectural Models," pt. 2, 29. One article recommended tracing linen for windows if the model was to be lighted from inside; see "Model Making by Architects: An Interesting Communication from a Reader Who Strongly Approves the Work Begun at Columbia University," *American Architect* 118 (December 8, 1920): 750. Isinglass was used in a model illustrated in Hoyt, "World's Fair Models," 426.

12. Celluloid windows were in use in 1914; see Berthold Audsley, "Miniatures and Their Value in Architectural Practice," *Brickbuilder* (bound with *Architectural Forum*) 23 (September 1914): 215.

13. For acetate sheet, see Waring, "Improved Techniques," 60. Acrylic was developed in the 1940s. Plexiglas was in use for modelmaking in 1949; see A. L. Aydelott, "Making a House Model," *Progressive Architecture* 40 (October 1949): 69. According to Hoyt, Conrad used "windows of synthetic resin"; "World's Fair Models," 422–23.

14. De Grey, interview.

15. Cited in Franz Schulze, *Mies van der Rohe: A Critical Biography* (Chicago: University of Chicago Press, 1985), 101.

16. The model is illustrated in *Peter Pran: An Architecture of Poetic Movement* (Windsor, U.K.: Andreas Papadakis, 1998), 74.

17. "Soleri's Cities on Display," *Progressive Architecture* 51 (April 1970): 29; "Soleri's Urban Utopia Comes to New York," *Interiors* 130 (August 1970): 6.

18. All material from this paragraph from "How to See Through Walls," *Economist Technology Quarterly*, September 22, 2001, 6, and http://www.metropolismag.com/html/content_0401/shulman/, January 2002.

19. Millon, *Triumph of the Baroque*, 484–85, 537–38.

20. John Wilton-Ely, "The Architectural Models of Sir John Soane: A Catalogue," *Architectural History: Journal of the Society of Architectural Historians of Great Britain* 12 (1969): 17.

21. Edward W. Hobbs, *Pictorial House Modelling* (London: Crosby Lockwood and Son, 1926), 9.

22. Ross Wimer, interview with author, May 19, 2000.

23. Mike Fairbrass of Richard Rogers Partnership, interview with author, May 22, 2002.

24. Michael Sorkin, interview with author, May 12, 2000.

25. Illustrated and discussed in Howard Colvin, *Unbuilt Oxford* (New Haven and London: Yale University Press, 1983), 9–11.

26. John Frederick Physick and Michael Darby, *Marble Halls: Drawings and Models for Victorian Secular Buildings* (exhibition catalog, London: Victoria and Albert Museum, 1973), 14–15.

27. See *Victorian Church Art* (exhibition catalog, London: Victoria and Albert Museum, 1971), 48–49.

28. Mike Fairbrass, e-mail message to author, December 11, 2001.

29. http://www.predock.com/clay.html, February 2001; the projects referred to are California Polytechnic State University and Agadir Palm Bay project, Morocco.

30. Sorkin, interview.

31. Elisabeth Kieven, "'Mostrar l'Inventione': The Role of Roman Architects in the Baroque Period; Plans and Models," in Millon, *Triumph of the Baroque*, 204.

32. Kenneth McCutchon, "Architectural Models," *Architects' Journal* 84 (October 1, 1936): 460.

33. LeRoy Grumbine, "The Use of Scale Models as an Aid to the Architect," *Western Architect* 34 (June 1925): 61.

34. Sorkin, interview.

35. Alec Vassiliadis, telephone conversation with author, December 12, 2001.

36. Jun Yanagisawa, "A Utopia Called Model," in *Toyo Ito: Blurring Architecture* (Milan: Edizioni Charta, 1999), 156.

37. Keith Mendenhall of Gehry Partners, e-mail message to author, December 7, 2001.

38. Mendenhall, e-mail.

39. Hani Rashid, interview with author, March 3, 2000.

40. West 8, project information.

41. Ethel Bartholomew, "Architectural Model Making as Part of the Technique of the Drafting-Room," *Architecture* 54 (September 1926): 284.

42. Daniel Libeskind, *Daniel Libeskind, Radix-Matrix: Architecture and Writings* (Munich and New York: Prestel, 1997), 18.

43. Fritz Neumeyer, "Beyond Narratives: The Architectural Object as a Representation of a Methodology of Making and Communication," *Architecture + Urbanism* 229 (October 1989): 36–38.

44. Alec Vassiliadis, videotaped discussion on models, NBBJ, Seattle, May 5, 2000.

45. Keith Mendenhall, interview with author, December 3, 1999.

46. Michael Schumacher, e-mail message to author, May 8, 2000.

47. Yanagisawa, "Utopia Called Model," 156.

48. Rashid, interview.

49. Mildred Friedman, ed., *Gehry Talks: Architecture + Process* (New York: Rizzoli, 1999), 50.

CHAPTER 8:
A PROCESS OF CHANGE

1. Harvey Wiley Corbett, "Architectural Models of Cardboard," pt. 4, *Pencil Points* 3 (August 1922): 17–18.

2. It is important to bear in mind that Corbett's cardboard models were probably among the finest of the time to be produced in-house.

3. Percy Collins, "Architectural Modeling," *American Homes and Gardens* 12 (August 1915): 261.

4. Jane Jacobs, "The Miniature Boom," *Architectural Forum* 108 (May 1958): 110; Jeremy Lebensohn, "Mighty Miniatures," *American Craft* 48 (June–July 1988): 35. In 1939, Conrad was already working with architects like Edward Durell Stone; see Robert I. Hoyt, "World's Fair Models," *Pencil Points* 20 (July 1939): 422, 425.

5. Jacobs, "Miniature Boom," 110.

6. Michael C. Pollak, "Master of Miniatures," *Bergen County Record* (New Jersey), February 3, 1986, B1.

7. George Gabriel, interview with author, February 2, 1999.

8. Gabriel, interview. For the diamond shop, see Pollak, "Master of Miniatures," B1.

9. Gabriel, interview.

10. John Wilton-Ely, "The Architectural Model: 1. English Baroque," *Apollo* 88:80 (October 1968): 253.

11. Sanford Hohauser, *Architectural and Interior Models: Design and Construction* (New York: Van Nostrand Reinhold, 1970), 10.

12. Hohauser, *Architectural and Interior Models*, 10.

13. Alec Saunders, e-mail messages to author, January 9 and 18, 2002.

14. John Rawson, "Small Beginnings: Modelmaking," *Architects' Journal* 191 (January 17, 1990): 68.

15. Mike Fairbrass of Richard Rogers Partnership, interview with author, August 18, 2000.

16. Emile Garet, report on the U.S. Capitol model and improvements, at the request of Elliott Woods, superintendent of the U.S. Capitol, n.d., U.S. Capitol Archives.

17. Willy Leichter, who set up the machine at Skidmore, Owings & Merrill in 1985, e-mail message to author, November 18, 1999.

18. Thomas Fisher, "P/A Technics: Lasers," *Progressive Architecture* 67 (June 1986): 109.

19. Described and illustrated in Marc H. Miller, *The Panorama of New York City: A History of the World's Largest Scale Model* (New York: Queens Museum, 1990), 32–35.

20. Rawson, "Small Beginnings," 66.

21. Janet Abrams, "Models of Their Kind," *Independent*, August 26, 1988, 18.

22. John Chisholm, "Rehearsal for Reality," *Architect and Building News* 2 (February 27, 1969): 27. The self-destruction of the model was in fact part of a long tradition. C. Du Bourg's (or Dubourg's) popular public shows in the late eighteenth and early nineteenth centuries consisted principally of models. His 1785 attempt to portray the effect of Vesuvius was a miscalculated experiment: it started a fire that destroyed the whole show; see Margaret Richardson, "Model Architecture," *Country Life*, September 21, 1989, 225–26.

23. Ross Wimer, interview with author, May 19, 2000.

24. Wimer, interview.

25. Jacobs, "Miniature Boom," 107.

26. Akiko Busch, *The Art of the Architectural Model* (New York: Design Press, 1991), 27.

27. Rawson, "Small Beginnings," 68.

28. Gitta Morris, "Kenneth Champlin Gives Life to Architects' Dreams Long Before the Engineers and Construction Crews," *Metropolis* 15 (January–February 1996): 70–73, 75.

29. Peter Pran, interview with author, January 25, 2000.

30. Annette Kreimeier at Atelier 36 and Monath & Menzel, both in Berlin, e-mail message to author, February 25, 2000. In Germany at that time, CNC milling was heavily relied on by both smaller and larger workshops, as these two firms exemplify.

31. Richard Armiger, "My Modelmaking," *Architects' Journal* 201 (February 2, 1995): 50.

32. Alec Vassiliadis, conversation with author, October 2, 1999.

33. The first rapid prototyping technology, stereolithography, was invented in 1984, but it was not used in architectural modelmaking until the 1990s.

34. Wimer, interview.

35. Ivan Harbour of Richard Rogers Partnership, interview with author, August 18, 2000.

36. Kimberley Holden, e-mail message to author, October 4, 2001.

37. Gregg Pasquarelli, e-mail message to author, January 28, 2002.

38. Project description provided by the architects, e-mail message to author, October 4, 2001.

39. Pasquarelli, e-mail.

40. Lester Fader and Carl Leonard, "Holography: A Design Process Aid," *Progressive Architecture* 52 (June 1971): 92–94; Tom Porter, *How Architects Visualize* (New York: Van Nostrand Reinhold, 1979), 111–14.

41. Keith Mendenhall of Gehry Partners, interview with author, December 3, 1999. See also B. J. Novitski, "Gehry Forges New Computer Links," *Architecture* 81 (August 1992): 105–10.

42. Mendenhall, interview.

43. Mildred Friedman, ed., *Gehry Talks: Architecture + Process* (New York: Rizzoli, 1999), 272.

44. Pran, interview.

45. Cesar Pelli, interview with author, February 2, 2000.

46. Peter Zellner, *Hybrid Space: New Forms in Digital Architecture* (New York: Rizzoli, 1999), 34.

47. Cited in Zellner, *Hybrid Space*, 34.

48. Philipp Ursprung, "The Transparence of the Model as the Model of Transparency: Jürgen Mayer Hermann's E.gram," *Daidalos* 74 (October 2000): 62–65.

49. Maurice Gauthier, "Studying in Three Dimensions," *Pencil Points* 7 (July 1926): 411.

50. Hani Rashid, interview with author, March 3, 2000.

51. Rashid, interview.

52. Jun Yanagisawa, "A Utopia Called Model," in *Toyo Ito: Blurring Architecture* (Milan: Edizioni Charta, 1999), 155.

53. Spencer de Grey of Foster and Partners, interview with author, August 16, 2000.

54. Pelli, interview.

55. Rashid, interview.

56. Steven Holl, *Parallax* (New York: Princeton Architectural Press, 2000), 114.

57. Pran, interview.

58. Rashid, interview.

59. Michael Sorkin, interview with author, May 12, 2000.

60. Keith Mendenhall, e-mail message to author, February 9, 2000.

61. Rashid, interview.

62. Stefan Behnisch, "Lob der Pappe: Modellbau im Architekturbüro," *Baumeister*, April 1992, 103, from the translated summaries.

63. Rashid, interview.

64. Michele Saee, interview with author, January 19, 2000.

65. B. J. Novitski, "Computer-Assisted Model Building," *Architecture* 81 (October 1992): 117. Novitski's conclusion is based on a comment made by Bertha Martinez of Zimmer Gunsul Frasca Partnership.

66. Wimer, interview.

67. De Grey, interview.

68. Pran, interview.

69. Richard Tenguerian, letter to the editor, *Progressive Architecture* 76 (November 1995): 14.

70. Timothy Johnson, then working for Ellerbe Becket, note to Richard Tenguerian, n.d. The model referred to was for the Elihu M. Harris State Office Building, Oakland, made in 1992.

71. Daniel Libeskind, response to after-lecture questions, National Building Museum, Washington, D.C., April 6, 2001.

INDEX

ILLUSTRATION CREDITS

Numbers refer to page numbers.